Newly-Qualified Social Workers

Newly-Qualified Social Workers

A Practice Guide to the Assessed and Supported Year in Employment

JONATHAN PARKER, IVAN GRAY,
ANDREW MORRIS and SALLY LEE

4th
Edition

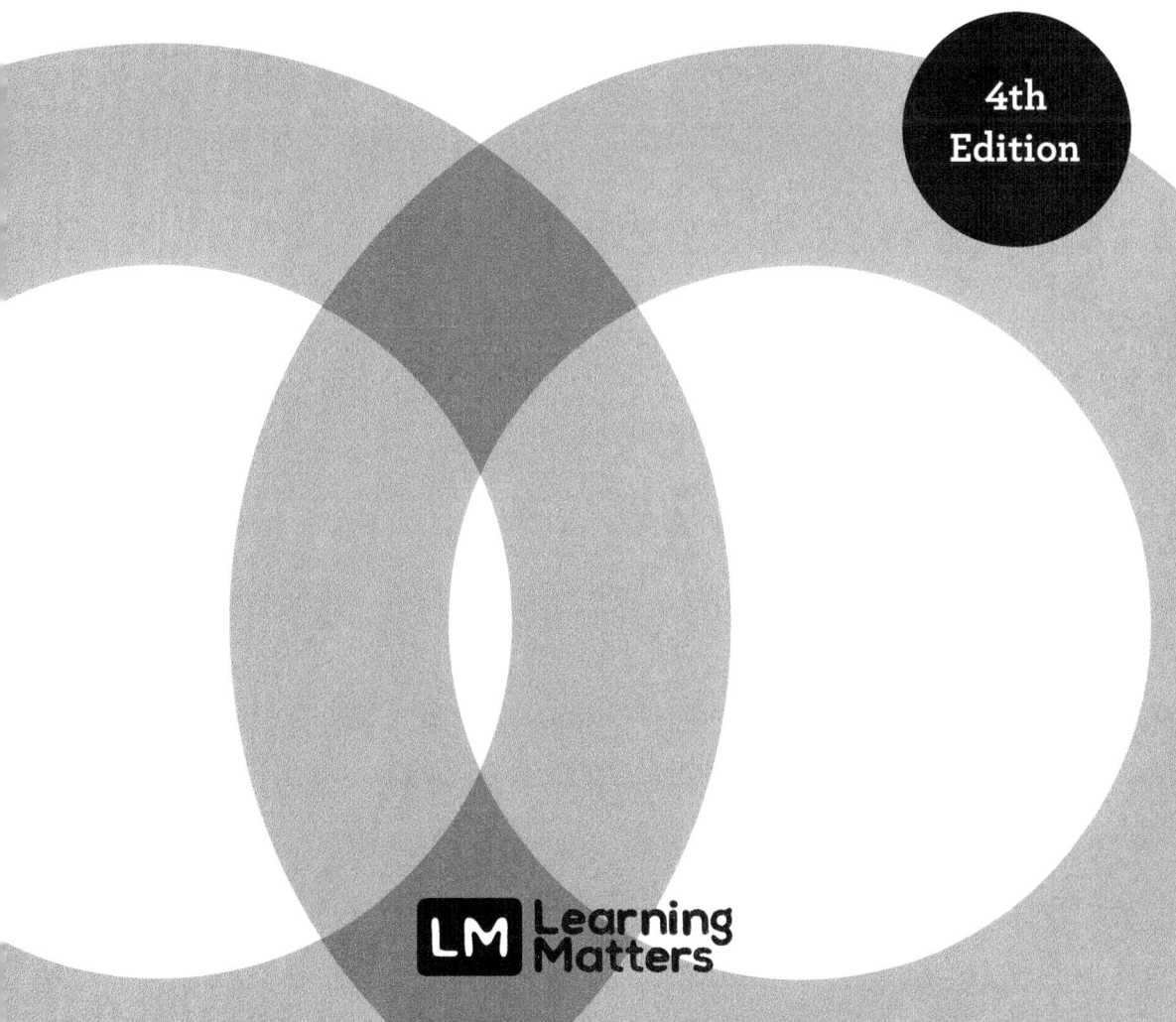

LM Learning Matters

3rd Floor
HYLO
103–105 Bunhill Row
London, EC1Y 8LZ
UK

2455 Teller Road
Thousand Oaks
California 91320

10th Floor, Emaar Capital Tower
2 MG Road, Sikanderpur, Sector 26
Gurugram, Haryana – 122002
India

8 Marina View Suite 43-053
Asia Square Tower 1
Singapore 018960

Senior publisher: Susannah Trefgarne
Assistant editor: Sahar Jamfar
Senior project editor: Chris Marke
Marketing manager: Ruslana Khatagova
Cover design: Bhairvi Vyas
Typeset by: C&M Digitals (P) Ltd, Chennai, India
Printed in the UK

Library of Congress Control Number: 2026930289

British Library Cataloguing in Publication Data

A catalogue record for this book is available from the British Library

ISBN: 978-1-5297-7674-4
ISBN: 978-1-5297-7673-7 (pbk)

Contents

Post-Qualifying Social Work Practice Series

Series Editor: Keith Brown

The Post-Qualifying Social Work Practice series from Learning Matters is aimed at busy social work and health care practitioners who are looking to enhance their skills and extend their knowledge.

These books cover a range of relevant topics in the field and enable professionals and students to engage critically and confidently with social work practice.

Each book is:

- Accessible
- Written from a practical point of view
- Skills-focused, with clear links to qualifying training and CPD
- Packed with up-to-date information on integrated health and social care.

About the editors

Dr Jonathan Parker, Professor Emeritus Bournemouth University, Honorary Professor University of Stavanger, Norway, and University of Hertfordshire. He was Chair of the Association of Teachers in Social Work Education (2002–2005), Vice Chair of the UK higher education representative body, the Joint University Council for Social Work Education (2005–2010), and is a Fellow of the Academy of Social Sciences. He is author of the best-selling book *Social Work Practice* (7th edition, SAGE, 2025) and series editor for Transforming Social Work Practice series (SAGE).

Dr Ivan Gray holds academic and professional qualifications in applied social science, social work, and management science. He has extensive experience across services as a social worker and social work manager and was director of a unit specialising in organisational and management development for public services. He has designed and led several social work and management programmes and whilst semi-retired is still active as a researcher writer and consultant.

Andrew Morris, Senior Lecturer in Social Work, Bournemouth University. Andrew teaches across human development, research for professional practice, and various continuing professional development units in social work education. His PhD research explores shame in the context of poor mental health, with a focus on reflective, ethically grounded practice.

Dr Sally Lee, Senior Lecturer in Social Work, Bournemouth University. Sally qualified as a social worker in 1993 and then worked in a range of services for adults in the south of England. Over a long career in social work, she reflects on the value of social work to effect change and support people who may be experiencing marginalisation or going through periods of transition. Sally now teaches social work and enjoys helping students as they develop into social work practitioners. Her research promotes participation and is focused on sexual wellbeing. She, along with Lou Oliver, is author of *Social Work Practice with Adults* (SAGE, 2023).

Book contributors

Jude Badmington-Fowler is a Senior Lecturer on the BSc Social Work Programme and Post Qualifying Programme and the Programme Director for Post Qualifying Social Work at Cardiff Metropolitan University. Over the last 18 years Jude has been continuously involved in teaching within the social work arena and worked in academia for the last 11 years. Prior to this, Jude worked a Senior Social worker in Adult Services teams in both London and Cardiff.

Mandy Cowden is a Professional Advisor within the Workforce Development Team at the Social Care Council (Northern Ireland). She has over 30 years of experience of social work across sectors and has worked at the Social Care Council for 5 years. Mandy has responsibility for supporting and monitoring career long Post Registration Training and Learning (PRTL) for social workers and social care practitioners and also oversees the implementation and quality assurance of the Assessed Year in Employment (AYE) for newly qualified social workers.

Dr Barry Fearnley is a Practice Educator and Associate Lecturer – Placement Tutor, with a professional background in children and families social work. During his career, he has held a range of roles in higher education, including Senior Lecturer, Head of Partnerships for Social Work and Social Care, and Placement Lead. Dr Fearnley has extensive experience supporting social work students across a wide variety of practice settings, including children and families services, adult services including mental health, schools, and the voluntary sector. He remains committed to developing high-quality learning opportunities that bridge academic theory and professional practice.

Dr Scott Grant is a social worker and a senior lecturer in social work based at the University of the West of Scotland. Scott has conducted research on NQSW experiences of social work education, as well co-leading a five-year longitudinal student of NQSW experiences of professional employment in Scotland. Scott has a background in adult and justice social work.

Catherine Maguire is Co-Director of Regulation and Standards (interim) at the Northern Ireland Social Care Council. She has extensive experience as a social worker in the justice sector and in the delivery, management and regulation of social work education and practice. Her current responsibilities include workforce regulation and standards along with regulation of social work education and training at qualifying and post-qualifying levels.

Dr Louise Oliver is a senior lecturer within the social work team. She teaches on both the qualifying and post-qualifying social work programmes. She is also a qualified social worker who has predominantly worked in children's and families within local authorities. Her interests are in Violence Against Women and Girls, family violence and abuse, particularly Domestic Abuse, Intimate Partner Violence, Child-to-Parent

Violence and Abuse, familial problematic communication, with a focus upon secrets and secrecy. As well as social work practice education, with a focus upon innovative pedagogical teaching tools and also critical reflection.

Richard Williams, formerly Senior Lecturer in Social Work, Bournemouth University.

Acknowledgements

Now in its fourth edition, it has been a real privilege to write and edit this book. We are extremely grateful to our editors, contributors and writers to the previous three editions whose groundwork has laid the foundations for an ever-changing text that will need to be reinforced, altered and updated as time exacts and demands important changes. Our extensive thanks are due to the contributors to this new edition. Alongside those acknowledged above, are those who helped with ideas, thoughts and opinions that helped to liven the text with an immediacy from practice. These include Kayleigh Chapman, Emma Crawford, Marianne Jackson, Marion Meyer, and Katrina Swain and many others. From Sage we are grateful to Kate Keers who started the journey towards the fourth edition and most ably continued and supported by Sahar Jamfar and Susannah Trefgarne. As editors, we are thankful and honoured to continue to take this project forward and hope, humbly, that we are helping the next generation of social workers.

Chapter 1

'Give everyman thy ear, but few thy voice'

*Jonathan Parker, Ivan Gray, Andrew Morris &
Sally Lee*

Introduction

In Shakespeare's play *Hamlet*, Polonius offers sage advice to his son Laertes before the latter sets off on a journey to France. At one and the same time Polonius is not only suggesting that it is important to listen and hear the words of others without offering quick judgement but also advises Laertes to reflect, take time and not to act impulsively. For social workers at the beginning their careers, this is wise advice. It is crucial that accepted givens are questioned and that you allow yourself to develop a reflective approach that immerses you in the worlds of those you are working with and not to seek to impose what you think is right on to the situations in which you find yourself. Of course, there are limits to this when there is an immediate need for support, safeguarding and so on, but in these contexts, you will be working with other more experienced social workers to whom you should also 'give... thy ear'. The speech is a call for endurance and quiet tenacity in respect of difficult and messy human worlds, which in social work practice are often replete with conflict at relational, organisational and sometimes national levels. It resonates well with social work practice. Post-Brexit, these messy global problems have extended internationally, especially in respect of education (Parker, 2025). So, social workers must gird themselves to practise alongside those they work with in their daily lives. As newly qualified and supported social workers it is hoped you will be protected from the worst and most conflictual aspects of the job. However, it is important to be aware of the contested environment you are entering. Indeed, you are more than likely to have seen, heard and experienced some of this during your qualifying education especially when undertaking practice education or placements. It is important to acknowledge the unalloyed realities of social work. Social workers stand between the recognised and established social order, whether one agrees with it or otherwise, and those people who for various reasons fall outside of its protection, recognition and acceptance. Seeing this with open eyes and developing a listening approach takes time and courage.

In earlier editions of this book, we called upon new entrants to social work to 'mind the gap', drawing on the safety advice to passengers on the London underground. This suggested there was a potential gap between one's education and training and the exigencies of real-world and real-time practice. This, of course, remains the case, but it is important to not only note the things we don't yet know but to accept

Polonius's advice to listen, reflect and internalise what is happening before we rush in to act. We hope this book goes some way to assisting in that development and transition from student to practitioner.

This chapter introduces the concept of the Newly Qualified Social Worker (NQSW), and briefly introduces the Assessed and Supported Year in Employment (ASYE) and Assessed Year in Employment (AYE). We recognise the differences across the four countries of the UK in their approaches to this foundational time in every social worker's career (see Chapter 2 for a fuller discussion). At the outset to the chapter, we will introduce ourselves as authors and editors, reflecting on what brought us into social work, practice and education, and some of the stumbles we took or revelations we experienced on our journeys towards enhancing our practice. In the complex, challenging arena of your newly qualified status it is important that we discuss some of the issues we faced and some of those core issues, conflicts and complexities that still remain and no doubt you will face throughout your career. Social work itself may have changed since we qualified, and the contexts of practice have evolved, but many of the things we needed to learn and cope with remain. Subsequently, we will introduce very briefly the standards and requirements expected of you in each country in your first year(s) as a qualified practitioner and indicate how this book can help point you to ways in which you might complete portfolio work or other requirements demanded of you in your respective countries. This will allow us to present you with the rationale underpinning the book, what we are covering and who we have asked to contribute to it. Prior to this, it will be useful to complete the following activity that will help you acknowledge your hopes and fears in becoming a social worker.

ACTIVITY 1.1

Naming your fears and anxieties

We all have fears and anxieties alongside hopes and dreams in our lives. Take a piece of paper, tablet or create a computer file and spend a few moments jotting down three to five core fears and anxieties you have in making the transition from student to NQSW. Alongside these, note down three to five hopes or aspirations you have for being a social worker.

Keep these alongside you, adding reflections and notes as you move through this book and, indeed, through the process of developing as a social worker. You may wish to construct a table with the following headings:

- Hopes and aspirations, with reflections and actions
- Fears and anxieties, with reflections and actions

'We know what we are, but know not what we may be'

Ophelia's statement to Claudius in *Hamlet* indicates her uncertainty about the future, suggesting flux and change as we move through our lives. As newly qualified social workers we may know 'what we are', perhaps referring to what our jobs are called such as 'social worker', 'case worker', as members of the social work profession, however that contested term might be defined (see Chapter 10), and we may know what it is to which we aspire, but we do not yet know how the journey will proceed. This is something that applies to us all, especially in the ever-changing social work world. We don't always know how things will turn out and, in this section, we introduce ourselves as authors, reflecting on our own complex journeys as social workers and the warps and wefts, twists and turns within these journeys.

Who are we?

When I (Jonathan Parker) qualified as a social worker I took a Certificate of Qualification in Social Work, a CQSW, alongside a master's degree. The CQSW was introduced in the 1970s following changes within local authorities and lasted until it was replaced by the Diploma in Social Work in 1991, which itself was replaced in 2003 by the degree level route to qualification. In the days in which I studied, students were expected to gain and develop their competence and confidence to practise through the assessed placements so that on day one of starting work you were assumed to be able to work in the same way as someone qualified for years. So, starting my first post as a hospital social worker I was given responsibility for a Cardio-thoracic unit, a general surgical ward and an appallingly named 'Department for Medical Elderly', or an older persons' ward. I had very little induction or explanation about what my responsibilities were and had to learn quickly that attending ward rounds, liaising with the consultants, who would often assume they could instruct me on work to be done, and ensuring I had good relations with the nursing teams who would request my involvement as appropriate, was fundamental to the role. When I moved jobs to a busy neighbourhood 'patch team' (really, child protection for the qualified social workers and everything else for social work assistants [unqualified social workers in the days before registration became mandatory] and domiciliary officers) six months later, I was given a desk with a pile of case files on it and told to get on with it. There was training in these roles but nothing mandatory and any joint initiatives where we would train with the police for joint interviewing were met with mutual suspicion and not entirely productive. This 'baptism of fire' encouraged me to offer more active support and supervision to any new employees starting with the team and for students as I began to take them on placements. The term 'baptism of fire' was something we returned to in our earlier research concerning the experiences of new social workers (see Bates et al., 2010). When I made my next move into a specialist multi-agency team for people with dementia, my role became split between practice, training and research. From this, providing education, training and support became something I was especially keen to develop. This imperative took firm hold as I moved into academia, leading a university-based placement unit and offering continued professional education and development.

I (Ivan Gray) am from a working-class family as well as one with a long history of rural servitude and so I am very conscious that I am the first of my family to have the privilege of a university education and a professional career. I am very much a child of the

Welfare State, aware of the opportunities it has given me and am now committed to extending its benefits to others. My experiences have led me to being an active social-ist strongly influenced by theories of alienation and understanding modern industrial society as alienating us from our true selves, from others, from our work and from the products and outcomes of our work. Social work, on the other hand, has always been for me self-actualising and liberating for both practitioner and those we work with. In trying to empower others, social workers also liberate themselves. Personal and self-development go hand in hand with the development of others and both demand social and political awareness and action.

I have enjoyed a wide-ranging social work career. I began as a hospital almoner with a traditional psycho-dynamic approach that assisted me in responding to those suffering grief and loss. Then in contrast to this in the Welsh valleys I worked as a welfare rights worker in a department where community work and community devel-opment were seen as the foundation of social work practice.

Later, when working in juvenile justice, I developed a foundation in court work and was able to develop my groupwork skills. I then worked with families in the com-munity as a generic social worker and then as a community-based psychiatric social worker where I was able to develop my individual and group therapeutic interven-tions in day care and hospital settings.

Promoted to Deputy Area Manager, I had significant responsibility for generic services and their co-ordination in an inner city. This included children's services encompass-ing child protection conferencing and I was one of the first managers to make use of risk management techniques and their application to child sexual abuse. I was also one of the few managers lucky enough to lead a community development team.

As my practice developed, I taught groupwork to residential and day care workers and as a practice teacher played a central role in leading and developing national policy that introduced training programmes for practice teachers. I developed and ran the first practice teacher courses in the country. In a joint university and local authority post I led a student unit that worked as a team in an area office as well as teaching on a social work programme. This very broad practice base and man-agement experience allowed me later in my career to specialise as a university tutor, mentor, lecturer, and programme leader, developing leadership and management courses across health and social care services.

As a management development specialist, the social and political beliefs that shaped my social work practice shaped my approach to developing leaders. My emphasis has always been on building enabling, participative and developmental leadership that respects pro-fessional independence and its importance to service quality. So, I have long struggled with 'managerialist' approaches that use practice standards, performance measures and practice protocols to manage professional practice. In my experience it is an approach to managing service quality that undermines professional discretion and disempowers the social work teams on whom service quality and any improvement depends.

The values and belief systems that are the beating heart of social work are in my view resilient and will weather the current crisis in our services. Whatever form they take in modernity and the seeming chaos that is replacing it, they are age old and will persist as long as human society persists. They are fundamentally a celebration of a caring community where everyone matters and has equal place and the vulnerable, disadvantaged and the traumatised are protected and nurtured to achieve their potential.

My Social Work Journey (Andrew Morris). School never felt like the right fit for me. I wasn't in any of the higher sets, and I left with a handful of underwhelming GCSEs. Without a clear direction, I drifted between jobs that didn't bring me much satisfaction. Deep down, I knew I wanted to do something meaningful, but I had no idea what that might be or how to make it happen.

Then one evening, I had a conversation that changed everything. I got chatting with a friend's sister – a bubbly, confident Children & Families social worker. As she described her role, I was struck by how fascinating and impactful her work sounded. In that moment, I decided I wanted to follow her path and do the same.

I returned to education, enrolling in a Foundation in Welfare Studies course. This experience was the most inspiring thing that had happened to me so far in my life. I loved every minute of it, and it ignited my passion for learning like a match to a bonfire. From there, I completed an Access Course, but university wasn't financially viable at the time. Instead, I pursued counselling training, qualified as a counsellor. I volunteered with a counselling charity for two years before finally taking the plunge and joining Bournemouth University to study for a BA in Social Work.

College had been invigorating, but university was even better. After graduating in 2007, I began my social work career with the Older Persons' Mental Health Team, where I was part of a project supporting individuals living with dementia. About two and a half years later, when the project came to an end, I transitioned to the Adults with Learning Disabilities Team. There, I qualified as both a Best Interests Assessor and a Practice Educator. This was my absolute favourite role in social work in my social work career. My enthusiasm for learning fuelled my passion for supporting and helping students on placement.

When my local authority set up a dedicated Deprivation of Liberty Safeguards (DoLS) Team, I was invited to join as the first Best Interests Assessor in the local authority. I worked there for over seven years, during which time I qualified as an Approved Mental Health Professional (AMHP) and even managed the team for a while. Alongside my practice, I pursued an MA in Advanced Mental Health Practice and qualified as a tutor, teaching creative writing and support work through the local adult learning service.

Though I loved social work, my drive to learn and share knowledge remained strong. So, when an opportunity arose to become a Lecturer in Social Work at Bournemouth University, I decided to make the leap from full-time practice to academia. I've been a lecturer ever since, combining my passion for social work and education, and loving every moment of it.

I (Sally Lee) always enjoy hearing from practitioners about their journey into social work as each path is unique but usually initiated by the individual's sense of compassion and their fundamental drive to embark on a career that is meaningful for themselves and the people with whom they work. This is true for me as, for as long as I can remember, I have been driven by the desire for social inclusivity.

I qualified in 1993 and started my professional career in an acute hospital social work team. It was a great place to develop skills of interprofessional working and learn an appreciation of the complex web of services which make up the UK's system of welfare. It was a dynamic environment to hone my embryonic practice, but it was also challenging to work in an environment that was dominated by the medical model and where the drive was to discharge people without always taking account of their circumstances. It was a place where I truly gained pride in being a member of a profession that cares for people's wellbeing in the round – for their physical, emotional, social, economic and other forms of health.

I moved to community-based social work in 1999 and until 2016 undertook a variety of social work roles with adults. Over the course of my practice career I have worked with older adults, many of whom were living with dementia, people at the end of their lives, adults with learning disabilities, adults living with mental ill-health and adults with physical disabilities. Some roles I chose, and some came to me through organisational restructuring, which is a common experience for social workers and something to be aware of. Key learning I gained is that no matter the focus or title of the team you are working with, be it mental health, older people or learning disability, social workers require wide ranging knowledge and skills. People do not fit neatly into the categories assigned by organisational structure, meaning that, for example, adults with learning disabilities may also live with poverty, substance dependency, parenting difficulties, mental health concerns, domestic abuse or any other concern. This means that practitioners need to be constantly alert and attentive, engaging with people to enhance their wellbeing in ways that are individually meaningful.

I have always approached my work with adults, their families and communities with a sense of curiosity and anticipation of working in partnership. Going back to my own drive for inclusiveness I have enjoyed the challenge posed by practice that social workers must operate in ways that may sometimes appear to be contradictory – for example, they must protect people whilst also promoting autonomous decision making; they must demonstrate care but also exercise their legal duties – successfully co-navigating a pathway through ethical dilemmas with individuals or managing risk in supporting them to exercise their rights is what I have loved in practice and found to be a privilege.

I was very fortunate to be able to undertake a part-time Professional Doctorate starting in 2010. My research was prompted by a practice dilemma around disability, sex and intimacy and in 2016 I moved into education. I now teach students on social work qualifying programmes and love the mutuality of learning – I know it is a cliché, but it is true, we never stop learning, and it really is a privilege to be in a position to learn.

ACTIVITY 1.2

Reasons for becoming a social worker

As you can see from our stories above, there are many personal, professional and political reasons for us entering social work. These underlying drivers often interlink and, at times, some take precedence over others. It is worth reflecting on your own journey so far. You will already have come a long way. So, write down the key reasons and drives for you wanting to become a social worker. Identify where these have changed and developed and think how these reasons seem to you now as a new social worker. This is something to reflect upon and adapt throughout your career.

What's in a name?

Since the 2010s, throughout the UK, there has been a concerted effort to ensure newly qualified social workers moving into their first positions are supported and continue to learn and develop as part of a career framework. Of course, this drive to support people relied on assumptions that the majority of social workers were employed in local authority or allied positions. By 2012, the focus on the newly qualified framework had changed and in the current four UK administrations we have a NQSW supported year in Scotland, in Northern Ireland we have an Assessed Year in Employment, in Wales we have a consolidation programme and in England we have an Assessed and Supported Year in Employment.

Definitions are, of course, important, but as Juliet opines to Romeo, names may differ to describe the same or similar things – *'What's in a name? That which we call a rose By any other name would smell as sweet'*. Much of what we say in respect of newly qualified practitioners in one of the UK administrations can transfer to the others, and where they do not do so exactly, our reflections offer the potential for deeper and wider learning. This transferability of learning and critical reflection on what we are doing is important and underpins the development of lifelong or continuing learning that is shared across the devolved professions. Whilst Chapter 2 has more detailed descriptions of the support offered in each of the four countries, we offer a brief summary here by way of introduction recognising the importance of each country's approach.

The supported year in Scotland seeks to build the foundations of continuing professional learning across set requirements for newly qualified social workers. The Scottish Social Services Council website provides information and guidance to guide people into social work (www.nqsw.sssc.uk.com/home/information-for-nqsw/#InformationforNQSWs). The focus in the website concerns registration and transition across the liminal state from student to social worker and how to use effective supervision to strengthen this development. There are eight areas of continuing professional learning to reflect on and develop over time comprising:

- Ethics, values and rights-based practice

- Communication, engagement and relationship-based professional practice

- Critical thinking, professional judgement and decision making

- Promoting wellbeing, support and protection

- Working with complexity in unpredictable and ambiguous contexts

- Use of knowledge, research and evidence in practice

- Self-awareness and reflexivity

- Professional leadership

There is recognition of different routes through the year with guidance, reflective activities and questions being developed to support the journey.

In Wales, the programme reflects a consolidation of learning, with the emphasis clearly on continued learning as social workers glide into practice and continue their development. Again, the responsible social care council, Gofal Cymdeithasol Cymru/ Social Care Wales (2018), has published its guidance and expectations for the consolidation programme as a beginning part of the continuing professional education and learning (CPEL) required for social workers in Wales. There are three core elements to the programme:

- Applying analysis in assessment to inform interventions

- Working collaboratively with people in need of care and support, their carers, other professionals

- Intervention and application of professional judgement in increasingly complex situations

Under each of these broad learning areas sit a number of more detailed learning outcomes which include developing knowledge and understanding of legislation, theory, partnership working, safeguarding, and risk; value-based approaches embedded in relationship-based working; interpersonal, administrative and technical skills; developing critically reflective approaches to practice; and managing one's self and one's professional development as a newly qualified practitioner.

The Northern Ireland Social Care Council published its revised guidance for NQSWs in 2021. Alongside registration, NQSWs in Northern Ireland must be employed 'in an agency that can provide practice that will offer consolidation and development in the six key social work roles/National Occupational Standards for Social Work 2011 ... and support for the AYE' ((Northern Ireland Social Care Council, 2021, 2.1.1). Evidence of competence in six key social work roles is required and, focusing on safeguarding and protection, must include:

- An assessment, including the assessment of harm or abuse and a related work plan

- A risk assessment and management plan

- The application and evaluation of a minimum of two methods and/or models of social work intervention to promote change

The six core social work roles are taken from the 2011 National Occupational Standards and comprise the following:

- Maintain professional accountability

- Practise professional social work

- Promote engagement and participation
- Assess needs, risks and circumstances
- Plan for person centred outcomes
- Take actions to achieve change

In England, the Assessed and Supported Year in Employment programme for NQSWs is offered by Skills for Care on behalf of the regulator, Social Work England, although NQSWs can take the programme during their first four years post-qualification. The programme again focuses on developing a continued approach to professional learning. Social workers undertaking it are assessed against either the Child and Family Post-Qualifying Standards (Department for Education, 2018) or the Adult Services Post Qualifying Standards (Department of Health, 2015) depending on area of practice. Social workers practising in children and families work should be able to demonstrate knowledge and skills in:

- Relationships and effective direct work
- Communication
- Child development
- Adult mental health, substance misuse, domestic abuse, physical ill health and disability
- Abuse and neglect of children
- Child and family assessment
- Analysis, decision-making, planning and review
- The law and the family and youth justice systems
- The role of supervision
- Organisational context

Adult social workers must demonstrate a wide range of assessment, planning, support and relationship-building skills, knowledge of wellbeing and the influence of intra/interpersonal, community and structural factors on individual wellbeing, risk management and safeguarding. There also remains a focus on effective assessment and outcome-based planning, direct work with people, supervision and critical reflection and analysis, understanding the organisational context of practice and the development of professional ethics and leadership.

The Professional Capabilities Framework (PCF) has been valued by many social workers as they move through the different stages of their careers. Although the PCF (BASW, 2018) only relates to English social work, its nine domains transect many of the requirements, standards and expectations delineated for NQSWs across the four countries. It could be useful to keep in mind those domains – professionalism; values and ethics; diversity and equality; rights, justice and economic wellbeing; knowledge; critical reflection and analysis; skills and interventions; contexts and organisations; professional leadership – as you work through your developing learning and through this book.

When you are completing your country-specific learning and development as a NQSW there are often assessment tasks and requirements to complete. The collection and presentation of evidence differs across the different care councils but the development of a portfolio of evidence represents a useful tool for critical and reflective practice and to maintain a picture of the journey travelled. Where used in a reflexive way it can help you continue to build your own understanding of your strengths and needs as a practitioner and to identify learning for the future. It will help you dig deep into the experiences you have had, how you have reacted to them and felt about them and what you now need to do to embed the learning positively within your own practice. Consider the following activity to explore your own country approach to newly qualified social workers.

ACTIVITY 1.3

Things I need to do and who can help me

Identify your own country requirements for the assessed year or consolidation programme. Make a note of the things you identify that you need to learn over the forthcoming year. Ask yourself and note down the opportunities that are available to you and identify potentially supportive people to assist you as move through the year.

Comment

These notes can be used to form a beginning action plan once you are ready to start. If you develop a table, you can keep a tally of your experiences and what you have learned and completed. You should include the following headings in your learning plan:

- *What do I need to learn or complete?*
- *What learning opportunities are available?*
- *Who can support me in this?*
- *What have I achieved?*

'This above all; to thine own self be true'

Throughout your qualifying social work course, you will have confronted stories of the alleged 'failures' of social workers and their organisations, poor practices, and the opprobrium of those seeking to lay the blame for public ills and private tragedies on social work and social workers so as to deflect attention from more pressing structural problems, discrimination and oppression. The unpleasant political arena in which social work takes place can exert a significant impact on individual social workers and this has been recognised for many years (Pearson, 1973; Parker, 2024). No doubt, you will have been versed in developing protective armour, critiqued the slippery concept of resilience and maybe faced that thorny question of personal or corporate responsibility for your own wellbeing, good practice and development. In this book, we are firmly of the opinion that blaming social workers for societal ills is a political artifice deliberately and callously employed to deflect blame from party political unpopularity or 'failure' (Parker, 2024). This is not to say that social workers do not make mistakes and sometimes monumental and life-changing ones. There are also some 'bad apples' in the barrel given that social work is a human occupation. However, to use the blame-card as the first stop when tragedy occurs helps no-one but simply creates an atmosphere of fear where solace is found in completing the systems and procedural work rather than focusing on the interpersonal, community and social work that is at the core of our profession. These worries are real, and it is important to confront them and develop strategies to cope at this early stage in your career.

Polonius's advice to his son Laertes, quoted at the outset to this chapter, concerned his conduct at university. Now you have moved from university to qualified professional practice the centrality of integrity, being true to yourself, and to the values of social work are no less important. Also, standing by the work that you do, the decisions you make and knowing how they fit within that ethical frame is something to continually develop through reflection on your practice experiences.

ACTIVITY 1.4

Exploring your values

Think back to Activity 1.2 concerning the reasons you wanted to become a social worker. Ask yourself what these say about your personal values and those of social work itself. Write down how these two sets of values overlap and where they might be in a degree of tension. Think about how this may affect your practice and identify ways you might deal with this whilst remaining true to yourself. After each chapter in this book, refer back to this activity.

Comment

Keeping a reflective diary is perhaps something you have been encouraged to do on placement or when completing an extended piece of academic work such as a dissertation. It is also something that is encouraged within qualitative research, intending to make sense of what is observed and experienced. It can be useful to incorporate the keeping of a reflective diary as a new social worker. It will help you identify development and outstanding learning needs.

'Suit the action to the word. The word to the action.'

We are writing this book because through our experiences and knowledge we have become passionate about encouraging the continued development and learning of, and support for, people as they move into one of the most important jobs in modern societies, social work. We want to address some of the mistakes we have made, experienced and have witnessed and to move to a new and brighter future. Throughout the present chapter we have emphasised the centrality of staying true to yourself and practising accordingly. This, of course, demands that we know ourselves and are able to deal with some of the complexities and discomfort that can arise when we do come to know ourselves, what we think and how we act in the world. Where we find ourselves unable to deal with these things we at least know that we should ask others and listen to their advice. One of the key ways of ensuring this is, as we have mentioned previously, to foster a critical self-reflection that is also compassionate to you as a fallible and learning human being. If you find yourself not agreeing with something that seems to be accepted by colleagues and others, allow yourself to ask why and not to either diminish yourself or to castigate the other. It is easy in the current socio-political situation we find ourselves in to draw hard and fast rules about things or erect clear unbending boundaries. Human realities are more complex than that and it is incumbent on us to approach the world around us with acceptance and understanding where possible. It is also appropriate to be angry and to seek change when we see clear injustices. In all our human-to-human interactions we need to ask ourselves what, why, and how questions to ensure we reflect honestly and remain true to ourselves.

Summary

In this chapter, we have introduced ourselves, the authors, as social workers and educators. We have done so as a means of 'humanising' the process of becoming a social worker. We all start from different perspectives and experiences, and it is important to recognise these and to accept there will be differences and even disagreements in the ways in which we approach our roles and our learning for them.

This introduction to ourselves has allowed us to present, briefly, the support and assessment you will experience in each of the four countries of the UK. We have offered our advice and suggestions distilled from many years' experience for each of us and hope you will find this book useful and supportive as you make that important transition from student to qualified social worker.

Further reading

BASW. (2018). *Student PCF level descriptors for pre-qualifying levels and ASYE*. British Association of Social Workers. www.basw.co.uk/resources/student-pcf-level-descriptors-pre-qualifying-levels-and-asye

Whilst a key element of social work in England, the domains identified within the PCF are useful for all four countries in the UK and often reflect universal requirements.

The following recommendations are specific to each country administration:

Department for Education. (2018). *Post-qualifying standard: Knowledge and skills statement for child and family practitioners*. Department for Education.

Department of Health. (2015). *Knowledge and skills statement for social workers in adult services*. Department of Health.

Gofal Cymdeithasol Cymru / Social Care Wales. (2018). *Continuing professional education and learning: A framework for social workers in Wales – Requirements for the consolidation programme for newly qualified social workers*. Social Care Wales.

Scottish Social Services Council. (2019). *Standards in social work education in Scotland*. https://learn.sssc.uk.com/siswe/siswe.html

Social Care Wales. (2023). *Consolidation programme for newly qualified social workers – Your questions answered*. https://socialcare.wales/cms_assets/file-uploads/Consolidation-programme-for-newly-qualified.pdf

Northern Ireland Social Care Council. (2021). *The assessed year in employment (AYE) for newly qualified social workers in NI*. Northern Ireland Social Care Council.

Northern Ireland Social Care Council. (2022a). *The assessed year in employment for newly qualified social workers in Northern Ireland*. https://learningzone.niscc.info/social-worker-assessed-year-in-employment-aye/

Northern Ireland Social Care Council. (2022b). *(Registration) Rules*. Northern Ireland Social Care Council. https://niscc.info/app/uploads/2020/09/20250310_Registration-Rules-2025_Final_Signed_CC.pdf

Chapter 2

Newly Qualified Social Workers around the UK

Scott Grant, Jude Badmington-Fowler, Mandy Cowden, Catherine Maguire and Jonathan Parker

Introduction

The central focus of this book relates to England and the Assessed and Supported Year in Employment (ASYE) in that country. However, it is crucial to acknowledge and to learn from the other three countries and their experiences in supporting newly qualified social workers. This chapter presents background information on social work and support for new practitioners in Scotland, Wales and Northern Ireland. The programmes described are continually revised and updated, just as they are in England, and so things may change. Having said that, what we can recognise is the support that is provided is embedded within the professional development frameworks for each country and supported by the Scottish, Welsh, and Northern Ireland social care councils. The necessity of supervision and critical reflection informs each of these programmes and research and evaluation is fundamental to each programme.

The NQSW supported year in Scotland

Let's first provide a brief historical introduction to the development of training and support for NQSWs in Scotland. Until recently, Scotland had no recognised scheme to support NQSWs in the first year of their employment. Previous arrangements required NQSWs to evidence 144 hours of learning and training by way of a written submission (a record of achievement known colloquially as a 'PRTL' – post-registration training and learning). At the time of writing, Scotland is currently rolling out a new and mandatory *NQSW Supported Year*. This took effect at the start of October 2024 and all NQSWs are now expected to meet the new requirements set by the Scottish Social Services Council (the professional regulator in Scotland).

At the last count, Scotland had 6,427 registered social workers employed across 32 local authority areas (Scottish Social Services Council, 2024a). There are approximately 1,700 registered social work students studying at different levels across nine Scottish universities. Approximately 500 social work students graduate each year in Scotland.

Support for NQSWs

Very little was known about how NQSWs were supported in Scotland until a study was commissioned in 2014 by the Scottish Social Service Council (SSSC). This became the first national study of its kind in Scotland since Marsh and Triseliotis included Scotland as part of a wider UK study into 'readiness' of social workers and probation officers in 1996. The authors of the new study in 2014 found that levels and quality of support for NQSWs in this critical phase were at times poor and often inconsistent across Scotland (see Grant et al., 2017a). The authors suggested that further work was required to understand the experiences of NQSWs beyond the snapshot they offered here – particularly what happens to NQSWs as they develop beyond this initial phase. Prompted by this and a wider review of social work education at the time, the SSSC commissioned a further study in 2016 to provide a longer and deeper view of NQSW experiences across Scotland. Until this point, no longitudinal data existed in Scotland. The SSSC funded a five-year project led by a larger team of researchers, including authors from the 2014 study. Initial findings from this longitudinal study confirmed that NQSWs continued to receive inconsistent experiences of support in their first year (Grant et al., 2017b). An emerging sense of complexity, nuance and contingency in the experiences of NQSWs led to suggestions from the authors for a more consistent, responsive and tailored approach to how we support NQSWs moving forward.

Alongside a longitudinal study on NQSWs, the SSSC also commissioned a range of work in 2016 to complement a review of social work education and a new initiative to prepare a set of 'standards' for NQSWs in practice, including an options appraisal for implementing a probationary year in Scotland (Gillies, 2016). A major Scottish Government report at the time, *Social Services in Scotland: a Shared Vision and Strategy 2015-2020* (Scottish Government, 2015), recognised the importance of consistent support and development opportunities for all staff across the country, but specifically noted that NQSWs required a 'more structured system of support in their first year of practice similar to other professions' (p17). The 'options appraisal' consulted employers, academics, NQSWs and students, and considered existing equivalent arrangements in England, Northern Ireland and Wales. It presented a range of possibilities for Scotland and led to pilot testing of different models across three sites from November 2018 to December 2019. Each site agreed to provide NQSWs with structured supervision, protected learning time, access to learning opportunities and a restricted caseload. Whilst supported by most, major concerns were flagged in a separate survey of stakeholder perspectives on introducing a probationary year. These included apprehension of introducing additional assessment at the post-qualifying stage, as well as funding and resource implications of imposing a scheme across organisations already hamstrung by existing budgets (Scottish Government, 2018). Nevertheless, a separate evaluation of test sites found that a staged and supported approach was seen to be better than current arrangements for inducting NQSWs into the workforce; although concerns about resourcing, particularly the amount of time required to complete paperwork, emerged here too (Gordon et al., 2020). The evaluation found little appetite for any type of formal 'assessment', preferring instead a model and process of 'verification' against agreed standards.

NQSW core learning elements

In 2016, the Scottish Social Services Council commissioned work on the development of a benchmark standard for NQSWs (Daniel et al., 2016). This work helped to shape current NQSW *Core Learning Elements*, also informed by Codes of Practice (SSSC, 2016), Standards in Social Work Education in Scotland (SSSC, 2019), longitudinal research on NQSWs (see: Grant et al., 2022), and new insights and understanding around the nature and importance of workplace learning for social workers (see: Ferguson, 2022a; 2022b). There are currently eight *Core Learning Elements* for Scottish NQSWs:

1. Ethics, values and rights-based practice

2. Communication, engagement and relationship-based practice

3. Critical thinking, professional judgement and decision making

4. Promoting wellbeing, support and protection

5. Working with complexity in unpredictable and ambiguous contexts

6. Use of knowledge, research and evidence in practice

7. Self-awareness and reflexivity

8. Professional leadership

NQSWs in the new Supported Year are required to evidence knowledge, understanding and competence across all 'learning elements', but there is clear acknowledgement that newly qualified staff are situated within a wide range of settings, and that attempts to provide evidence of meeting each 'element' should be considered holistically and within the organisational context of their own particular setting (SSSC, 2024b).

The NQSW supported year

The agreed approach for the Supported Year puts responsibility on supervisors and employers to evaluate progression of each participant against 'core learning elements' at three points: within the first six weeks; at six months; and finally at 12 months. A core mechanism for reviewing progress and capturing evidence will be the provision of structured professional development discussions between NQSWs and supervisors, in addition to regular supervision sessions. The process is designed to capture an 'incremental consolidation' of knowledge, skills, values, and experience mapped to core learning elements. The nature of feedback should be formative, developmental, and strengths based. NQSWs must meet all mandatory learning activities to meet registration requirements. Progress here is validated and endorsed by employers.

Before the point of qualification, social work students in the final stage of their education should produce an Individual Learning Plan (ILP). This document is designed to capture learning needs relating to areas of knowledge, skills and experience that NQSWs are hoping to enhance within their first year of qualification. At the time of writing, most universities in Scotland have either implemented or are planning to implement a transitions curriculum in the final year of undergraduate and postgraduate education where students are encouraged to reflect on their learning, progress and development of professional identity as a NQSW. These aspects should also be captured in the student's ILP before they leave university.

The ILP will be presented to employers who will consider the learning needs and areas for development identified by each NQSW. Employers will work with each NQSW to create an Individual Development Plan (IDP) to help address current learning needs and plan for future development. Employers should provide formal induction, professional development planning, consistent and accessible support, professional supervision, and continuous professional learning opportunities to enable NQSWs to meet their registration requirements and make progress against core learning elements (SSSC, 2024c). NQSWs will maintain a record of progress and evidence on a Continuous Professional Learning (CPL) review template (the IDP will be incorporated here). It will be the responsibility of employers and supervisors to validate and endorse the evidence presented by NQSWs, and it will be the responsibility of the individual NQSW to maintain a record of learning and upload required documents when prompted (by the SCCC) at the end of the Supported Year. A summary of key tasks for NQSWs, employers and supervisors is provided in Table 2.1 below (adapted from NQSW Supported Year Overview and Guidance SSSC, 2024c: 27):

Table 2.1   Supported Year – summary of key tasks and responsibilities

Responsibility	Task	Timescale
NQSW	Confirm SSSC registration details	On starting role
Supervisor/employer	Identify peer support and/or mentor	Before/on starting role
Supervisor	Set timeline and dates for initial, mid and end of year professional development reviews	On starting role
Supervisor/NQSW	Orientation into approach	As part of initial induction – within first 4 weeks
Supervisor	Supervision sessions arranged	No less than 4-weekly
NQSW	Maintain a record and evidence of mandatory CPL activity	Ongoing
NQSW	Collect feedback from minimum five people	Ongoing
NQSW	NQSW share individual learning plan with supervisor	Share with supervisor a minimum of 5 working days in advance of initial review
NQSW	Complete self-assessment against core learning elements	Share with supervisor 5 working days in advance of reviews

(Continued)

Table 2.1 *(Continued)*

Responsibility	Task	Timescale
NQSW/supervisor	Initial professional development discussion and agreeing IDP	No later than 6 weeks from registering/starting post
NQSW/supervisor	Mid-year professional development discussion and IDP review	At 6 (9) months
NQSW/supervisor	End of year professional development discussion and IDP review	At 12 (18) months
NQSW/supervisor	Agree and sign initial and mid-year sections of NQSW Continuous Professional Learning review template	Within 10 working days of professional development discussion
Supervisor	Agree and sign copies of completed end of year section of NQSW Continuous Professional Learning review template Validation by supervisor	Within 10 working days of end of year professional development discussion
Employer	Endorsement by employer	Within 20 working days of receiving documentation
NQSW	Submission of required forms to the SSSC by NQSW	Within 2 months of end of Supported Year

NQSWs should submit the following documents to the SSSC at the end of their Supported Year in practice: (a) a completed and signed CPL review template, and (b) a completed and signed validation and endorsement form from their employer. The SSSC will then update the applicant's registration to demonstrate that requirements have been met. The SSSC will not review every submission, but a sample will be selected for assessment. The onus is therefore on employers to ensure that each NQSW has met core learning elements of the Supported Year at the final stage. Non-completion of the Supported Year will result in potential removal from the register as continuous professional learning requirements have not been met as a condition of registration.

The writer is not aware of any official plans to evaluate the NQSW Supported Year in Scotland at the moment; however, it is presumed that the SSSC or Scottish Government will consider October 2025 as the end of the first full year of national implementation. Evaluation and subsequent amendments are therefore likely after this point.

Supporting NQSWs in Wales

Since the establishment of the Welsh Assembly in 1999 under the Government of Wales Act 1998, following voting in favour of devolution in the 1997 referendum, social work practice and its context in Wales has significantly altered (Gwilym, 2023). Here we will outline how NQSW support has developed for the early period of post-qualifying practice. The Welsh Government adopted a distinct approach, often referred to as the 'Welsh Way', to policy making (Williams, 2011). As a result of devolution, newly qualified social workers practise within a very different legislative framework to their counterparts in England, Scotland and Northern Ireland, and work in accordance with, inter alia, the Social Services and Well-being (Wales) Act 2014 and the Well-being and Future Generations (Wales) Act 2015 (Gwilym, 2023). However, it is important to note that UK legislation still informs practice in areas such as mental health and mental capacity.

In addition, owing to devolution, the regulation of social workers along with social care workers, is different in Wales from other UK nations, with the profession being regulated by Social Care Wales (previously known as the Care Council for Wales), in accordance with the Regulation and Inspection of Social Care (Wales) Act 2016 (Thomas, 2023). This act provides the structure for the regulation and inspection of social care in Wales, and this included the regulation of education and training of social workers and students (Thomas, 2023). In Wales, social workers must practise in accordance with National Occupational Standards (SCW, 2011), which stipulate the agreed standards of competence required by the profession, and the Code of Professional Practice for Social Care Workers (SCW, 2017), which outlines the required regulatory standards for both social care and social workers. Furthermore, *The Social Worker Practice Guidance for Social Workers Registered with Social Care Wales* (Social Care Wales, 2019b) provides more in-depth guidance, based on the Code of Professional Practice for Social Care (Social Care Wales, 2017), for the registered profession and newly qualified social workers.

With the introduction of the Wales Act 2006, the Welsh Assembly were able to pass laws in Wales and a referendum in 2011 facilitated the enhancement of these powers (Gwilym, 2023). In 2007, *Fulfilled Lives, Supportive Communities: A Strategy for Social Services in Wales Over the Next Decade* was produced to modernise social services in Wales (Williams, 2011). In 2011, The Welsh Government published a White Paper, *Sustainable Social Services: A Framework for Action* (Welsh Assembly Government, 2011) which again demonstrated the drive for modernisation and indicated an evident commitment to enhancement of the professionalism of social workers, identified career pathways and post-qualifying requirements for registered social workers within Wales.

The development of support for newly qualified practitioners

Following the publishing of *Sustainable Social Services: A Framework for Action* (Welsh Assembly Government, 2011), in 2008, the Care Council for Wales (now known as Social Care Wales) developed the *Continuing Professional Education and Learning: A Framework for Social Workers in Wales* (CCW, 2012) (initially referred to as CPEL).

The CPEL framework stipulated the minimum requirements designed to enhance the standard of social work practice, identified the minimum arrangements for post-qualifying learning and training of social workers within Wales, as well providing social workers with support through their career progression (CCW, 2012). The framework commences with the Consolidation Programme designed for newly qualified social workers within their first period of registration as qualified practitioners and this usually takes place in the second and third year of practice, builds on and complements the first year in practice. In the same year, the Care Council for Wales introduced a guide entitled *Making the most of the first year in practice: A guide for newly qualified social workers* (CCW, 2008) which was designed to support NQSWs in their early years of practice and manage the transition from student to practitioner. Prior to this, there was no formal structured process that outlined the arrangements for continuing professional education and learning of social workers following their initial qualification and support for NQSWs; therefore, this marked a significant turning point in post-qualifying requirements and support for social workers in Wales.

Being mindful of the pertinence of a well-defined, supported and co-ordinated transition to the social work profession for newly qualified workers, and the essential components of an personalised induction, robust supervision and mentoring, and the opportunity for continuous professional development (CPD), CCW and CSSIW (Care and Social Services Inspectorate Wales) jointly developed guidance for social work employers entitled *The First Three Years in Practice – A framework for social workers' induction into qualified practice and continuing professional education and learning* (CCW, 2017). This brought all elements of the first three years in practice, viz, Induction to professional social work; Growing in competence and confidence; and Consolidation Programme and renewal of registration with the regulatory body, into one document. In 2019, this was updated and *The First Three Years in Practice – A framework for newly qualified social workers' induction and continuing professional development* (SCW, 2019a) is the current guidance for social work employers to produce their models of support during the first three years of a newly qualified social worker's practice. This, and preceding guidance, would make certain that the transition from graduate to a professional social work practitioner was efficient with the expectations being clearly stipulated. The development of this model is in line with the Code of Practice for Social Care Employers that stipulated that that employers should:

> *Provide a robust and accessible induction, learning and development opportunities to help workers do their jobs effectively and prepare for new and changing roles and responsibilities. (SCW, 2018a)*

The identified model contains four different sections:

- induction
- growing in competence and confidence
- Consolidation Programme
- renewing registration

(SCW, 2019a)

The first stage of the framework is the 'induction' phase, designed to take place within the first three months of practice, and stipulates what this stage must encompass and includes, inter alia: an introduction into the organisation as well as the local community, ensuring that the newly qualified worker is knowledgeable of the Welsh context (SCW, 2019a). The importance of the induction process in assisting individuals to settle into and become familiar with the organisation is well documented (Maclean and Lloyd, 2008; Gray, 2009; Maclean and Harrison, 2009; Williams and Rutter, 2010; Showell Nicholas and Kerr, 2015). At this stage, SCW recommend that each practitioner should possess a personal development plan that they completed during their degree that specifies their strengths, achievements, as well as their learning needs as a newly qualified social worker. If practitioners are successful in completing this stage, which is sometimes connected to the probationary year, they can progress to the new stage of their induction (SCW, 2019a).

The second phase of the framework is 'growing in competence and confidence' and generally takes place within the first year and an individual plan is developed, identifying the newly qualified worker's learning and development needs, considers the learning priorities of the organisation and indicates how support will be provided to facilitate reflection upon individual personal and professional development (SCW, 2019a). Consideration is given at this stage as to how the social worker will be supported to facilitate progression and when the social worker will be ready to undertake the Consolidation Programme, the third phase of the framework. SCW stipulate that the plans should include the following components:

1. *A learning and development programme*

    To facilitate the development of knowledge and skills, individualised learning opportunities, the undertaking of training associated with the requirements of the Consolidation Programme learning outcomes, along with specified training to meet priorities of the organisation, local and national, are recommended by SCW (SCW, 2019a). The importance of CPD in facilitating social workers to carry out their roles effectively and developing knowledge is recognised by Laming (2009), Munro (2011) and Megginson and Whitaker (2007) (cited in Halton et al., 2013).

2. *Supervision*

    The provision of supervision for newly qualified social workers, to facilitate the development of confidence and personal development, support wellbeing as well as the management of challenging work situations is recognised by SCW (2019a). Early discussions regarding the purpose of supervision, along with the length, frequency and recording of supervision is suggested by SCW (2019a). The responsibility of the employer to provide supervision is illustrated in the *Code of Professional Practice* section 7 (SCW, 2017) and the accountability of social workers to utilise supervision to facilitate development and reflection is stipulated in *The Social Worker: Practice Guidance for Social Workers Registered with Social Care Wales* (2019b), paragraph 7.3.

3. *Complexity of work*

    The plan also considers the complexity of work and expectations are set in relation to allocated work and the need to '… balance developmental opportunities with experience and levels of confidence.' (SCW, 2019a, p.6). By the end of the first year, assessment of the NQSWs' competence in managing complex work is considered by managers to identify readiness to progress to the Consolidation Programme.

4. *Mentoring*

    In addition to the support provided through supervision, SCW recognises the role mentoring can play in the first three years of practice (usually between 4–6 sessions) in enabling newly qualified workers to consider 'best practice', reflect and develop both confidence and resilience (SCW, 2019a). The importance of this 'multi-faceted activity' (Mullen, 2009, cited in Fletcher and Mullen, 2012, p.508) in the provision of adequate support, self-growth and the development of resilience and confidence is additionally recognised by Mullen (2009, cited in Fletcher and Mullen, 2012) and Fletcher (2007).

5. *Obtaining feedback from people receiving care and support*

    Feedback from observing visits with newly qualified social workers, along with feedback from individuals who use services, and their carers, are deemed to be invaluable methods of informing the development of newly qualified workers and this forms the final element of the individual plan (SCW, 2019a).

SCW (2019a) stipulates that the newly qualified social worker's plan needs to be reviewed every six-months to facilitate consideration of the practitioner's progress as well as providing the opportunity for the recognition of additional learning and developmental needs.

The consolidation programme

The third phase of the framework, the consolidation programme, builds on the first year in practice and is for all newly qualified social workers. This programme '... establishes a culture and expectation of career-long learning and development for the social work profession' (SCW, 2023). Newly qualified social workers are not able to commence the programme until their managers are satisfied that they have completed the previous two phases of the framework, as outlined above (SCW, 2019a). *The First Three Years in Practice: A framework for newly qualified social workers' induction and continuing professional development* (SCW, 2019a) stipulates that every social worker in Wales who qualified on, or after 1 April 2016, must undertake the mandatory Consolidation Programme, within the first three-year registration period, which facilitates the embedding of professional knowledge and skills and the increase in the complexity of work (SCW, 2019a). In addition, renewal of registration is dependent upon having successfully fulfilled the requirements of the programme. The document *Continuing Professional Education and Learning: A Framework for Social Workers in Wales. Requirements for the Consolidation Programme for Newly Qualified Social Workers* (SCW, 2018b) outlines the requirements of the Consolidation Programme and includes the Programme's Learning Outcomes to be met and how the learner can demonstrate the meeting of these.

The Programme's learning outcomes, which reflect the key roles identified in the National Occupational Standards for Social Work (2011) (SCW, 2011), incorporate the three significant areas identified by SCW that newly qualified workers need to consolidate their practice and develop further their knowledge and skills which are:

- Applying analysis in assessment to inform interventions

- Working collaboratively with service users, carers and other professionals

- Intervention and application of professional judgement in increasingly complex situations (SCW, 2018b).

In Wales, there are two Consolidation programmes approved by Social Care Wales, Porth Agored, in association with University of Wales, Trinity St David and Consortiwm Y De – South Wales Consolidation Programme delivered through a partnership between Cardiff Metropolitan University and the University of South Wales.

The fourth phase of the framework is renewing registration. It is at this stage of the newly qualified support framework that social workers who fulfil the requirements of the Consolidation programme are able to renew their registration (SCW, 2019a).

It is, therefore, evident that, in Wales, newly qualified social workers are afforded a structured robust employer-led framework to support their transition from a student social worker to a newly qualified social worker and assist with the development of confidence, competence and growth as practitioners. The *Continuing Professional Education and Learning: A Framework for Social Workers in Wales* (SCW, 2018b) as well as identifying the minimum arrangements for post-qualifying learning and training of social workers within Wales, provides practitioners with invaluable support through their career progression and beyond their experience as newly qualified social workers. This framework is currently under review by Social Care Wales; however, it is anticipated that such a robust post-qualifying framework will remain, albeit, in a potentially altered and updated guise.

The following is a case study of a newly qualified social worker who reflects upon their experiences of the Consolidation programme and their future continuous professional development.

CASE STUDY 2.1

Johanna's story

In July 2021 I qualified as a social worker and started my first role in children services where I rapidly began experiencing the demands of frontline social work. In October 2022 I commenced upon the Consolidation programme and was keen to get this completed as quickly as possible. I didn't expect to find the process beneficial, which on reflection sounds arrogant but I viewed it as an exercise that I needed to complete, one more hurdle to overcome whilst

(Continued)

(Continued)

trying to manage a busy and demanding case load. However, the Consolidation programme provided me with the time and tools to reflect upon what I had experienced during my first 15 months of practice, and I had experienced a lot! CPEL gave me the opportunity to consider how my practice had developed, how my Welsh culture contributed towards my experience and how I wanted to develop moving forward in terms of future goals. Completing the Consolidation programme has been incredibly beneficial, I feel I now understand what kind of social worker I am and what I want my future social work self to look like. I believe it has re-focused me after what was an intense first year in practice and really grounded my social work values. I'm due to start my Enabling Practice Learning programme this October and I'm really excited about this path CPEL has placed me on.

The AYE in Northern Ireland

The development of NQSW support and training in Northern Ireland (NI) is again similar but slightly nuanced ensuring the specifics of the country are considered. In NI, responsibility for social work policy and workforce planning sits with the Department of Health (DoH). Approximately 60 per cent of the 6,843 registered social workers in NI are employed in the five integrated Health and Social Care Trusts. Social workers also work in the criminal justice, education and voluntary and community sectors (NISCC, 2023).

In 2001, the DoH announced a policy for the Reform of Social Work Education in response to a major review of professional training across the UK. As part of the suite of changes that followed, social work qualifying training was established as an undergraduate degree and all newly qualified social workers (NQSWs) were required to undertake an Assessed Year in Employment (AYE) linked to registration with the Northern Ireland Social Care Council (Social Care Council).

The reform programme was announced at the same time as the Social Care Council was established by the DoH to set standards for practice and professional education and to regulate social workers and professional training. In NI, a social worker's relationship with their regulator commences at the outset of their professional training through registration as a social work student and continues throughout their career. Like other parts of the United Kingdom, in NI social work is a protected title.

The delivery of social work education and training in NI is supported by formal partnership arrangements with government, approved programme providers, employers and those who draw on services. The partnership arrangements enable a more responsive system and the regulator to have a handprint on quality across the continuum of social work education and training from qualifying level, through the AYE and the Professional in Practice CPD framework for post-qualifying education and training.

Recent analysis of social work practice in NI has focussed on the challenge to the profession of working during the conflict known as 'the Troubles' (Duffy et al., 2019) and the intergenerational legacy of trauma that still affects the wellbeing of individuals, families and communities (Duffy et al., 2022). A newer challenge has been that of delivering social work in a society on which COVID-19 has had a significant impact, compounded by a cost-of-living crisis and under-investment in health and social care services. NI is also becoming a more culturally diverse society (Northern Ireland Statistics and Research Agency (NISRA), 2024) and social workers must practise cultural humility and understand the intersectionality of discrimination.

Each year just under 250 social workers graduate in NI (DoH) and are registered as newly qualified social workers with an Assessed Year in Employment (AYE) condition of registration. A small but growing number of internationally qualified social workers also apply to join the NISCC register.

The role of the Northern Ireland social care council

The Northern Ireland Social Care Council is the workforce regulator for social work and social care in Northern Ireland and is an arm's length body of the Department of Health. There are over 49,000 social care practitioners registered with NISCC of which 6,800 are social workers. The Social Care Council's strategic vision is to have a 'thriving, capable and compassionate social work and social care workforce providing the highest quality of care, protection and support to people in need' (NISCC Strategic Plan 2023–2027). The primary role of the Social Care Council is to protect the public through the regulation and development of the workforce, ensuring that social workers are equipped with the right knowledge and learning opportunities to practise social work and deliver safe, effective care that meets the Standards of Conduct and Practice (2015) (O'Rourke et al., 2023). The Social Care Council do this through collaborative partnership working and by listening to social work registrants, their employers and the people who draw on services.

The Social Care Council has adopted the International Federation of Social Workers (IFSW) (2014) definition of the role of social work which is to be concerned with 'social justice, [and] human rights' and to work for 'social change and development' and the 'empowerment and liberation of people', thus positioning social workers at the forefront of helping to address complex societal issues impacting on individuals, families and communities and balancing issues of risk whilst respecting human rights. It is a complex and skilled role and a deeply rewarding vocation.

Supporting learning and development for early career social workers in Northern Ireland

The Assessed Year in Employment (AYE) was first established by the Department of Health in 2004 and the current AYE structure was revised and updated in 2015 (DHSSPS, 2015; NISCC, 2022a). The AYE was designed to help social workers make the significant transition from being a student to a newly qualified social work practitioner by continuing to build on learning though practice, consolidating skills including assessment of risk, support planning and exploration of current models of practice interventions and ensuring protected time for training and development days (see Chapter 9).

In Northern Ireland all NQSWs must complete the AYE and then achieve a minimum of two requirements within the Social Care Council's continuous professional learning and development Professional in Practice Framework during the following three-year period of registration (see Figure 2.1).

Social Work in Northern Ireland

How your continuous professional development is supported through regulation.

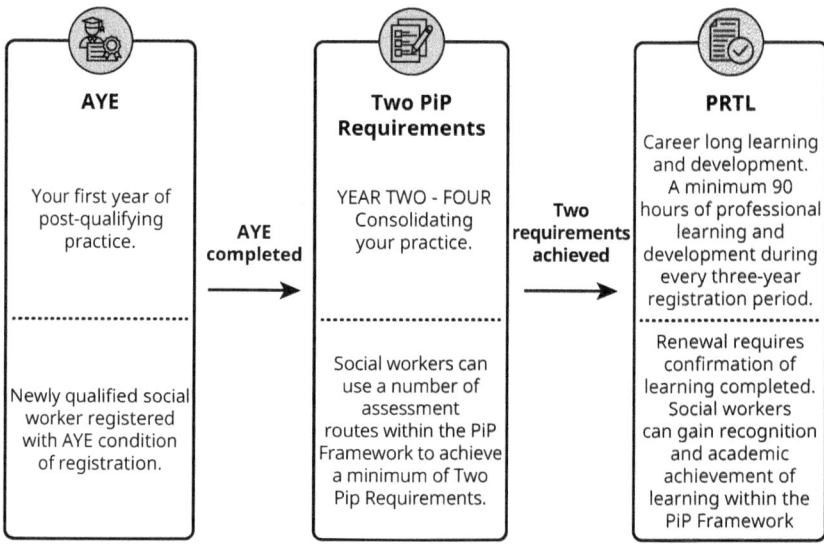

Figure 2.1   Social work in Northern Ireland

The assessed year in employment

Research suggests that the first one to four years of post-qualifying practice are significant in forming emotional coping and resilience mechanisms in social workers, as well as developing practice, supporting wellbeing and leading to better retention rates for staff (Grant et al., 2022; McFadden et al., 2022; Hamill et al., 2023). The AYE marks the start of a career-long journey of professional learning and development and a commitment from the Department of Health, the Social Care Council and employers to supporting NQSWs right from their first year in practice.

NQSWs must complete 198 days of social work practice during which their progress and competency is assessed against the six key social work roles identified in the Social Work National Occupational Standards (2011) (https://niscc.info/app/uploads/2023/11/Social-Work-Occupational-Standards.pdf). In order to meet the requirements of the AYE, social work employers must ensure that NQSWs have access to:

- a named social worker as their line manager or supervising social worker
- fortnightly supervision for the first six months of employment and monthly supervision for the remaining six months

- a minimum of 10 learning and development days linked to a Personal Development Plan (PDP)

- a mid-point (6 months) and final (11 months) appraisal

NQSWs are required to evidence their competence in practice, including identifying and managing risk and implementing a range of models of practice. At the appraisal points NQSWs are required to critically reflect on their learning and practice development (see Chapter 4). Social workers will sometimes need extensions to the AYE assessment period if competence levels are not fully met within the timeframe and the assessing manager can seek approval for these from the Social Care Council.

The AYE policy provides a framework and sets minimum standards by which employers can assess competence, ensures opportunity across all sectors and areas of practice and reassures the public of the quality of professional development of NQSWs. To explore the structure in more detail, visit The Social Care Council Learning Zone AYE Resource, https://learningzone.niscc.info/social-worker-assessed-year-in-employment-.

Understanding and supporting the AYE journey

The Social Care Council are required to carry out an annual audit of a range of employer evidence used to evaluate AYE competency including reflective statements from social workers (NISCC, 2022a). Findings from the audit are used to highlight key themes and recommend improvements in the arrangements and promote regional consistency. The AYE audits during and post pandemic identified a range of factors that presented particular challenges for NQSWs entering the workforce at that time. These included the impact of the pandemic and working in health and social care systems under pressure. There were examples where these challenges could be mitigated by support from experienced team colleagues and line managers with regular access to supervision. A Northern Ireland based service evaluation of an AYE mentoring programme initiated during Covid explored the emotional and psychological pressure of becoming a social worker at this time. The evaluation evidenced the significant positive impact of introducing mentoring, in addition to supervision, on resilience building and improved wellbeing (Hamill et al., 2023).

The Social Care Council co-chair an AYE Leadership Network which is a regional, cross-sector group with lead responsibility for supporting AYE social workers within their organisation. During the pandemic the network led a range of initiatives to support AYE social workers which included online peer support meetings and resources, theory to practice learning sessions and mentoring and coaching models of support (O'Rourke et al., 2020). The opportunity to share experiences and challenges faced by NQSWs in this way increased capacity for shared learning and problem solving for those charged with supporting AYE across the system. The AYE Leadership Network have continued to build on the promotion of shared learning and regionally consistent approaches to support AYE.

Recent research studies have indicated the importance of employer attention to emotional and psychological wellbeing and supportive structures to help early career social workers' development of resilience and suggests that such enhanced organisational supports have the potential to improve retention of staff and improve outcomes for people drawing on services (McFadden et al., 2019; McFadden et al., 2022; Roulston et al., 2022; Roulston et al., 2024). Further research is exploring the concept and definition of 'safer staffing' to inform safe and effective staffing legislation in NI and support the retention and development of social work staff to include guidance on what a suitable caseload for a NQSW should be (McFadden et al., 2024).

The professional in practice (PiP) framework and the two PiP requirements

Social workers who successfully complete their AYE are then registered with a mandatory condition of registration to complete a minimum of Two Requirements in the Professional in Practice (PiP) Framework within the next three-year renewal period (NISCC, 2022b). The AYE and the Two Requirements conditions of registration provide a strong foundation for Continuing Professional Development (CPD) in the vital first four years of post-qualifying social work practice.

The PiP Framework is the formal continuous professional development (CPD) structure for social workers in Northern Ireland, https://learningzone.niscc.info/professional-in-practice-pip/ . The Framework has been designed to enhance the competence and expertise of social workers throughout their career by enabling access to a wide range of opportunities for academic, work-based and independent learning. The Framework is delivered through a partnership model with employers, academics and service user and care involvement. Social workers can engage with the PiP Framework via a range of routes and work towards achieving recognition for their learning at postgraduate level choosing from one or more of the four PiP Awards: Consolidation; Specialist; Leadership & Strategic; and Advanced Scholarship Awards. PiP achievement is a benchmark and evidence of professional competence and quality of practice (O'Rourke et al., 2023).

The Social Care Council recognises the critical importance of social workers' CPD as the means to ensuring that registrants are encouraged to assimilate new learning and new ways of working to benefit the people they support. The Framework enables social workers to engage in learning and development using their practice experience, combined with professional knowledge, skills and values for the purpose of assessment at postgraduate level.

Post registration training and learning

Career-long commitment to learning and development after achievement of the Two Requirements is evidenced by social workers through confirmation of Post Registration Training and Learning (PRTL) of at least 90 hours within every three-year renewal period in order to proceed with renewal and remain on the register. The Social Care Council quality assure the professional learning being undertaken by carrying out twice-yearly auditing of a sample of social workers' PRTL. The Social Care Council provide a range of Learning Zone Resources to support social workers' learning and development, see https://learningzone.niscc.info/ and encourage practitioners to share their practice knowledge and experience through regular practitioner-led Lunchtime Seminars, see https://niscc.info/lunchtime-seminars-presentations-and-videos and by taking part in the Social Care Council Care to Chat Podcasts, see https://niscc.info/care-to-chat-podcast/.

ACTIVITY 2.1

Exploring your country's expectations

We have waited until we have completed the overview of different country approaches to the support and assessment of newly qualified and early career social workers before asking you to undertake some reflection on your own position. So, depending on your country of work and the specific programme you are undertaking, consider what is expected of you in the forthcoming year. What do you need to do in order to achieve these expectations and where and from whom can you gain support? Write down your thoughts, add to them and adapt them as you work through the book and keep checking them as you progress through your supportive programme and assessment.

Summary

This chapter has presented an overview of the ways in which NQSWs are supported and provided with professional development programmes in Scotland, Wales and Northern Ireland. It usefully highlights the importance of the Care Councils in each country, something that the English system could benefit from rather than the fragmented approach taken currently, where the ASYE is supported through Skills for Care, not the professional body Social Work England. It is also important to note the centrality of critical reflection and good supportive rather than managerial supervision. Sharing the professional standards and practices across the four nations has the potential to help us all in enhancing our support and development activities for NQSWs. In the next chapter, Barry Fearnley will help you to explore the complex and challenging transitions that you will make from student to qualified practitioner, something important in whichever country you are practising.

Further reading

We suggest that you use the further reading recommended in Chapter 1 to underpin this chapter, especially the following.

The following recommendations are specific to each country administration:

Department for Education. (2018). *Post-qualifying standard: Knowledge and skills statement for child and family practitioners.* Department for Education.

Department of Health. (2015). *Knowledge and skills statement for social workers in adult services.* Department of Health.

Scottish Social Services Council. (2019). *Standards in social work education in Scotland.* https://learn.sssc.uk.com/siswe/siswe.html

Social Care Wales. (2023). *Consolidation programme for newly qualified social workers – Your questions answered.* https://socialcare.wales/cms_assets/file-uploads/Consolidation-programme-for-newly-qualified.pdf

Northern Ireland Social Care Council. (2022a). *The assessed year in employment for newly qualified social workers in Northern Ireland.* https://learningzone.niscc.info/social-worker-assessed-year-in-employment-aye/

Chapter 3

From social work student to newly qualified social worker

Barry Fearnley

Introduction

This chapter will begin by exploring your changing landscape from education, social work student, to employment, newly qualified social worker, and will prepare you for your continuing journey of learning and subsequent professional growth and development. Following your final year of study, and the commencement of your social work career, your identity will change from a social work student to newly qualified social worker. As a newly qualified social worker in the United Kingdom (UK) you will undertake your Assessed and Supported Year in Employment (ASYE) or equivalent. In England, the ASYE is a 12-month, employer-led and employment-based programme of support and assessment for newly qualified social workers (NQSWs) (Skills for Care, 2024). In Wales (Social Care Wales (SCW), 2012) the Consolidation Programme for Newly Qualified Social Workers is part of the Continuing Professional Education and Learning (CPEL) framework. In Scotland (Scottish Social Services Council (SSSC), 2024b) there is a dedicated website for the support of Newly Qualified Social Workers (NQSW). In Northern Ireland (Northern Ireland Social Care Council (NISCC), 2021), newly qualified social workers complete the Assessed Year in Employment (AYE) followed by the Professional in Practice (see detailed country descriptions in Chapter 2).

Through a series of activities, this chapter will guide you to consider your learning journey thus far. This will include identifying your strengths, areas for further development and gaps in knowledge and skills. This will assist you with applying for jobs in addition to preparing for an interview. Additionally, this will support you in developing skills of critical reflection necessary for the ASYE and the annual renewal of your registration with one of the four United Kingdom's professional bodies. The chapter will then explore reflexivity and becoming a reflexive social worker. Finally, the chapter will look at the importance of working collaboratively and building networks.

Considering your learning journey

When you started your social work course and thus your learning journey to become a social worker you were actively building on, and developing, your cultural capital (Bourdieu, 1996). Bourdieu's theoretical construct 'cultural capital' includes the accumulation of knowledge, skills and behaviours. Acquiring such knowledge, skills and behaviours can be multi-dimensional and, therefore, could be through both personal and/or professional endeavours. Indeed, when we consider the ecology of human development (Bronfenbrenner, 1979) we can see the interconnectedness between the personal and professional undertakings. However, in this chapter the focus will be on the development of professional capital (Bourdieu, 1984).

Within the discipline of social work, the development of cultural capital (Bourdieu, 1984) is essential and ongoing throughout the social worker's career. This is a necessity and can be clearly identified through the United Kingdom's (UK) four Social Work Professional Bodies: Social Work England (SWE) (England), Scottish Social Services Council (SSSC) (Scotland), Social Care Wales (SCW) (Wales) and Northern Ireland Social Care Council (NISCC) (Northern Ireland). These four professional bodies refer to 'continual professional development' and you will need to demonstrate this through critical reflective practice (see Chapter 4). For instance, '(A)s a social worker, you must develop social work practice through supervision, consultation, reflection and analysis' (NISCC, 2019). Thus, in qualified practice, there is an emphasis on the continued learning journey. Although the landscape may have changed from a social work student at university, to a social worker within an employing agency, importance will be placed on you exploring your professional growth and development through the lens of critical reflection. Reflection will enable you to:

- review a process to see if it achieved the desired goals or outcomes
- make learning visible
- complete the learning cycle for each incident in our lives
- give a more considered response to an event
- achieve meaning and understanding inside actions
- add value to self and to performance
- move us from novice to expert

(Butler, 1996, p. 271)

To begin the transition from social work student to newly qualified social worker let's consider your social work learning journey. The social work qualifying course is the beginning of your social work career. This programme is designed to equip you with the knowledge and skills to undertake social work practice and register with one of the UK's four Social Work Professional Bodies. Your professional growth and development should continue throughout your social work career. However, we will begin by exploring, reflecting upon, and mapping your learning journey thus far (see Activity 3.1).

Mapping your learning journey

Reflecting on your learning journey as you progressed through the social work course begin by listing the modules undertaken including your skills days and placements (see Figure 3.1).

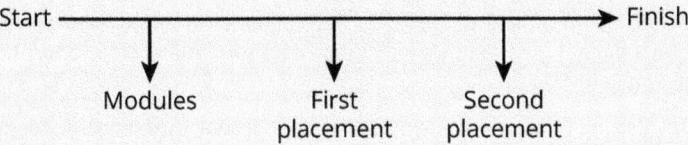

Start ──────────────────────────────────────▶ Finish

Modules	First	Second
	placement	placement

Figure 3.1   Reflecting on the social work course

Reflecting on the list of modules:

• Which module stimulated you the most? Why?

• Which module challenged you the most? Why?

• Which module presented a 'significant' (light bulb moment) learning opportunity? What learning did you take from this module?

• Which theories, models and approaches influenced your practice during placement? How did you apply these in practice?

Reflecting on the skills days including your shadowing experiences and observations:

• What skills did you develop? For example, communication including verbal, non-verbal, written and digital, active listening and observations.

Building on your reflections in Activity 3.1

During Activity 3.1 you reflected on your learning journey and social work course. Let's now explore those reflections a little deeper in relation to your practice learning placements. When considering your placements, think about where they were based, for example, working with children and families or adults. What work did you do during your placement? This might have included working with individuals. Who were these individuals – service users, colleagues, other professionals? What was the purpose of your involvement and what knowledge informed your practice? What skills did you use? Did you apply different knowledge and skills when working with adults, children, young people, team members and other professionals? An example might be an assessment you were asked to undertake and complete. An assessment will include assessing risk, strengths and needs along with writing and completing any associated documentation. These areas offer a wealth of opportunities for reflection, along with subsequent learning and development.

Using Rolfe et al.'s (2001) model of reflection – What? So what? What next? – and reflecting on your placements, now complete Activity 3.2.

ACTIVITY 3.2

Reflecting on practice learning placements

What? During practice learning what have you learned and developed a greater understanding of? How did you apply this knowledge in practice during your placement? What feedback did you receive following the completion of modules and placements?

So what? Reflecting on a piece of work you have undertaken during your placement what went well? What did not go as anticipated? What were you feeling at the time? How did you manage your emotions?

What next? Reflecting on your placements, what gaps in your knowledge could you identify? Are there any gaps in your skills? What areas could you identify for further development? For example, communication skills, observation skills or time management.

Following on from Activity 3.1 and Activity 3.2, you now have a list of knowledge and skills gained during the social work course, including your placements. Now we will develop this further to identify areas for development and any gaps.

Knowledge and skills audit

Now complete Activity 3.3 noting your knowledge and skills in addition to areas for further development. This will be a valuable exercise which will assist you in completing job application forms and during the interview.

ACTIVITY 3.3

Identifying your knowledge and skills

Continuing to think deeply about your social work course, explore what knowledge and skills you have acquired, and what requires further development or constitutes gaps in your learning. Create a table of reflection with the following headings:

- Knowledge and skills identified

- Knowledge and skills to be further developed

- Gaps in knowledge and skills

Complete the table with your reflections.

Think about the learning you have taken from the course and during your placements, what have you learnt through your experiences?

This could be your intervention, assessment or report writing skills along with your interpersonal skills. For example, when undertaking direct work with children, what knowledge and skills did you apply? What theories, models and approaches did you use? What knowledge and skills do you need to develop further, when undertaking assessments? When writing assessments and reports did you identify any gaps in your knowledge and skills, for example, analysis?

Identifying your knowledge and skills

Using critical reflection to identify knowledge, skills and areas for enhancement is of enormous benefit to your continued professional development and provides a foundation for applying for employment and preparing for the interview. The activities above will enable you to gain a greater understanding of your strengths, while, at the same time, you will be able to consider areas for further development. Additionally, you might also identify gaps in your knowledge and skills. Identifying, recognising and acknowledging such gaps is a strength, and, again, central to your professional growth and evolution.

Let's clarify, a strength is something you are good at, but even so you will need to consider continual professional development of these strengths and reflect on the skills you have and how you can develop these further. Nevertheless, these are strengths. You are likely to be aware of the areas you need to consider for further development; however, these areas require a little more thought. It is important to reflect on these areas, create an action plan and find opportunities to advance your knowledge, understanding and skills in those identified areas. Gaps in your knowledge and skills, on the other hand, are a little more difficult to identify because sometimes we don't know what we need to know.

Reflecting on your learning journey, did you experience being asked to do something you did not know how to do, or had no previous experience of doing? What did you do in these circumstances? Such gaps in knowledge and skills often come to our attention through reflection, observation and/or feedback from tutors, practice educators, work-based supervisors, other team members, mentors or managers and/or other professionals alongside those people using social work services. Let's explore some of the ways in which you could develop your knowledge and skills.

Developing your knowledge and skills

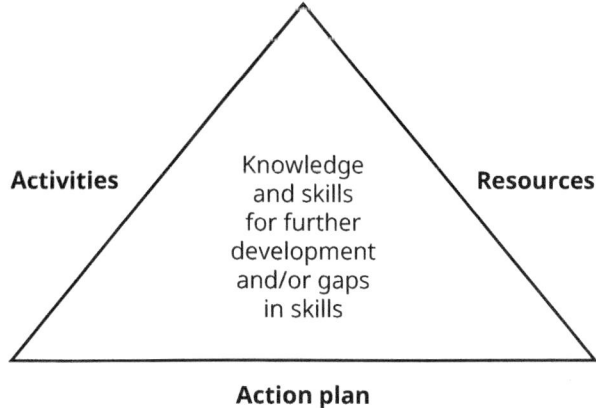

Figure 3.2   Areas for further development

Following on from Activity 3.1 and Activity 3.2, and the identification of areas for further development and/or gaps in your knowledge and skills, we will explore a three-step process (see Figure 3.2). This will include an action plan that takes into consideration activities and resources. An action plan will help you to focus on your strengths and areas for development. These were identified in Activity 3.1, Activity 3.2 and Activity 3.3 and will also benefit you when applying and completing an application form for employment as a social worker.

Your job application form

When completing your application form remember to include your strengths alongside your areas for further development. You should be prepared to discuss these during an interview. With regards to strengths, and respecting confidentiality, provide examples from your involvement and engagement of the social work course or from your placements and don't forget previous experience; think about transferable skills. Here, consideration could be given to goal planning, working to timescales and using your initiative to achieve results, which might include overcoming obstacles to achieving your goals. In relation to areas for further development, consider what you need to develop; for example, mentoring, training, shadowing, or co-working to develop your practice experience. And remember, supportive supervision is vital to your growth as a social worker in all aspects of your professional development.

Discussing your strengths will inform the interviewer(s) what you can bring to the team and organisation and to those who use your services. The identification of areas for development, and how you could develop these areas further, is demonstrating and acknowledging an awareness of where you need to develop your knowledge and skills and that you are prepared to engage with this. Indeed, this could also be regarded as a strength. During the interview, when you are asked if you have any questions, opportunities for development in addition to enquiring about the Assessed and Supported Year in Employment (ASYE) Programme could be one of the areas to focus on.

Furthermore, when completing your application form you need to consider any additional needs you might have. When considering additional needs, think about your previous experiences and ask yourself 'how did I manage different situations and circumstances previously?' Reflecting on your previous experiences, you can draw upon and highlight the strategies you have used and developed in your application form, and during your interview. Think about transferable skills and provide examples. Additionally, ask yourself:

- What can I do to support myself?
- How might I help my manager/mentor in supporting me?
- What can the team/organisation do to support me?

Be open and honest and demonstrate your communication skills and transferable skills when discussing what support you need. Again, this can be counted as a strength.

Let's start with the action plan (see Figure 3.3).

Figure 3.3   Action planning

An action plan would consist of you setting yourself goals and the identification of activities or tasks and timescales to complete the goals. Create a table with the following headings:

- Knowledge and skills to be developed

- Goals

- Tasks to be undertaken

- When will you do this? (timescales)

- Reflecting on your learning

Goals should be challenging, but achievable, and include a wide range of learning opportunities. Any activity undertaken could be a learning opportunity. Each goal can have a number of learning activities with the purpose of developing your knowledge or skills. Allocate a different timescale for each goal so that you do not overwhelm yourself. It is essential with any action plan that the goals are small and broken down into achievable tasks where you can critically reflect, identify further learning opportunities and develop further goals (see Parker, 2025). In this way the cycle continues:

- Goal

- Identifying tasks to meet the goal

- Identifying activities to complete the task

- Goal achieved

- Critical reflection on learning

- Areas for further learning identified

- Set goals (the cycle continues)

This cycle of learning and development is demonstrated through Walker et al. (2008), although writing about practice education, who consider the continuous spiral of professional development and learning throughout your career. The spiral takes you on a learning journey, which includes developing confidence, new knowledge, increasing understanding, embedding this knowledge in practice, exploring new ideas, generating and engaging in explorative discussions and identifying areas for further development. However, when setting goals and timescales do remember that you need to be realistic.

When you have completed your action plan, you can then move towards thinking about the activities you need to undertake to meet your goals. These should include a wide range of learning opportunities. We now turn to explore these activities further (see Figure 3.4).

Figure 3.4   *Activities to meet your goals*

Activities are those learning opportunities that enable you to complete the tasks you set yourself and thereby meet your goals. These could include face-to-face or online training, shadowing and observations of practice. Observations are part of placements and the ASYE, and are beneficial following the ASYE for continuous professional growth and development. Observations could also include you observing your practice educator, work-based supervisor, colleagues or other professionals. Whether observing someone else or they are observing you, be specific in what you want to focus on and what you want to be observed doing. Think about the wider picture, this will help with contextualising the situation or circumstances, along with exploring multi-perspectives.

When considering activities, ask yourself: what is the purpose of the activity; what would you like to learn or skill you would like to develop; reflect on Activity 3.2 along with your table, and any feedback you would you like in relation to your practice. An example could be your communicative approach when undertaking an assessment including the questions you asked and how could these be developed. As discussed previously, could you have asked different questions to gather the information required? Likewise, when shadowing what is the purpose and what do you hope to gain? Shadowing and observations are excellent learning opportunities, especially when followed by critical reflection. Following any activity always revise your action plan. It is best used as a living and organic thing that changes and develops alongside you. Another consideration when creating your action plan is resources. Let's explore what we mean by resources (see Figure 3.5).

Figure 3.5   Identifying resources

There are a wide range of resources available to you. Resources include your practice educator, your tutor and your manager/mentor. Additionally, resources include reading materials such as the books you used during the social work course, articles, study notes, podcasts and reflective journals. Organisations also have a wealth of resources, for example, training and online guidance in addition to templates for assessments and reports. They also have policies and procedures which provide an abundance of information. Supervision is an excellent resource. Remember that colleagues and other professionals are excellent resources with experience and specialist knowledge.

An example of the importance of resources in the development of your knowledge and skills could be the undertaking of an assessment. To complete an assessment, you read the policies and procedures, complete the assessment, whole or part of, and ask for feedback from your practice educator/manager/mentor. You might consider shadowing or observing a colleague, as discussed previously. A reflective journal is key to advancing your development and recording your reflections; at each point in the process think about your thoughts, feelings and what you might do differently next time.

Professional growth and development: The transition from social work student to social worker

Before we begin to consider professional growth and development, let's explore the transition from being a social work student to a qualified social worker, followed by your changing identity. Here we need to acknowledge that the 'transition from education to practice is probably the most important transition in professional educations' (Henriksen, 2023, p.794).

The social work course equips you with the knowledge and skills to be a social worker and therefore there is coherence and thus connection between education and practice. Social work is underpinned by theories, research and legislation with a strong emphasis on critical reflection and continuing professional development through reflection. This is congruent with Schön's (1983) notion of the reflective practitioner (Henriksen, 2023). What is important within the transition from student to social worker, from education to employment, is that the knowledge and skills gained through your education journey are applied in practice, reflected upon and new knowledge gained. Here we see a cycle of continual professional growth and development, which can be linked to Dreyfus' (2004) five-stage model of adult skill acquisition. The five stages are:

Stage 1 – novice,

Stage 2 – advanced beginner,

Stage 3 – competent,

Stage 4 – proficient,

Stage 5 – expert.

'Novice' is the beginning of your professional social work journey and as you gain experience you will develop your knowledge and skills further and progress through the five stages. The ASYE programme will support you, through critical reflection, in the development of your skills and knowledge along with the application of theory to practice, through the initial stages. As you progress through your social work career you will work through all the stages.

The transition from student to social worker can be an exciting and fulfilling time – a sense of achievement – but it may also invoke many emotions including feeling overwhelmed and anxious. Duchscher (2009) refers to this as 'transition shock' which links to four psychosocial elements. These are what you might experience as you transition from being a student to social worker:

Emotional – *stressed, anxious, feeling overwhelmed, scared, fearful and having self-doubt. If supported by the team, you might also feel excitement and confident.*

Physical – *physical exhaustion can be increased towards the end of the first three months as a direct consequence of excitement and over stimulation.*

Sociocultural – *the time it takes you to feel part of the team, beginning to trust your judgement, and ultimately leading to an appropriate work–life balance.*

Intellectual – *your ability to recall theory to apply to a practice situation. Initially, you may need longer to recall information when making decisions. You may need time to recall information which might impact on your time management.*

Your social work identity

Your identity as a social worker starts when you commence the social work course. However, 'social worker' is a protected title, and you cannot call yourself a social worker until you are qualified and registered (The Social Workers Regulations, 2018). Nevertheless, as you progress through the course and during your first placement you will start to develop your identity. During the final placement, an emerging identity will evolve progressing to a social worker's identity whose practice is underpinned by professional standards (see SWE (2019), SSSC (2020), NISCC (2019), SCW (2017)). Professional growth and development begin when you start the social work course. This then continues throughout your social work career and is referred to as continuing professional development (CPD):

> *You should always be looking for ways to improve your practice so you can provide the best possible support. CPD is not just about attending training courses, it can be any activity you feel would improve your practice. This could include learning from podcasts, webinars, project work, articles or reviewing your own practice in a particular area. It could also be the work you have done through programmes such as the assessed supported year in employment. (SWE, 2024)*

Or continuous professional learning (CPL):

> *Continuous professional learning (CPL) is the learning we do for work which helps us develop our knowledge, skills and professional behaviour so we can deliver our best practice. (SSSCa, 2024)*

One of the distinct differences between a social work student and a social worker relates to your responsibilities. Upon successful completion of the social work course, you will be able to register with one of the four United Kingdom Professional Bodies. This brings significant responsibilities with regards to caseload management, decision making and safeguarding. As a student, you are responsible and accountable for your actions and practice; however, your practice educator is ultimately responsible. As a qualified and registered social worker, you are now the allocated social worker and thus undertaking and completing assessments, report writing, gathering evidence, decision making and working in partnership and collaboratively with other professionals is your responsibility. This includes your social work practice being underpinned by theories, models and approaches and within a legislative framework. For example, see 'Be accountable for the quality of my practice and the decisions I make' (SWE, 2019, p.6f); As a social service worker, 'I am accountable for the quality of my work and will take responsibility for maintaining and improving my knowledge and skills' (SSSC, 2020, p.26f); 'Be accountable for the quality of your work and take responsibility for maintaining and improving your knowledge and skills' (NISCC, 2019, p.17f); 'be accountable for the quality of your work and take responsibility for maintaining and developing knowledge and skills' (SCW, 2017, p.15f) . This brings us to a consideration of whether social work is, indeed, an art or a science.

Is social work a science or art?

To answer this question, we can refer to Samson (2015) who observes that 'the origins of social work were based upon women of privilege conducting charity work with the less fortunate. This work forged a new profession that became focused upon achieving professional status and legitimacy, turning to science to establish a solid knowledge base' (p.128). Social work as a science or art is debatable but we rehearse some arguments below. You could argue that social work is a science because you are observing, assessing and evaluating. The relationship between science and social work is the evidence-based, or evidence-informed, approach to practice. Social work practice that is underpinned by research and theories. This also includes ethical-based decision making where decisions are based on evidence, are non-judgemental, and underpinned by ethical principles. Social work could also be defined as an art when contextualised within a practice perspective; there is an emphasis on building, developing and maintaining relationships, communication and interpersonal skills, for example see 'Establish and maintain the trust and confidence of people' (SWE, 2019, p.4f). Thus, a social worker should be able to integrate the two, science and art. The integration of research and theory to practice; see 'Maintain an up-to date knowledge and evidence base for social work' (NISCC, 2019, p.22f).

Additionally, and equally important, there is practice wisdom. Practice wisdom is 'a system of personal and value-driven knowledge emerging out of the transaction between the phenomenological experience of the client situation and the use of scientific information' (Klein and Bloom, 1995, p.801). Practice wisdom is your experience. This experience could be personal, along with being gained from previous employment and from your social work course including skill days, shadowing, observations, and placements, in addition to the experience gained during the ASYE Programme and from 'doing' social work. Thus, we can see:

> *Practice wisdom emerges as a core feature in a practitioner's developed professional experience and serves to translate both empirical and theoretical knowledge and previous practice experience into present and future professional behaviour.*

> (Klein and Bloom, 1995, p.803)

The implications of integrating knowledge gained through research, theory and practice experience is that you will be a social worker undertaking best practice. Furthermore,

> *Reflection is the prerequisite for the articulation of practice wisdom, which not only allows the translation of theories to specific contexts for personal use but makes it possible to determine what constitutes the good in a particular time and space for the users or clients.*

> (Chu and Tsui, 2008, p.51)

Professional growth and development is part of a continual process of theorising and evidence building including building new knowledge and developing skills:

- New knowledge

- Apply to practice

- Reflection

- New knowledge and understanding

- Apply to practice

- Reflection

- New knowledge and understanding (continuous cycle)

Here we can see in action the spiral-like twists and turns of professional development and learning, that we discussed previously. Likewise, this could reflect a similar process in relation to developing your skills. An example could include your knowledge and understanding of the assessment process and subsequent development and application of skills to ensure that you have all the appropriate and relevant information. This would also include all aspects of the service user's strengths, needs and risks that you have identified and will inform your decision-making skills in ethically and evidence-based ways. Evidence-based is a contentious term but can be understood as meaning information gathered from as many sources as possible through partnership and collaborative working. It is not just undertaking an assessment, part of the assessment process includes evaluating, analysing and synthesising information, writing your assessment, making recommendations, and presenting your assessment (Fearnley, 2022). Thus, written and verbal skills are essential. Such practice and subsequent development of knowledge and skills should continue through your social work career:

- Professional growth and development

- Social Work Professional Bodies/Professional Standards

- Registration/Re-registration

Organisational context

As stated previously in this chapter, the ASYF programme in England and cognate programmes in the other three nations focus upon the support and development

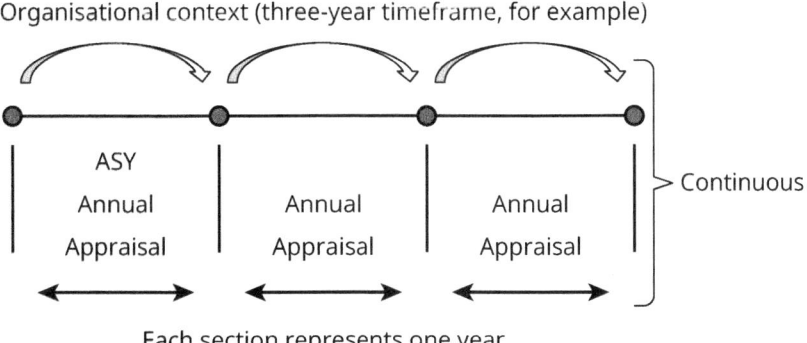

Figure 3.6   Organisational context

of you, a newly qualified social worker, and thus is a substantial contribution towards your professional growth and development in your first year(s) in professional practice. An essential component of professional growth and development is critical reflection and is a central part of the ASYE programme. Additionally, annual appraisals can be significant factors in your professional growth and development. An annual appraisal consists of setting clear objectives, goals, which are achievable, measurable and realistic. The objectives are set by yourself alongside your mentor/manager and may comprise a range of opportunities for you to advance you knowledge and skills in addition to increasing your exposure to different experiences (see Figure 3.6).

Personal/professional context

Short-term goals are identified through reflection and supervision. Each goal, again, should be clear and achievable. To meet these objectives, tasks are identified with clearly defined timescales, and through the completion of activities, resources and training. In addition to your professional growth and development, this also demonstrates continuing professional development which is a requirement with Professional Bodies. Further, this contributes to the organisational appraisal process. Thus, resulting in demonstrable continuous personal and professional growth and development to advance your social work career. A record of your CPD activities is necessary for your annual social work renewal. This enables you to demonstrate your CPD but also can be used when applying for career progression.

Your professional growth and development should include exploring different:

- theories
- models
- approaches

together with a critique of these aspects, in addition to investigating and identifying:

- emerging issues
- underlying issues/concerns
- safeguarding matters

This, in turn, should assist you in developing skills and knowledge in areas such as:

- managing uncertainty and change
- caseload management
- implementing and reviewing interventions
- time management

- prioritisation of practice

- developing professional curiosity

- developing professional assertiveness

Critical reflection is a key component of professional growth. Through regular and thoughtful reflection, you can evaluate your experiences, identify areas for improvement, and build on your strengths. Further, these reflections will enable you to demonstrate your continuing professional development not only as a practitioner but also for renewal of your registration where appropriate. A reflective journal is essential for this purpose in addition to comparing previous critical reflections with new ones. Within your reflective journal you should be able to see your development and progression, along with identifying strengths and areas for further development. Additionally, you should include what you might do differently when you find yourself in a similar situation or set of circumstances. Reflection to action, reflection in action, and reflection on action (Butler, 1996) may be undertaken in many different ways including writing reflective accounts, during discussions with colleagues, tutorials and supervision sessions. Following your reflections, it is the learning you have accrued that is significant. This will inform your action plan and subsequent professional growth and development. Here we can see a cycle of reflection along with the continuous spiral of professional development and learning discussed previously. There are many different models of reflection; however, we are going to explore the Dramaturgical Approach to reflection.

Dramaturgical approach to reflection

The dramaturgical approach to reflection is a fluid model, which encourages deeper reflection within different contexts. The dramaturgical model of social interaction is most associated with Goffman, and you may have encountered his work during your qualifying course. Goffman (1959/1990) applies theatrical language to everyday life where individuals perform like actors. Goffman refers to terms such as scripts, scenes, frontstage and backstage, all of which you will recognise as being the language of the theatre. The 'dramaturgic' relates to the self in addition to social interactions; our performance as individuals in the wider world – the frontstage (to an audience) or the backstage (when we are not preforming to an audience but are still actively engaged in the performance as a whole). Within our student and/or social work role we are performing to a wide range of audiences.

The dramaturgical approach to reflection is presented through a series of seven scenarios which presents the scenarios in a flow-chart representation; however, reflection within these scenarios is not necessarily undertaken sequentially or cyclically. You can choose a particular scenario to focus your critical reflections on, or alternatively more than one scenario, or of course, all of them. If choosing all of them, your reflections could be in any order and determined by what you are reflecting upon. You do not have to start with the script.

- The script

- Language

- Characters/Actors

- Roles

- Venue

- Audience

- Editing Process

We will explore the dramaturgical approach of reflection through two examples. First, through a case study where a social work student is adopting the approach in preparation for completing an application form and interview. Second, we will explore each of the seven scenarios in relation to the social work role.

CASE STUDY 3.1

Zara

Zara is a final year social work student. She has attended a careers fair which included a workshop focusing on the Assessed and Supported Year in Employment. During the workshop the facilitators, who were social work team managers, talked about the importance of planning and preparing when applying for jobs. This included reflecting on the social work course and placements. Zara was excited about applying for jobs but felt a little overwhelmed and anxious. Zara had a good working relationship with her academic mentor and decided to request a tutorial. She thought that maybe they could help her overcome some of her feelings and provide a few ideas of where to start. During the tutorial Zara's academic mentor suggested adopting the dramaturgical approach to reflection. They reminded Zara about how she had used this approach in one of her assignments and how she had used it when reflecting on her placements.

The tutorial helped to allay some of Zara's anxieties, and she felt more confident about writing her application forms. She used the seven scenarios to help plan and complete the application forms.

The script – Zara thought about the script in the context of the job specification, application form and statement and how she could map her knowledge and skills, along with the experiences from her placements to the Essential Requirements on the job application form.

Language – reflecting on the careers fair, Zara remembered the managers talking about the importance of being clear and concise when writing the statement, in addition to being factual and providing examples. This helped her to consider the language she needed to use and important areas from practice that she needed to include. This included writing about risks, strengths and areas for development, along with values and equality, diversity and inclusion. Zara recognised that listening is also a significant factor when being interviewed.

Characters/actors – Zara thought about who the characters/actors might be who would be reading her application form and interviewing her for the job. She recalled from the careers

---

fair that there might be a senior manager, a team manager, a representative from People Services (Human Resources) or a social worker. Zara reflected on how she might approach the questions being asked, considering the language, but also providing answers that were appropriate for each of the panel member's different roles.

Roles – here Zara reflected on the different roles of the interview panel and her own role. This included how she should present herself; a social work student or newly qualified social worker. She had limited experience but was motivated and enthusiastic. She thought about how she could present herself as confident while at the same time being nervous.

Venue – Zara thought about the geographical location of the interview and the practicalities of travelling to and from the office. When she received an invitation for the interview, Zara visited the building, explored car parking and considered the time it would take to travel from home to the venue.

Audience – Zara reflected about the audience and who would be reading the application form, along with how, at the interview, she would need to give her best 'performance' to be successful and be offered the post.

Editing process – Zara recognised that this was an important part of the application process. She knew that she must meticulously proofread her application form and ensure that she had written to all the Essential Requirements and, as many as possible, the Desirable Requirements too. She was aware that this was an opportunity for her to impress the panel and therefore knew that she needed to provide examples from practice, highlighting her strengths and areas for development. As she re-read her application form, she realised that she needed to include a sentence about why she was applying for the post and why she wanted the job. Through the editing process, Zara had been able to refine her application form, strengthen it and give herself the best possible opportunity to be invited to an interview.

ACTIVITY 3.4

Reflecting on the case study

Having read the case study, now consider the activities you have undertaken so far in this chapter identifying knowledge, skills and areas for development. How would you apply the dramaturgical approach of reflection when writing application forms and preparing for interviews?

We will now explore the seven scenarios of the dramaturgical approach to reflection in relation to social work practice.

The script – the script contextualises the situation and/or circumstances. This could include the telephone call, home visit, direct work with the child(ren) or individual or family. It could also include working with colleagues or other professionals. Additionally, it is important to consider digital communication within this. Here the scene is set, and might be, for example, a referral, gathering a piece of additional information, or presenting a report. It could also be an assessment. Reflection in relation to this scenario could include reflecting on the initial referral. You could consider the process you will follow, the knowledge you will draw upon, and the skills you will use prior to the next steps following the initial referral. You could also reflect on action subsequent to the initial telephone call or home visit. Say, for example, it was an initial referral, you could consider reflecting on your first thoughts and feelings of receiving the referral, any assumptions you might have made and whether these informed your practice. These reflections are personal, but linked directly to professional practice and thus span both domains. Here we can see how deeper reflections may be achieved, facilitate professional growth and development, while at the same time contribute towards a personal consciousness of your own beliefs and assumptions. These could be reflected in your presentation of self, questioning approach or demeanour.

Language – reflection here is undertaken in relation to how you use language to engage, encourage and enable in addition to provide and collect information. You, the social worker, need to avoid jargon, acronyms, colloquialisms, euphemisms, and clearly articulate the purpose of your involvement, reasons for actions, recommendations and what will happen next. You could reflect upon how you adapted your language when speaking to parents, children, colleagues, managers and other professionals. Consider the context and audience to whom you are presenting information. Language also refers to tone, level, and the way the words are spoken. Also consider both verbal and non-verbal communication, written including digital communication, and body language. Furthermore, listening is essential to ensure you have a thorough understanding of the situation, circumstances and what is being said.

Characters/actors – tools such as ecomaps and genograms (Fearnley, 2022; Parker, 2025) are essential in establishing the identity of all the characters/actors. However, not all the characters/actors will be identified immediately. Nevertheless, there are likely to be many different characters/actors including your manager, other team members, parents, children, grandparents, wider family members, friends, senior managers/directors, other professionals, judges, lawyers, barristers, foster carers, the list is endless; and don't forget you as both social worker and individual actor. We can see therefore that you, as the social worker, performs to a wide range of audiences, and how each individual acts will be determined by the script. Indeed, each individual will be performing and, therefore, as Goffman (1959/1990) suggests, the performance will be what that individual(s) wants us to see, their frontstage performance. However, we also need to consider the backstage and what the performers are not saying, doing, or hiding from us. The tools you use, the engagement with each individual, the meetings, along with your role – what part did you play, do you play – are all areas for critical reflection. For example, you may reflect on the tools by considering how you completed the genogram (reflect on each task including introducing the piece of work, who to include, did you exclude anybody and why, what were you feeling at the time), how did you communicate and engage with individuals and what did you learn?

Roles – within any given situation there are always a number of individuals or characters as discussed above, each of whom are playing their role. Each member of the family, parents, children, grandparents, have their role to play within the context of family life. Each professional you work with will have their role. Here we observe a myriad of interconnected relationships, which you, as the social worker, need to be aware of, recognise and acknowledge. The social work role is complex, there are many different roles including undertaking assessments, protecting and safeguarding, supporting and advocating on behalf of children and adults and, at times, simultaneously. However, social workers do not work in isolation. They work within a multi-agency and inter-professional approach and as such work in partnership with other professionals too. Once again, we can see a myriad of interconnected relationships. When reflecting on the roles, consider each individual as a character/actor, and ask what their role within the performance is, within the story, along with their narrative. Now, reflect on your role; what was the purpose of your involvement, how are you managing the various relationships, what knowledge are you drawing on and what skills are you using? Are there any gaps in the areas of assessment, managing people, working with complexity, and balancing and prioritising pieces of work. These reflections and the learning taken from them, contribute towards your professional development in addition to the gaps in knowledge and skills which can be added to your action plan.

Venue – the venue will change and be determined by each piece of work, your role, the characters/actors, and the script. You may be undertaking your role in the office, the family home, a school, a hospital, a court. Critical reflection might include a consideration of the etiquette of each venue. The courtroom, for example, will have its own customs, dress code, a way of addressing the judge, the barristers and other members of the courtroom. During visits to the family home, you need to respect the family's space while at the same time undertake your work such as completing an assessment. Also, within these reflections consider power and language, especially your own in relation to those with whom you are working. Thus, the expectations change as the venue changes; nevertheless, whatever the venue, it is important to remember confidentiality.

Audience – you, as the social worker, will be presenting a variety of different pieces of work to a wide range of audiences. Your audience might be a family, a multi-disciplinary meeting, or your manager. Therefore, the audience is the individual or individuals who you are working with or addressing or presenting to. Each individual is a character/actor, playing their role, in the venue. Their performance varies depending on their audience and on the other characters/actors. Your language changes as you present yourself to others. You recognise, acknowledge and value the audience whether you are presenting information to an individual or a group of individuals. You are non-judgemental, use language that is not patronising, and that is easy to understand. Adhering to the professional standards and/or codes of practice you are respectful, polite and courteous; at all times demonstrating professionalism. Reflecting on the various pieces of work undertaken, or are undertaking, you need to consider who your audience was, is. Indeed, this includes all the scenarios discussed thus far; however, when critically reflecting on this scenario think about presentation of self, conduct, behaviour, your performance. Additionally, think about your identity as a social worker. Think about what your audience sees, and what you would like them to see. How do they see your performance?

Editing process – you may share your assessment, report or other documentation with families, your manager, other professionals to name a few. During the writing and sharing of these pieces of work you will edit your communication, language, presentation of self, depending on the message you wish to convey. You will present an edited version to your manager of what you observed during a home visit, what the parents reported, what the children reported. You will write an edited version of the case notes, chronology, assessment and report. During this editing you will use a different language for the various audiences, notwithstanding the information must remain factual so that consistent information is being presented. It is worth scrutinising your editorial process and ask yourself, why did you include some things, but exclude others, why use some words, but not others, and importantly, are you presenting an authentic picture of situation and/or circumstances.

The importance of engaging in critical reflection is that your learning continues, your self-questioning develops and, through the dramaturgical approach to reflection, you explore social work practice through multiple perspectives. Additionally, when using the dramaturgical approach to reflection, within each scenario, you could consider using another model of reflection, for example Rolfe et al.'s (2001) model – What? So what? What next? – as discussed earlier in the chapter. Therefore, each of the three questions could be used within each scenario. This would provide an added dimension and further in-depth reflective element. Another area of significance is reflexivity. This is what we will explore next.

Reflexivity

Becoming a reflexive social worker is a skill that will develop with experience. This is likely to have started during the social work course and particularly during placements. Reflexivity includes observing the role of emotions and how emotions might influence, or have an impact on, our social work practice and decision making (Ingram, 2015). A critically reflexive social worker is one who questions and self-examines their own assumptions, values and beliefs along with the presentation of self on others. Critically reflexive social workers apply a critical questioning approach evaluating their interactions and actions including verbal and non-verbal communication, written and digital communication, and their relationships with others.

D'Cruz et al. (2007) identifies three variations of the meaning of reflexivity. The first variation relates to the individual's ability to process information and create new knowledge. From a social work student to a newly qualified social worker, you will have been, and continue to do so, developing, building upon, and creating new knowledge. You will have been doing this through critical reflection, critical thinking and critical analysis. Through the process of critical reflection, identifying strengths, areas for development, and gaps in knowledge and skills, as explored previously, you will continue in your learning journey and subsequent professional growth and development. Here you see how your new knowledge and skills could be demonstrated through the dramaturgical approach to reflection and in particular the 'Script' and applied to a job application form and interview as illustrated in Case Study 3.1. The ability to process information and create new knowledge also relates to the social worker's ability to understand information, knowing what processes and proce-dures to follow. For example, the social worker thoroughly understands the referral and thus the purpose of their involvement, what they need to do next and why, and through the assessment process can generate new knowledge and understanding in relation to the situation and circumstances in which they are working. Once again, we can see how the dramaturgical approach to reflection engages a deeper under-standing of the various aspects of social work practice and thus will support you in completing your ASYE programme.

The second variation describes reflexivity as an individual's self-critical approach. This is where you question your beliefs and assumptions and explore the world around you from multiple perspectives. The dramaturgical approach to reflection, explored in Case Study 3.1, is invaluable in this context. Additionally, the reflexive social worker is self-examining, questioning what they are doing including why and how. They would also explore power between relationships, including relationships between individuals and between individuals and organisational structures. The dramaturgical approach to reflection could be used to critically reflect on all seven scenarios or alternatively one scenario in relation to values, beliefs, and assumptions or power dynamics. This would support the writing of an application form (see Case Study 3.1) or completing the ASYE programme.

The third variation examines how emotions influence a social worker's practice. The reflexive social worker is likely to have a greater understanding of how they present themselves and how their emotions might influence their ability to build, develop and maintain relationships. Again, the dramaturgical approach to reflection is worth considering. For example, think about 'Language', the spoken word, the emotional impact of words, tone of voice along with timing and context. Within this drama-turgical scenario, we could also consider listening. Listening to what is being said is especially important, being comfortable with pauses, and enabling individu-als to have their say, tell their story, or contribute to the wider picture, for example within an assessment. Within Case Study 3.1, listening is very important within the context of the interview; having a clear understanding of what is being asked will enable you to answer the question thoroughly and possibly with demonstratable evi-dence. Additionally, we can also see 'Characters/Actors' and 'Audience'. This variation demands a self-exploratory look at relationship development, building and mainte-nance. Here we can see the importance of relationship-based social work (Ruch et al., 2010). Additionally, we can use the seven dramaturgical scenarios to reflect upon how our emotions might influence our relationships, and how our practice might impact the emotions of others within their respective roles and in different 'Venues'. Further, as you will have observed during your social work course, a significant aspect of social work is working collaboratively. This includes working in a multi-agency/inter-disciplinary approach. Thus, developing these working relationships is essential.

Developing your networks

One of the essential requirements within social work is working with other profes-sionals. Thus, your social capital, an individual's social network (Bourdieu, 1996), is as important in your professional world as in your personal world. In your personal world, your social capital includes networks of support and influence such as family, friends and group membership. In your professional world, your social capital will include colleagues, other professionals and community networks. Building this network is a skill. Activity 3.5 might assist in both developing this skill and building your network.

ACTIVITY 3.5

Developing your network

Whether you are a social work student or newly qualified social worker, on placement or employed, ask each team member, including the manager, for the name of three partner agencies they work with. Follow this by asking the team member to introduce you to a member of that agency.

The identification of different agencies will enable you to develop your network and this will be further advanced with introductions to individuals. Here you will you be joining a community of practice (Wenger, 2000; see Chapter 6). The benefits of participating within a community of practice are enormous and include sharing knowledge, experiences, resources along with developing your skill of exploring multiple perspectives. Additionally, there is the building of your identity, your identity as a social worker. All these aspects, along with critical reflection and becoming a reflexive social worker, will enhance your professional growth and development.

You might work with some professionals only once whilst you may work with others on many separate occasions. The skill is engaging these individuals in the social work process, which relates back to communication and interpersonal skills. These professionals are also a resource. Within their own professional role, they have a wealth of knowledge and therefore building relationships provides you with a valuable source of knowledge. No, we are not talking about sharing confidential information, but a question about an illness, a mental ill-health concern, a substance for example illicit drugs, could help you understand the potential impact, internal/external stressors, and provide an opportunity to explore wider consequences. Here we can see the development of your social capital (Bourdieu, 1996), and subsequent sharing of knowledge and experience, which contributes towards your professional growth and development.

Summary

This chapter has explored your learning journey and how this continues to advance your professional growth and development. You have reviewed your learning journey through the social work course, identified learning and through critical reflection demonstrated professional growth and development. Therefore, your learning is much more visible. The seven scenarios of the dramaturgical approach to reflection enable a more in-depth reflection including multi perspectives from seven different, but interrelated scenarios. Each scenario could be presented on its own, from a single perspective or from multiple perspectives. Alternatively, several scenarios might provide the opportunity to explore a piece of work from different, but a specific outlook. Indeed, all seven scenarios could be reflected upon, and in any order. Thus, this approach to reflection is flexible, adaptable and multi-dimensional. Undertaking such critical reflection will add meaning and understanding, along with creating new knowledge, to enhance and advance your social work practice. Through the process of critical reflection, in addition to your increasing experience, your practice wisdom will grow. An important thing to remember is that your learning journey is continuous throughout your social work career. We build on these ideas in Chapter 4 which considers critical thinking and reflection as part of your continuing professional development.

Further reading

Ferguson, I., Ioakimidis, V., & Lavalette, M. (2018). *Global social work in a political context: Radical perspectives*. Bristol University Press.

This book provides global perspectives of social work including inequalities and economic problems. Case studies, projects and approaches from different countries provide additional insight into international social work.

Ingram, R. (2015). *Understanding emotions in social work: Theory, practice and reflection*. Open University Press.

This book provides a greater understanding of how emotions might impact our relationships including social work practice. There are activities which support reflection along with 'key learning points' at the end of each chapter.

Rutter, L., & Brown, K. (2019). *Critical thinking and professional judgement for social work* (5th ed.). Sage/Learning Matters.

This book provides a wealth of information in relation to critical reflection and writing. There are chapters on professional judgement and using knowledge in practice. This is a very good resource for students and newly qualified social workers completing the Assessed and Supported Year in Employment (ASYE) programme.

Chapter 4

Managing CPD and critical thinking throughout your assessed and supported year in employment (ASYE)

Andrew Morris

Introduction

Congratulations on qualifying as a social worker!

The transition from student to newly qualified social worker, and then on to experienced social worker, will see you grow and develop as a professional. Chapter 2 discussed the process for supporting newly qualified social workers and how this is different in each of the four countries in the UK. Chapter 3 considered your transition from student to newly qualified social worker. The information in this chapter will be relevant to all four nations, and over the following pages, you will learn how to effectively use your continuous professional development (CPD) opportunities to make the most of your time as a newly qualified social worker. You will also be asked to consider CPD and how you can make this as beneficial to your development as possible. The final section of the chapter looks at critical thinking and discusses its importance for both experienced and newly qualified social workers and identifies top tips on how to practise it. The chapter will end with some suggestions on self-care and how you can look after yourself during your newly qualified year in practice.

CPD and Critical Reflection during your assessed and supported year in employment

The assessed and supported year in employment is employer-led and designed in each country to ensure that you, as a newly qualified social worker, are sufficiently supported and assessed.

As well as you, there are three other stakeholders who support you in your mentorship and CPD requirements during your ASYE year. These are your allocated assessor, your employer, and the service users you will be working with each day.

1. The main role of the assessor is to ensure effective support and assessment arrangements are in place for you. In the end, they will make a professional recommendation that will be moderated 'internally' by your employer. The relationship with your assessor/mentor is key to a successful ASYE and it is important to make the most of the relationship by… building mutual respect; being open and honest; and remember that it is a two-way relationship.

2. Some employers provide further guidance on how to build the relationship effectively. Remember that no one individual alone will take responsibility for your final ASYE assessment, essentially, it's all about trust. The more you trust your assessor, the more they will trust you to do a good job. The key to trust is open and honest communication.

3. Your employer is responsible for delivering your ASYE unit, arranging training and CPD opportunities, providing case management for your work, and ensuring you have a mentor/assessor.

4. Service users can provide you with feedback that forms part of your portfolio and highlight areas for development that you may wish to focus on to help develop your practice.

ACTIVITY 4.1

Effective communication

Please think of three things you can do to ensure effective communication, trust and respect with your:

Assessor

[For example, being open and honest about making mistakes or getting things wrong]

1.

2.

3.

Employer

[For example, recognising and telling your employer when you need help]

1.

2.

3.

(Continued)

(Continued)

Service user

[For example, clarifying expectations about what you can and can't do for them]

1.

2.

3.

Finally, consider any challenges, issues or factors that could prevent you from doing these things. What strategies could you use to minimise them?

There is no one standard way to complete the ASYE year because the requirements for the course vary from one local authority to another, and the programmes differ in each country, as discussed in Chapter 2. Therefore, it would be beneficial to find out how your employer's [or future employers'] NQSW programme supports newly qualified social workers (see Chapters 1 and 2).

ASYE programmes in England aim to ensure newly qualified social workers can evidence that they are meeting the relevant standards of the Professional Capabilities Framework [PCF] (British Association of Social Workers 2018) and the Knowledge and Skills Statements [KSS] (Department of Health 2015; Department for Education 2018). In England, registration is not linked to your newly qualified status. Instead, each care council requires you to meet specific qualifications and CPD criteria. You can register without holding newly qualified status, as long as those requirements are met. Depending on your country of work, you should familiarise yourself with the requirements and expectations.

Once you have qualified as a social worker, you can apply to register with the relevant professional body. For social workers in England, this is Social Work England. Once registration is complete, you will be entitled to use the term 'Social Worker', regardless of whether you have completed your newly qualified programme or not. ASYE programmes are run by employers, and they are open to all newly qualified social workers, whether you are working in a social work role in a statutory setting, voluntary, independent, private setting, or elsewhere. It also includes social work with all service-user groups, including children and young people and their families, adults with learning disabilities, mental health concerns, physical disabilities and older adults. As discussed earlier, each country of the UK has its own version of the newly qualified social worker programme, which will determine the particular CPD routes taken. (see Chapters 1 and 2).

Why do we need CPD in the newly qualified programmes?

The transition from being a university student to a professional social worker is not always an easy one. Social work is challenging – it requires skill, specialist knowledge, and emotional resilience. Social workers who had just qualified reported the transition from classroom practice to be especially challenging with some reporting feelings of frustration and unhappiness (Jack and Donnellan 2010). These feelings can leave newly qualified workers with a sense of disillusionment, and they are cited as reasons for leaving the profession (Csiernik et al. 2010). Further studies suggested there was a need for formal support mechanisms put into place to help newly qualified workers manage the transition into practice (Smith and Pilling 2007; Bradley 2008; Csiernik et al. 2010).

In order to address these issues, the governments of the United Kingdom developed NQSW programmes for social work graduates. They are all slightly different in Scotland, Northern Ireland, England and Wales, but they all feature a formalised programme of support (Moorhead et al. 2020). This support may include regular supervision, mentoring, training, and protected caseloads. However, resources in local authorities have often been constrained, leading to training that was *ad hoc* rather than focusing on professional standards (Moorhead et al. 2020). Further criticism was identified by Stevenson (2018) who found that nearly half of the newly qualified social workers surveyed reported not having protected (lower, less complex) caseloads. Regardless of the challenges of implementing formal support for newly qualified social workers, research suggests it has a positive impact on social worker confidence, recruitment and retention, and outcomes for service users (Carpenter et al. 2012; Moorhead et al. 2020). Let us now take a look at those who help make the newly qualified programmes effective.

Firstly, there is the student. You will take part in the programme, engage in supervision, and reflective learning, and complete your portfolio to evidence what you have learned and achieved. Most employers in England will ask you to write reflective pieces of between 1000-2000 words, focusing on a piece of work you have undertaken. Your assessor will carry out observations of your practice and provide feedback for you, which you will in turn reflect on. Statement 12(d) of the Knowledge and Skills Statements for Adults (Department of Health 2015) says you should complete three observations of your practice. You will also receive feedback from three service users, and you will reflect on these too. This can be the most useful feedback because it is from the people who are on the receiving end of your interventions and decisions. Their feedback will help identify gaps or blind spots in your knowledge or skills.

Your employer will support your learning through your ASYE year, and your assessor will check your work to ensure you have met the relevant criteria set out by your employer. You will then submit your portfolio to a university to ensure your work meets the required academic standards.

As the lead for the ASYE programme at Bournemouth University, I run regular induction sessions with new ASYE students. During these sessions, I talk about the assessed and supported year in employment, the academic learning outcomes, critical reflection, and assignment writing, and I take them on a virtual tour of our online library. Throughout the year, we also run workshops for students to help develop their knowledge and skills.

When you come to write your critical reflective logs or practice analysis, you will need to consider a piece of work you have completed. Ideally, it will be a recent piece of work so it is still fresh in your mind. Many ASYE students choose to base their critical reflections on an assessment with a service user or carer, or a review of someone's support. You will be expected to reflect on your work. This may involve a consideration of your thoughts and feelings about the person/situation. Some people explore issues of bias or prejudice that they become aware of during their reflection. Sometimes the person or situation reminds the social worker of things from their personal history, and they explore that and how it affected their work. Identifying your thoughts and feelings about a service user and then analysing them is key to critical reflection. Some people like to ask themselves questions such as: Why was I feeling this way? What could I have done differently? How can I use this insight to help my practice in the future? Putting yourself under the microscope and being brutally honest with yourself is a useful, albeit potentially uncomfortable, strategy. This will be a key feature of your CPD activities, and the more open you are with yourself, the more valuable your reflections will be.

Many clever people have developed many clever models of reflection. Two of the most common ones are Gibbs' Reflective Cycle (Gibbs 1988), and Kolb's Experiential Learning Cycle (Kolb 1984). Both models see learning as a process, rather than a one-off event. I will give a brief overview of them both here.

Kolb's model is based on theories about how people learn. The model focuses on the concept that people develop their learning and knowledge best through practical experiences. In other words, we learn best by 'doing'. Kolb suggests there are four stages we go through when reflecting on a situation.

1. The model starts with a 'Concrete Experience'. When you're writing out reflective pieces, this is where you may wish to write a brief summary of the situation you are reflecting upon. You may want to say why you were in a situation, what your role was, who else was there, etc. This stage also includes consideration of your thoughts and feelings at the time.

2. The next stage is entitled 'Observations & Reflections Stage'. Here you reflect on what happened; noting down any experiences you haven't come across before. You will ask yourself what went well in the situation, and what didn't go well. Why?

3. Next, you move into the 'Abstract Conceptualisation Stage', or Making Sense stage if you prefer. You start to develop new ideas. You ask yourself why something happened the way it did. You can draw on theory or research to help answer these why questions, and begin to develop a hypothesis/conclusion about the event.

4. Finally, you move into the Action Planning Stage. During this stage, you will consolidate your learning and hypotheses about the situation, and you have a plan to test them. You may try something different in a similar situation in the future, or you decide that what you did worked, and you'll employ that approach again. Either way, you will be applying your learning to new situations and then begin the cycle again to further develop your skills.

Gibbs, on the other hand, has a slightly more detailed approach.

Like Kolb, learning is seen as a process which begins with a Description.

1. The Description Stage will see you discussing the situation. You will most likely consider your role/what you did, when and where it took place, who else was there, and how did it go?

2. For the next stage, you will consider emotions, both yours and other people's. You may ask yourself what you were feeling before, during and after the event. You may speculate on what other people were feeling before, during and after.

3. Next, in the Evaluation Stage, you will consider how the event went. Was it successful? Did you get what you wanted out of it? Did it all go according to plan? Or were there any problems? Any challenges? What didn't go the way you expected, or hoped it would?

4. We consider these issues as we move into the Analysis Stage. Here we ask *Why?* Why didn't things go well? Why did things go well? We also consider why you [and possibly other people there] were feeling the way you were. You will apply theories and maybe look at research findings to help explain these issues.

5. Once you have your hypotheses and possible explanations of why things went the way they did, you move into the Conclusion Stage. During this stage, you consolidate what you have learned. You summarise what you've ascertained and consider the question: what have I learned from this experience? What could you have done differently?

6. We consider the last question in practical teams during the final stage of Action Planning, when you try out something different. If you said or did something, or used a theory or research finding that wasn't as helpful as you'd have hoped, this is where you can experiment and try again with something else. When you are next in a similar situation, do something that you didn't do last time and see what the outcome is. You will repeat the cycle, and your learning will develop.

7. You will be experiencing a lot of learning during your first year of qualifying, and reflective models like these will help you unpick your experiences and start to build your practice wisdom.

There will also be an element of critical analysis. You will be expected to critically analyse theory, research and legislation in relation to this piece of work. We will look at these aspects in more detail later in the chapter. There could be a final section looking at anti-oppressive practice, where you can demonstrate how you identified potential areas of oppression/discrimination and what you did to address them.

When you have completed all the assignments for your portfolio, they will be signed off by your employer, and then marked by a university academic. Most other higher education providers who run newly qualified programmes run them similarly. I do want to stress that not everyone passes their ASYE year the first time around. The main issues are around critical reflection or analysis in their reflective pieces. Critical reflection is covered later in the book, so I strongly recommend that any newly qualified social workers read the chapter on critical reflection.

How to make the most of your newly qualified year

Whichever way your employer has chosen to deliver the ASYE, clarity over assessment procedures is critical. Your employer is ultimately responsible and accountable for assessment decisions and determining any appeals or complaints from students. Remember, though, you are still responsible for your professional development. That's why it is important to look out for employers who will support you through your newly qualified year, and beyond, as you become a more experienced and, later, senior social worker. A good employer will have a well-established CPD framework for its staff, which ideally works in partnership with a university, as these will offer you nationally recognised awards that will be valued as such (Keen et al. 2016). Additionally, you may wish to look at whether your employer/potential employer provides dedicated time for CPD activities for newly qualified social workers. Alongside this point, find out about formal learning activities available for newly qualified people. You need the time, and you need meaningful things to do. Supervision will also be an invaluable resource in your learning. Having a protected caseload is also important. I have met many students who have ended up taking on additional pieces of work because of the pressures on the team. However, having a protected caseload is important when you are a newly qualified social worker, and you may wish to explore how this can be achieved before you start.

Supervision is also important. Make sure you have regular supervision sessions booked, and that they are run in a consistent format. As a former manager, it can be easy to slip into case management activities with supervisees. You and your supervisor need to make sure there is time built into your supervision sessions to reflect on your work. Critical reflection in supervision, in my opinion, is more important than case management. This is because it requires the use of more skills for both the supervisor and supervisee, and you will need to ensure the session doesn't turn into a counselling session, as that is not what either of you are there for. Instead, you want to strive for open, honest reflection on your work and learning needs. If you don't have this kind of relationship with your manager, there's nothing to say you have to do it with them. Maybe there's a colleague or peer in the team you could have this form of supervision with? It's something to think about anyway when you are considering your CPD options with potential employers.

ACTIVITY 4.2

Questions to consider about your employer's ASYE programme

Reflect on the following questions and note down your answers.

- How would you describe the key elements of your employer's or prospective employer's ASYE programme?

o   Partnership? Flexible? Professional confidence? Competence? Capability? Support? Assessment?

- How will you be supported throughout the year?

    o   Proformas? Induction period? Probation period? Reviews? Observations? Link to academic qualifications? Reduced workloads? What frequency of reflective supervision? Link to pay and progression? Moderation? Final assessment/outcome?

- What are the arrangements for probation, induction, appraisal, and resolving appeals and complaints?

    o   Pass/fail predictions? Extensions? Action plans? Probation?

Comment

Table 4.1   Questions and reflections to consider

You may have written something like the following:	
How would you describe the key elements of your employer's or prospective employer's ASYE programme?	Collaborating on the work Sharing learning Offers a variety of learning and support systems Close ties with a university
How will you be supported throughout the year?	Supervision every two weeks Protected caseload [remember Stevenson's (2018) research – see references at the end of the chapter] Access to online and in-person training A named mentor in the team
What are the arrangements for probation, induction, appraisal, and resolving appeals and complaints?	A planned induction process Regular reviews are built into the programme Opportunities for feedback, comments and complaints

Managing your newly qualified year in practice

As you start and then progress through your newly qualified year, you will be required to manage your time well. You will need to balance studying alongside your caseload. The rest of this chapter will consider some top tips on how to achieve your work/study/home life balance.

Firstly, start planning early. Think about how you study best. Do you leave things until the last minute? Or do you like to start early? Knowing this will help you plan your time better. One of my tutees at university always liked to leave things until the last minute. She tried to start an assignment early once but really struggled to get motivated. She said she needs the adrenaline of knowing she's only got a day left to complete the work – that's what helps her through her assignments. Another student, on the other hand, preferred to get the work done early. The stress of the approaching deadline was too much, so he liked to crack on with his work as soon as it was set. That way, if anything went wrong, he'd still have time to finish it before the deadline.

If you can, set aside time each day for some writing or reflection. This needs to be the time when you will not be disturbed. It can be for ten minutes or an hour – it's up to you. Remove distractions, e.g. switch off your email. Hide your phone. If you're in the office, it might be useful to find a quiet room away from other people; otherwise, their conversations will draw you in, or they will come and talk to you. Once you have your physical and mental space prepared, you can begin studying.

Set yourself studying goals each day. It could be something small like watching a YouTube video or reading an article from *Community Care*. Or, it could be something a little bigger, such as writing up some reflective notes. Again, these don't have to be extensive. Setting yourself a goal of 500 words, or even just 100 words, will be useful. Getting yourself into the habit of doing some uninterrupted studying each day will help you focus. It'll soon become second nature, and it doesn't matter if your reflective pieces never see the light of day – it's the process that is useful. You'll soon begin to think and reflect automatically, so when you come to write your reflective pieces in your portfolio, it'll come naturally to you.

It might be handy to find an ASYE Buddy. If you know of another ASYE student or group of students, you should consider connecting with them. You can support and motivate each other, and also commiserate and complain about all the work together too. You'll all be in the same boat after all!

Finally, make sure you look after yourself. It's too easy to get into bad habits of working in the evening and at weekends. If you find yourself saying you'll just write up one more thing in the evening, or you'll do a bit of work at the weekend, STOP! You're not paid to work 24/7, and your mind and body will take a huge battering if you don't look after yourself properly. Take breaks. Take time away from the screen and take your weekends off. You won't regret it. Remember, these tips are all about working smarter, not harder.

As you progress through your ASYE year there will be one main theme running through it – your CPD.

Managing your CPD

The purpose of this section is to explore CPD – what it is and why we need it. CPD in social work can be defined as:

> … *a term for the reflection and learning activities that social workers do through-out their career. CPD should maintain and improve a social worker's practice. (Social Work England 2022)*

As social workers, CPD is a concept that accompanies us throughout our professional careers. It will guide you down different paths to develop your knowledge and skills. It will always be there, underpinning training courses, referred to in supervision sessions, and it will come up in job interviews, as you move around in organisations. Wherever you are and whatever role you're in, you will be learning. As human beings, we begin learning from the moment we're born, and we don't stop until we reach the end of our lives. The famous science-fiction author Isaac Asimov once said,

You are never too old to learn more than you already know and to become able to do more than you already can. (Asimov 1985)

We can learn things for pleasure, such as how to cook, how to paint, and how to sing. We also learn things for work, such as how to carry out assessments, develop our understanding of legislation, and develop our time management skills. Learning is a process that began when we were born and carried on through school, adolescence, college and university, and it will continue throughout your life. Each of these stages gives us different types of learning, and our professional social work CPD will involve three different types of learning (Brown and Rutter 2019) (see Box 4.1).

BOX 4.1

Types of learning

Formal learning: This will meet nationally recognised standards and involve further academic study, e.g. post-qualifying stand-alone units at the university that could be used to help build a Bachelor's or Master's degree. These higher education programmes will be validated against nationally agreed standards, which will be recognised throughout the UK.

Informal [or non-accredited] learning: This includes in-house training and workshops, induction programmes, secondments, mentoring, or e-learning modules provided within your organisation.

Experiential learning: This is an area where we may learn the most. It includes activities such as peer discussions, coaching others, case study reviews, and supervision. It also covers the learning we develop from our practice with service users, carers, family members, and other professionals.

As social workers, we need to develop our learning because the profession is constantly changing. We need to maintain our skills and keep up to date with the ever-changing landscape of social work. To ensure we don't get left behind, both we and our employers have a responsibility to ensure our skills are up-to-date and relevant to the job at hand. This principle is enshrined in social work principles and policies. For example, the Professionalism and Professional Leadership elements of the ASYE level of the Professional Capabilities Framework (British Association of Social Workers 2018) explicitly talk about professional development, as does the Knowledge and Skills Statements (Department of Health 2015; Department for Education 2018). It is also a requirement of our continued registration as social workers. This reflects the fact that social work is always evolving and we need to evolve with it.

Once you have undertaken the activity, there will be an expectation that you will reflect on what you have learned. Social workers are encouraged to write a short piece of reflective writing to explore what you learned from the learning activity and how it will help your future practice. This is the key feature, not only of your NQSW year but of your ongoing CPD. So, how does this help the newly qualified social worker?

The Benefits of CPD

Before we look at the benefits of CPD, let's first ask ourselves, why do we learn stuff? Generally, we set out to learn new things to increase our knowledge, develop our skills, adapt to change, and understand the world better (Laal and Salamati 2012). Learning helps us become better social workers. While doing your newly qualified year, you will be learning constantly, and sometimes you won't even be aware of it. Thinking of you as an individual social worker, reflect on the following:

- Why do you want to achieve your ASYE?

- What do you want to learn/gain from it?

- Which areas do you feel confident in?

- Which areas don't you feel so confident in?

- How familiar are you with the latest thinking, discussions and/or developments in your area of work? How do we know what we don't know?

One simple answer to the last question is that we get feedback from others. This is the simple and most effective answer. While you are undertaking your first qualifying year, you are constantly being assessed. Receiving feedback and reflecting on it can feel awkward at first. You may feel exposed and criticised, and you may doubt your abilities. Rest assured, though, this is normal. Feedback from professionals and colleagues will usually be couched in supportive terms, and all feedback you receive will help you grow and develop.

This is where we take advantage of CPD opportunities. Every piece of constructive feedback provides a new area of CPD to explore. Imagine you are standing on one side of a river, which is where all the newly qualified social workers live. You want to get to the other side because that's where all the experienced social workers live. Each piece of feedback highlights something you need to work on – so think of it as a stepping stone to becoming an experienced social worker. Seek out feedback from people and identify your areas of development. This will form the foundation for a new stepping stone, and once you have identified an area of development, you can take part in CPD activities to address your knowledge gap. Once you have done this, you will have a new stepping stone to take you closer to your goal of becoming an experienced social worker.

CASE STUDY 4.1

Maria

For example, Maria was a newly qualified social worker in an adult social care team. She went out with a colleague observing her to visit a service user, James, who was living with a brain injury. Maria carried out her assessment. James answered all of her questions and said he was perfectly happy and content, and he didn't need any support. Afterwards Maria asked for some feedback from her colleague. Her colleague sensitively shared their thoughts. They asked Maria about James' insight into his care needs. She suggested James may have given the right answers to her questions, but the evidence in his home suggested he wasn't looking after himself very well. This led to a discussion around mental capacity. Maria became aware she was not that knowledgeable around mental capacity. Maria booked herself on some Mental Capacity Act training and so stepped onto another metaphorical stepping stone.

Now, I'm going to let you in on something that you may not be aware of at this stage of your career. The other side of the river is an illusion. It's always moving away from you. Those experienced social workers you see on the other side – the ones who know everything and who can handle everything – they're not on that side. They're actually still making their way across the river. They're a little further ahead of you but there are still things they are working on. They still have blind spots in their practice or in their thinking. There are things they want to develop or they want to learn. They'll never get to the other side of the river and neither will you because as we said earlier, social work is always changing and new things are coming out all the time. Everyone's CPD journey will be different and it will never end.

This means you will always be learning and developing and growing both as a professional social worker and also as a human being. As part of your journey, you'll be given a personal development plan. It may be called something different where you are but you will have one. It is a document that records the learning you have done so far, and it also records the learning that you wish to pursue in the future.

What I want to learn	What I have to do	What resources or support do I need	How will I know I've been successful	Date to achieve this learning by
Understanding the pressures faced by carers	*Spend time with carers, listen to their stories and needs*	*Attend the carers forum. Complete carers assessments.*	*Feedback from carers* *I will feel more confident in this area*	*30th June*
How to apply attachment theory in my assessments.				
How to develop effective studying strategies.				

Figure 4.1   Example of a personal development plan

During your newly qualified year, there will be lots of learning. Some people will be in a team with much more experienced colleagues and feel a sense of inadequacy because they seem to know so much. Everyone is on their individual journeys of learning and development, so carry with you the words of William Faulkner, 'Always dream and shoot higher than you know you can do. Don't bother just to be better than your contemporaries or predecessors. Try to be better than yourself' (Stein 1956).

Setting Goals for CPD

So now we know you – we are all learning and growing and developing ourselves. This is central to being a social worker in the contemporary world. It would be useful, therefore, to come up with a development plan. As mentioned above, your employer will have one for you, but there is no harm in taking the initiative and identifying your own learning needs. Your employer will have a range of courses which will form part of your induction and your first year after qualifying. I would suggest taking advantage of all of these. It will also be useful to reflect on your own experiences, strengths and areas of development and note these down. Make a list of topics that you would like to learn about or practise, and make sure these are included in your personal learning and development plan. Be aware that learning and development shouldn't always be easy or comfortable.

ACTIVITY 4.3

Start your personal development plan

Design your own personal development plan and list five things you would like to develop during your first year as a qualified social worker.

- What I want to learn
- What I have to do
- What resources or support do I need?
- How will I know I've been successful?
- Date to achieve this learning by

Learning can be a painful process. Some would argue that the most effective learning takes place when we move outside our comfort zones. This is not to say that will always be the case (Leberman and Martin 2003). You will find yourself feeling anxious if you are in a situation where you do not feel you are that confident when there is an issue you are not familiar with, when your responsibility increases, and you are under pressure from service users or carers (Williams and Rutter 2023). So, how can we best manage these feelings of anxiety while continuing to develop as a social worker?

One way you can do this is to keep your end goal in mind. Even the most experienced social workers still feel anxious when they are encountering things outside their comfort zones. For them, it may not happen as frequently, or as intensely to them as it does to newly qualified workers, but that feeling is still there. Experienced social workers feel nervous but they have a goal in mind. I remember attending some court training many years ago. It was run by a barrister and he invited people to 'take the stand'. He gave us a scenario and questioned us about it. The questions were challenging and he got everyone tied up in their answers. It was a very nerve-racking scenario but very useful as it helped to prepare us for being cross-examined if we had to go into court ourselves. In that example, we wanted to learn something, which would be useful in the future, and we had to keep our end goal in sight.

Another example from my practice comes from my role as an approved mental health professional [AMHP]. I had been a social worker for about seven years before I undertook my AMHP training. Despite my experience, I would always feel nervous when a referral came through. When I was given the referral I would have to gather background information, find two doctors to assist with the assessment, speak to the patient's nearest relative and advise them of the assessment, as well their legal powers under the Mental Health Act. Then I would have to visit the person and carry out the assessment with the doctors. Afterwards, if the patient needed to be admitted to hospital, the doctors would leave and I would be left with the patient while I waited for a bed to be found and then wait for an ambulance. Quite often I would have to draw on all my social work skills of assessment, building rapport, risk assessment, coordinating services, managing a crisis, and ensuring I was following strict procedures outlined in the legislation, all while working alone with a patient who was extremely unwell, anxious, confused, and sometimes hostile.

I managed my anxiety by breaking down the task and focusing on the goal of getting my patient safely into hospital. I attended all the AMHP forums and training courses. I read articles and blogs by experienced AMHPS and I shadowed colleagues whenever I could. For me, the fear was of the unknown – asking myself 'what if..?' As I developed a repertoire of different approaches and anecdotes from my colleagues I began to feel less like I was drowning and more like I was navigating a stretch of water. If something unexpected came up, I often had an example, a story, or a piece of knowledge that I could draw on to help me decide how I should respond. The more I practised, the more questions I identified about possible scenarios. In other words, I discovered more learning goals, which lead to me gathering more resources to help manage the role.

Once you have identified your learning goals you will be able to go out and find your own resources to meet them. This leads us to another useful question – what do you want to learn?

ACTIVITY 4.4

Take control of your CPD

The following activity has been developed from the previous edition of this book (Keen et al. 2016).

How might you develop a personalised and meaningful approach to CPD? Here are some topic areas and related questions to reflect on.

The context of CPD: Are you clear about why you are participating in a CPD session/activity? Is it all about registration, job chances, improving job satisfaction, or outcomes for your service users? Is it about improving your work environment or supporting others in the workplace?

Partnership: Who is involved in your likely CPD partnerships? What are these partnerships like and how can they be improved? Is it all 'in-house' or do you need to network with other professionals? What CPD opportunities is your employer offering?

Reflection: Are you able to stop and reflect on your practice? What barriers stop this process? How might you remove or lessen these barriers?

Motivation: What is your motivation to learn? What factors might improve your motivation to learn in the future? What might erode your motivation, and how could you address this?

At this point, it might be useful for you to draw up an action plan. Include a timeline in your plan for the skills, knowledge and experiences you wish to develop. What activities might help you achieve your professional development goals?

It might also be useful to draw up a list of key partnerships you might like to develop and consider how you might develop them.

- Think about what you are good at and what you like to do.

- Think about where you want to be, and/or where you want to work, in one to five years.

- Think about what skills and knowledge you would like to develop during this time. Feel free to revisit your undergraduate professional development plan or skills analysis.

Critical thinking and reflection

In this section, we will define critical thinking and reflection and identify tools to help you develop your skills in this area. Critical thinking and reflection form the foundations of your CPD activities. As social workers, we need to do more than cite research and memorise theories and pieces of legislation. We need to understand them and how they relate to the people we work with. Critical thinking and reflection help us develop our understanding and engage in deep learning. There are many definitions of critical thinking. One interpretation is that it involves '...analysis, evaluation, and the construction of an argument' (Lim 2011, p.88). Some may describe it as purposeful, reasoned, and goal-directed thinking (Deal and Pittman 2009). While others may argue it is the...

> *...ability to engage in purposeful, self-regulatory judgment that includes thinking about important problems within disciplinary areas as well as in the social, political and ethical challenges of everyday life. (Abrami et al. 2008, p.1102)*

To Sheppard et al. (2018), how social workers think is an issue that is just as important as *what* they should know. Critical thinking, or looking at the world through a more critical lens, is something we should be doing all the time, as it helps us in our assessment and decision-making. It is useful, or even vital to social work when we are looking at a referral, reading case notes or previous assessments for a service user, when carrying out an assessment and when planning support for someone.

Mathias (2015) looked at critical thinking in social work and identified two different approaches. The first is associated with scientific approaches and avoiding logical errors in judgement. It is a form of practical reasoning, which is a thinking process that identifies shared values and looks at how to meet these values. This approach complements evidence-based practice and is intended to promote positive outcomes for learners. It involves looking at facts and designing interventions that provide the best outcomes for the individual student. Authors who subscribe to this approach include Gibbs and Gambrill (1999), Gambrill (1993), and Gibbs (1991). However, like many things in the world of social work, this isn't as straightforward as it may appear. When considering this approach, it might be useful to ask yourself the following questions:

- Who defines what counts as evidence?

- Who benefits from having *this* as a piece of evidence? [and who misses out?]

- How useful is evidence that highlights what needs to be changed, if it doesn't also tell us how to change it?

- What isn't being counted as evidence? And what are the implications of this?

- Are we looking for evidence to support our position? Or as we looking to structure our position based on the evidence?

- How easily does evidence based on one person/situation fit with another person/ situation?

(Based on Hargreaves and Fullan 2012)

In contrast to this approach, Witkin (1990) and Gibbons and Gray (2004) suggest that critical thinking in social work should be aligned with social constructivism. Social constructivism focuses on the collaboration of learning. Students are encouraged to question and explore ideas to help build on the knowledge they already have. Here, teachers and educators are more like facilitators of learning, rather than the fonts of all knowledge, ready to impart their wisdom upon the grateful student. Students learn through collaboration, discussion and exploration of topics.

If you are taking this approach to your learning, it can be useful to ask yourself these questions:

- How do I ensure my learning/exploration of a topic is focused? One of the criticisms of social constructivist learning is that it can lack focus.

- Measurements of learning with this approach are based on your progress with a topic. If you are working to an agreed set of measures, there is a risk you will not meet them in a timely manner, due to the unstructured nature of the learning.

- Assessors/educators who come from a social constructivist approach are often focused on the *what* of learning, but less on the *how* of learning. What can you do to ensure your learning meets your preferred learning style?

- When looking at learning activities, how suitable are they for you as a learner, and the topic at hand?

(Based on Brophy 2006)

One of the aims of critical thinking is to help social workers identify the values inherent in any understanding of reality (Mathias 2015). Social workers ensure their decisions are informed or guided by social work values. We need to know why we are doing something and how this reflects the power in society. It helps us ask how this intervention/outcome impacts our service users or group of service users, and it helps us become more aware of our anti-discriminatory practice.

Both approaches to critical thinking bring value to social work. The practical reasoning approach promoted by Gibbs and Gambrill is beneficial in that it is intended to help avoid bias and assumptions in decision-making. It aims to distinguish facts from values (Gambrill 1993) and it, therefore, seeks to ensure our objectivity. Whereas, the social constructionist approach of Witkins, Gibbons and Gray is more in line with adhering to the relativist value base of social work. It could be seen as a reflection of the radical theme of social work from the 1970s. It requires more creative thinking and interpretation, but is seen as being less *scientific* (Bronson 2000). For example, we can question ideas, knowledge and *the usual way of doing things* by asking 'why'. Why do we use this method of assessment? Why is the person-centred approach seen as the ideal way of working in our team? Why are practice learning sessions structured in this way? We can develop this approach by asking more hypothetical questions, such as, 'What if we did things this way?' 'What does this approach mean to the service user?' [How useful is it to them?], 'What is another way of structuring this session?'

During your ASYE year, a blend of the two approaches will help you develop your own particular style and help to inform your thinking and decision-making skills (Mathias 2015). Indeed, by reflecting on both approaches, you will become more aware of the social construction of reality and where social work sits, and your decisions will be more defensible when following the practical reasoning approach. With that in mind, I would like to invite you to reflect on critical reasoning and social constructivism and consider which approach appeals to you the most in terms of learning. Which is the most helpful in terms of your learning style? Which one are you drawn to the most? Which one makes the most sense?

Now that we have seen what critical thinking is, let's consider why you should use it during your newly qualified year in practice.

Why use critical thinking?

One of the aims of critical thinking and reflection is to create some doubt and critique of one's actions and thought processes (Brown and Rutter 2019). It helps us to question our thinking and identify our blind spots. Critical thinking can help us to identify, avoid and/or address issues or practices that could be oppressive or discriminatory. By adding a critical element to our thinking, we see things from different perspectives and we are more open to recognising issues of social injustice.

As human beings, we are imperfect information processors. We are susceptible to bias and cognitive distortions. When dealing with information, our brains look for shortcuts which means we sometimes miss key points if we are not paying attention. We have all been human beings far longer than we have been social workers, and so we are susceptible to bias and cognitive distortions. Critical thinking can act as a way of identifying and acknowledging our biases to reduce their impact on our work.

In England, you will be working within the Professional Capabilities Framework [PCF] (British Association of Social Workers 2018). The PCF framework provides a single set of standards for all social workers from initial qualification to advanced practice. Critical thinking can be seen as a factor underlying all nine domains of the PCF. The other countries of the UK have slightly different standards. Social workers in Wales have the Code of Professional Practice; Social workers in Scotland have the Health & Social Care Standards; and Social Workers in Northern Ireland have the Standards of Conduct & Practice. However, critical thinking skills are central to achieving the standards in all four countries. Without the ability to critically think about and draw upon our professional knowledge, our skills/interventions, and our social work values, we would not be effective social workers. Indeed, without critical thinking and reflecting on what we could/should be doing, we would just be glorified form-fillers; ticking boxes and taking a procedural-based approach. This, I imagine, is not what you signed up for when you began your training!

Instead, critical thinking helps us see the world and the people we work with differently. We can use our critical thinking to help build our professional knowledge and skills. Going back to the practical reasoning and social constructionist approaches, both of these approaches increase our knowledge and awareness. When we are faced with a decision, a procedural approach may have us looking at a flow-chart where we begin at point A, move to Point B, assess a situation, and then move to Point C or D. This doesn't involve any great level of thinking, and it doesn't help to develop our knowledge through our practice. However, by using the social constructionist and/or practical reasoning approach, we are encouraged to think of other possibilities. We think outside the box. We consider the situation from different points of view, and by doing this, we may discover options that we would not otherwise have thought of.

This is not only useful to our practice, but I would also suggest it is vital to our practice. Consider for a moment, anti-oppressive practice. This value is one of the foundations on which contemporary social work is built. Discrimination and oppression can be experienced by anyone. Policies and ways of working can inadvertently discriminate against people or treat them unfairly. By engaging in critical thinking when undertaking our assessments or planning interventions, we can help to avoid any discrimination. Critical thinking helps us to become more aware of our values, as well as stimulating our creativity and curiosity. To put it in a nutshell, it helps to develop our decision-making skills, which are useful to us as social workers! Without the ability to critically reflect on our work, our planning, and our interventions, we will be at a great risk of poor decision-making. Poor decision-making can be the result of cognitive bias, where we focus on one particular piece of information or evidence and neglect other viewpoints. We may miss or even avoid other perspectives, such as the carers' views or the individuals' wishes. There is also the risk that we would take information at face value, without necessarily questioning it. This can lead to oppressive practices. For example, when I worked in an older person's team, a colleague had a telephone call from a GP. The GP was concerned about one of their patients who was living with dementia. They had been called out to see the patient that afternoon because they had run out of medication and were physically unwell. The GP believed the patient was no longer safe living at home because of the risk of self-neglect, and they needed to be placed in a care home. They listed several occasions where they had been called out to see this person, as well as the numerous visits from the district nursing team. The patient, the GP explained, was at risk of malnutrition, falls, becoming lost in the local community, not managing their personal care, and they also presented a risk of fire due to confusion about how to use their microwave. The GP gave my colleague a letter of support to help access funding for the care home placement.

On the surface, these concerns are all legitimate and pose significant risks that could result in serious harm. My colleague considered the GP's advice and engaged her critical thinking skills. She went out to assess the individual and, after some work with the person's family, carers, and an occupational therapist, they managed to support the patient to live at home, which was their wish, for another six months before they eventually had to go into a care home due to declining physical health. If the social worker had just accepted the GP's assessment and placed the individual in a care home, they would have been miserable.

So, I hear you ask, can we develop our critical thinking skills? One simple exercise is a SWOT analysis: SWOT stands for Strengths, Weaknesses, Opportunities, and Threats (see Table 4.2). The idea is to note down as many points as you can in each square. This will help to ensure you cover all perspectives and points of view. You can then assess the strengths and weaknesses of a particular plan and decide whether the benefits outweigh the costs. And, you can look at the threats – the potential problems – and come up with ways of managing each of these. Let's use the example above to see how it may look:

Table 4.2   Example of a SWOT Analysis

SWOT Analysis – whether to move into residential care or not

Strengths	Weaknesses
• Physical safety would be improved • The GP believes this is best for her • Reduced risk of malnutrition • Personal care would be managed well	• She doesn't want to go into a care home • She'd have less freedom • Unable to go to the shops/see friends when she wishes • She has memories in her current home • Residential care is expensive for the local authority
Opportunities	Threats
• If she had a fall, carers could attend to her immediately • Increased social opportunities	• She will likely feel miserable and experience a decline in her mental health. • Loss of identity • Sense of loss from moving into a care home. • She could be supported at home with a package of care

ACTIVITY 4.5

Reflecting on decision-making

Think of a service user you are either currently working with or someone you worked with on placement. Reflect on a decision you had to make as a social worker, and using a SWOT Analysis as a framework, jot down the various factors that may influence your thinking.

How can we develop our critical thinking?

One of the main components of critical thinking is the notion of self-awareness. Self-awareness – knowledge of ourselves – how and why we think and feel in certain situations (Carden et al. 2021) aids our critical thinking skills. Having a deeper level of awareness of ourselves helps us to become more open-minded and thoughtful (Walker and Finney 1999). We can question knowledge and situations more easily, and with practice, it becomes second nature to us. Ask any experienced social worker and they'll tell you, that as their critical thinking skills develop, they no longer watch films or they don't watch films and television programmes in the same way. They are looking beneath the surface, making links with theory, and recognising oppression and discriminatory attitudes. Critical thinking requires us to change our mindset and not take things at face value. To quote the wise Master Yoda, 'You must unlearn, what you have learned' in the 1980 Star Wars film *The Empire Strikes Back*.

Sometimes when we visit someone or talk to a service user, we get the sense that something is amiss. Critical thinking and reflection help us engage with our intuition. We become more aware of the subtle messages from our intuition that tell us when something isn't right. We can use supervision to help unpick and explore these experiences. Your supervisor or mentor will help you to go over what was happening and make links between the inner world of your thoughts and feelings, and the outer world of your service users and carers. They can help you become aware of new insights, biases, blind spots, or gaps in your skills/knowledge. This in turn becomes a form of practice wisdom which, according to Samson (2015), is the foundation of professional social work practice. Everything we've learned both formally and informally contributes to our practice wisdom. Over the next few years, you will build your repertoire of knowledge and wisdom about all things social work. It will help underpin your relationship skills as well as your assessment skills and critical thinking skills.

One of the main benefits for service users when you engage in critical thinking is that you look at situations from multiple points of view. It can be useful to help recognise whose voice is not being heard in decision-making. This could be during a meeting with a family, carers, service user, and/or professionals, or when you are gathering information for an assessment or when reading a report. Some people's voices or opinions will overshadow others and this could lead to their view being seen as 'the truth'. Their opinions may be louder and carry more weight, but as social workers, we need to ensure all voices are heard, and that all points of view are considered. Critical thinking helps us recognise whose voice or opinion is not being heard, and with that recognition comes awareness and we can turn our attention to the other perspectives.

How can we develop our critical thinking and reflection skills?

As mentioned earlier, most ASYE students are required to write critical reflection pieces at various points throughout their first year. These pieces of work generally follow the following format: An introduction that sets out the intervention or referral you will be talking about; a description of the service user and their situation; a discussion of theories, legislation and sometimes research that is informing your practice; followed by a conclusion which looks at the outcome for the service user and what you have learned as a social worker. It is important to remember that critical thinking isn't about memorising facts, finding evidence to support other people's conclusions, or blindly accepting what those in authority tell us. It's about being sceptical, examining our own and others' assumptions/biases/faulty logic. It's about exploring issues in order to see things from multiple perspectives. Here is a list of questions to help get your mind into critical-thinking mode:

1. When considering information ask yourself how do we know this? Was it an observation? Word of mouth? Common knowledge? Gossip? How valid is the source?

2. How does this look from the service user/carer perspective? How do they see my role and intervention?

3. What are three points that support my perspective? And what are three points that go against it?

4. Why now?

5. So what?

6. What if?

7. What don't I know?

8. Why is this important?

9. How will you know if your intervention is successful or not?

10. What do I want to achieve here?

11. What biases or assumptions could be made here?

12. What are some other possibilities?

As critical reflections focus on events that have happened in the past there is often a tendency for students to retell the story – to describe the events and what the student did to help the person. A lot of the time, this is too descriptive and some students fail to demonstrate their critical thinking skills in any great detail. To address this, we can be more curious about what happened and why. This is where our critical thinking comes into play. For example:

- When describing concerns raised in a new referral, we could ask ourselves why these concerns are significant. Why are they happening now? What might this mean for the service user?

- When writing about the recent history of a service user, we could ask why these previous events occurred? Why are the new concerns coming about now? Is there a link between then and now? What is different this time?

- Instead of listing options, we should explain the pros and cons of each option *for this particular person* (we are all different after all). Show the reader how the service user feels about each option. If they are unable to express an opinion, how does each option relate to their previous wishes or choices?

- When describing an intervention that you did or are thinking about, you could explain why this intervention was appropriate. Why was this the best outcome for the person? How did your social work values inform this decision?

- Then, at the end of your reflection/report/assignment/assessment instead of just summarising what happened and what you did, demonstrate to the reader why you made the decision that you did. If you are writing a reflective piece, tell the reader what you learned from this piece of work. What worked well? What didn't work so well? What will you do differently next time? What is one thing you will take away from this piece of work?

It might be useful at this stage to consider how we can think critically about theories and legislation. Here are some useful questions to help you critically think about the theories you use to underpin your practice and the legislation you are guided by.

Questions to ask when critically thinking and reflecting on theory

- Why did I choose this theory?

- Why did I reject another theory?

- What are the strengths and limitations of this theory?

- How successful was it?

- What will I do differently next time?

Questions to ask when critically thinking and reflecting on legislation

- How helpful is this piece of legislation, in this particular situation?

- Are there any grey areas in its wording?

ACTIVITY 4.6

Critically thinking about legislation

I have been marking reflective assignments for newly qualified and experienced social workers for many years. During that time, the one area that people tend to struggle with when engaging in critical thinking/reflection is legislation. Most people say they are following the Children Act 1989, the Adults with Incapacity (Scotland) Act 2000, the Social Services & WellBeing (Wales) Act 2014, or the Mental Capacity Act (Northern Ireland) 2016. They might quote the odd section from it to explain what they are doing. However, this is very descriptive, and it does not show your critical thinking or reflection skills. One way that you can showcase your critical skills is by considering the legal wording. Legislation often has quite woolly words and phrases, which are necessarily open to interpretation.

Consider the following phrases and reflect on what they mean to you, as a social worker, and what they might mean to your service user. Are there any differences? And if so, how do you decide who is right?

- *Within a reasonable period of time*

- *At risk of harm*

- *Consult with the SU/family*

- *Suffering from...*

- *The needs of the child*

- *Aim to work in partnership*

- *It is necessary to act*

- *Reasonable to believe...*

For example, reflecting on *Within a reasonable period of time* may be be interpreted as a referral for support, which could refer to a period of four to six weeks. In terms of how a service user may interpret it, a referral for support may refer to a few days.

Summary

In this chapter, we have explored the ASYE year – what it is, why we've got it, and how it works. It will help you make the transition from student to social worker as smoothly as possible and help you get the best start to your new career.

The main theme of the ASYE is your continuous professional development. We have seen that all social workers are always learning, all the time! Things rapidly change in our profession, and we need to stay on top of things. This means engaging in learning and constantly striving to develop our skills. One of the key skills you will need as a social worker is critical thinking skills. This involves questioning what we do and why we do it. It will be the focus of a lot of your CPD activities, and it will help you get the most out of your newly qualified year. Critical thinking will help you identify what you don't know or haven't been aware of. It will help you find the foundations or even reveal the next stepping stone on your never-ending journey of being a social worker. It is by no means an easy journey, but it is an extremely rewarding one, and the ASYE year will help you be as prepared as you can be.

This just leaves me to wish you the best of luck with everything in your future careers.

Further reading

Research in Practice. (n.d.). *Learning resources, activities, articles and research studies*. Retrieved October 3, 2025, from www.researchinpractice.org.uk

Has many learning resources, activities, articles and research studies that can help further your knowledge and give you valuable CPD experience.

Social Care Institute for Excellence. (n.d.). *Articles and resources for continuing professional development*. Retrieved October 3, 2025, from www.scie.org.uk

Has a huge collection of articles related to all fields of social work. You'll find no end of resources to help develop your CPD evidence.

Maclean, S. (n.d.). *Siobhan Maclean YouTube channel* http://www.youtube.com/@siobhanmaclean9614

An experienced social and worker and educator. She has published many books and her channel of YouTube is very popular.

Social Work Sorted. (n.d.). *Social Work Sorted: The Podcast* https://www.socialworksorted.com/podcast

This podcast is aimed at newly qualified social workers in the UK. The presenters discuss various topics to help recently qualified social workers reflect on their learning and grow as a professional.

Chapter 5

Managing your own induction, probation and supervision

Ivan Gray

Introduction

It's what is says on the tin; *in ducere* – 'to lead into'. Often it is done to you, but our stance is that a professional should lead themselves and that in fact this is one essence of professionalism (see Chapter 10). So, this chapter is about how you lead yourself into your new working community or organisation. You may ask, why not just let the organisation and its managers get on with it? Just go with the flow maybe and relax. Because you never know what you are going to encounter is why. It will be great if you are looked after, but you could find yourself left to your own devices lost in an unfamiliar community. And even if you are being helped this has its limitations. Being clear on what you want to achieve and why allows you to control and steer the process. Also, being clear about your expectations from the out-set, at induction, lays the foundation for your future practice and your health and wellbeing. The same goes for supervision. You can't assume good practice in your supervisor. You may be lucky, but you may not, or your supervisor could simply be terribly distracted by a crisis of some kind that distracts them from good supervision. Independence of thought and action on your part is good for you, good for the community of practice you are joining and good for the service.

Whilst initiatives such as the refreshing of the standards for employers have undoubt-edly improved the induction of newly qualified social workers in England in all four countries, it is still important that you take professional responsibility for and man-age your own induction and probation periods. This is why the first two sections of this chapter, on induction and probation, seek to provide you with models of good practice. Tailored information on supervision forms the final part of this chapter. High-quality reflective supervision is at the heart of social care and has been and will be crucial to your success.

Induction

The induction of newly qualified social workers can vary considerably (Bates et al., 2010; Grant et al., 2014, see Chapters 2 and 4). You may be warmly welcomed and provided with a well-structured, carefully planned experience that responds to your individual needs; or you may be offered a 'baptism of fire' that leaves you virtually to your own devices (Bates et al., 2010, p21). There is, however, some consensus on the value of a good induction and its key features (Fowler, 1996; Maher et al., 2003; NSWQB, 2004; Moriarty et al., 2011; Grant et al., 2014; Banks et al., 2021); good induction processes have been found to allow workers:

- to become effective more quickly;

- to settle into their teams more quickly;

- to be less anxious in new roles;

- to create realistic expectations of the job and the organisation;

- to reduce misunderstandings and grievances;

- to have confidence in new employers.

There is even a likely correlation between the quality of your induction and how long you stay in your new post. Fowler (1996), in an Institute of Personnel and Development publication, suggests a strong link between induction and employee retention and identifies the heavy costs to an organisation of early leavers, in other words, those who leave in the first few months of employment. This is confirmed more recently in teacher education by Reeves et al. (2022). Two older studies on the induction experiences of social workers (Maher et al., 2003, and an Irish National Social Work Qualifications Board study (NSWQB, 2004)) also note the importance of a good induction to retention. So, it may well be that if you start happy, you stay happy.

Good reasons abound for you viewing induction as *your* professional responsibility, accepting that a good employer should meet you more than halfway.

- Even if organisational practices do improve there will always be some posts and small organisations where a newly appointed social worker finds themselves virtually on their own with little option but to plan and manage their own induction.

- Whatever the policy initiatives, organisational practices are still likely to vary. If you have your own model of good practice you will be able to build on whatever is on offer.

- Professional social workers have considerable independence and responsibility in their work. Your induction sets the foundation for the effectiveness of your future practice and needs to be managed by you from the outset.

- Induction needs to be personalised so that it responds to your needs (Bradley, 2006). This is more likely to happen if you can take control and shape it.

This part of the chapter aims to ensure you are equipped to manage your own induction, even if organisational practices related to ASYE largely dictate your first year as a social worker.

Be clear

Be clear about what you want to achieve from your induction at the outset. This is best done by determining your aims and objectives. An aim identifies the broad purpose of an activity, and objectives break this down into manageable 'chunks' that help both plan and review progress.

ACTIVITY 5.1

Thinking about induction

Spend a little time thinking about your induction. What are the aims and objectives for your induction period? One way of thinking about this is to see yourself as an explorer about to enter exciting new territory. You are on a journey to find out what you need to live in this new land. Most of your exploration will consist of locating and obtaining information from the people who already live here. But it is not just an exercise in data collection – it is an emotional experience as well. You want to be accepted by the locals. You are going to work with them and will probably want them to like you and your work. In turn, they are likely to want you to respect them and their work.

See how your aim matches up with our suggested aim of induction:

To determine your role, your responsibilities and the rules, procedures, expectations and goals of the organisation you have just joined, whilst building the relationships and identifying the resources that you will need to practise effectively.

Depending on organisational practice, your induction could last just a few weeks or, more likely with the introductory programmes, a year or more. In a broader sense, one could argue that your induction never really stops as you will be always finding out about your place of work. Nevertheless, remember the land of work is complex and well-populated. It is very common to feel overwhelmed and swamped by the number of people you meet and the amount of information you have to assimilate. Your first few days can be exhausting and chaotic. Some things might not make complete sense, and you may even have doubts about how well you fit in. Recognise that this complex land, and your practice within it, will be subject to and affected by local and national political changes.

As such, your land of work is likely to have a formal and informal culture. For instance, there will be formal procedures that say how you *should* behave and then there will be the informal ways that people *actually do* behave and get things done. There will be some procedures you must follow to not put people at risk, but there is more choice than is often recognised around this essential core. It may be helpful to realise there will not be a fixed set of people you must know or a comprehensive set of procedures identifying the *right* way to do things. Build your own view of this land and your own way of doing things. We explore more of these imperatives and Fletcher's 'situational ethics' in Chapter 10 (Fletcher, 1966).

As with most journeys into unknown lands, a guide is invaluable. During your ASYE year or equivalent it is likely that your line manager, supervisor or assessor acts as one, working out with you who you need to see and the information you need to be given. Take any questions or clarifications to them for discussion – they might not be able to answer them immediately, but they should be able to identify others that can. You may find your guide has a structured induction plan waiting for you when you meet, clarifying your responsibilities in terms of caseload, your record of assessment or equivalent, appraisal, supervision and the newly qualified programme process in general. You may, however, need to build your own induction plan, and agree it with your line manager and/or supervisor. If this is the case be mindful that corporate induction programmes tend to be very general and can too easily deteriorate into a tick-box experience. Check out what is expected and what is on offer and incorporate it into your plan. If you are managing your own induction you only need one initial contact to set the ball rolling. Once you have made contact with one key person in your network, find out from them their key contacts and what they view as essential information and then locate their contacts and arrange to meet them. Gradually, by following up on these 'threads', you will identify and make contact with everyone in the network. Either way – structured or unstructured – it is important for you to take responsibility for the process and be proactive, as induction is deceptively complex – and this is why we suggest you approach it methodically.

As you chart your passage through the land it can be helpful to take notes on the information and people you come across. You should be able to find time in your first few days and weeks to think, reflect and write notes. Keeping notes of who you meet,

Figure 5.1   An example of a stakeholder map

what they do, how you might work with them (e.g. how you make referrals) and their contact details can be invaluable. Also note any questions you have and/or points for clarification. Keeping an induction file that includes both your notes and the information you collect can help you gradually build a picture of your new land. This file can then be used as an ongoing resource. Just finding your way around can be important too. Some newly qualified social workers have found it helpful to buy an A–Z or to use a satellite navigation tool. However, it is now possible to do this with a smart phone.

You will see by now that we view the process of induction as a creative space for you to fill. It is an opportunity for you to establish yourself and to shape your place in the organisation. We now explore in more detail the key dimensions of induction to help you do just that (see Figure 5.1). You can, if you wish, use these four dimensions to structure your induction file and to organise your induction plan and experience. In effect, these are the broad objectives to go with your aim. We have broken down each key dimension into its component parts and these constitute our suggested objectives of induction that you will need to achieve to meet our suggested aim of induction (see Activity 5.1). We will take each of the key dimensions in turn.

Key dimension 1: building relationships with those who support your practice

This dimension is built around two themes that develop relationship building within your practice as a new social worker.

1.1: to identify, make contact with and build initial relationships with those within the organisation that will support your practice

Getting to know who in the organisation makes things happen and who to go to for advice is crucial. The best source of this information is your team or others doing a similar job. Aim to meet the people they work with on a daily basis. Ask your team how they are best approached and the best way to work with them. Methodically build up a list of people in your file, make contact with them and introduce yourself. Sometimes a telephone call is enough but with really key players you may need to go and visit them. It may pay to build a map of crucial contacts – like the one in Figure 5.1 for example. This can be called a 'stakeholder map', as you are identifying all those who have a stake in your practice. Shadowing or a mini-placement can be useful for getting to know teams or sections you will work with on a daily basis, such as assessment or emergency teams. These methods can allow you to build relationships that can make a big difference to your effectiveness in the long term.

1.2: to identify, make contact with and build initial relationships with those outside of the organisation that support your practice

There may be as many people outside of your organisation that you will need to make contact and build a relationship with as within it. Health and social care provision is a complex and ever-changing network of voluntary, independent and private sector organisations, groups and even individuals. Any care plan in any sector will inevitably demand that you mobilise this network and co-ordinate their activities.

As above, talk to your team about who they regularly work with and ask about how to get the best from them – perhaps even what sort of problems they experience and how they get around them. If there are any formal referral mechanisms, be sure you know what they are and check on waiting times. As within your organisation, visit any key organisations, groups or individuals and introduce yourself. Again, shadow or placement opportunities can be invaluable. It will be essential for you to talk to people who use services and carers too. Ask colleagues for advice about people who could help. Like Karen in Case Study 5.1, they often have the best local knowledge about support and resources.

CASE STUDY 5.1

Karen's experience of meeting new social workers

G is our foster child and has lived with us for 27 years, since he was two weeks old. He has Down syndrome and autism, as well as a serious heart condition. As such we have presented an 'interesting case' for newly qualified social workers. For a period of about 10 years, when he was younger, we had a series of them. Even when they had left us, many of them would continue to ring me for advice and information for other clients.

I have built a fair knowledge of local resources over the 27 years. I am always willing to be helpful, but I often wonder why this sort of knowledge is not recorded somewhere central.

G loves meeting new people, so it was never a problem for him to meet new social workers. He greeted everyone the same, climbing on their laps and giving them a sloppy kiss. Not all new social workers were prepared for this and had to work out how they would deal with it. One lady had very prominent teeth and G was transfixed by them and kept talking about them, much to my embarrassment, and hers. Be prepared for children to be frank and completely natural!

It is always refreshing meeting someone enthusiastic and raring to make a difference. They usually go away full of things to find out and ready to learn. The ones I appreciate most are the ones who are honest about both their own capabilities and the system within which they are working. Some promise the earth and deliver nothing. The one that impressed me the most was a lady who confessed to knowing nothing and went away on a mission to find out, always admitting when she failed and never forgetting to come back to keep me informed. She was always honest, modest and treated us as the experts in G's needs and habits.

I also remember being lectured in childcare by one new social worker. I had G and two other young children of my own. I was offended that she chose to speak to me in this way and discovered on asking that she had only a five-month-old baby! I did not appreciate her theoretical knowledge being delivered in this way. Theory is all well and good but there is nothing like a healthy respect for experience.

Key dimension 2: establishing relationships with your immediate team and supervisor

The second theme continues to consider relationship building and now develops this wihtin your professional setting.

2.1: building an effective working relationship with your supervisor/s

It is worth noting at this point that at the heart of induction and probation is your interaction and relationship with your supervisor/s. In general terms the effectiveness of induction and probation, and your work generally, will be determined by the quality of your supervisory relationship. Although good practice around managing supervision will be explored in more detail in the third and final section of this chapter, it is worth making some initial points here.

Find out about your organisation's formal supervision policy. Talk to managers about their expectations and ask colleagues for advice about what has worked (or not) for them. Try asking managers and supervisors how they like to work and establish the 'dos and don'ts'. Think about sharing a little about yourself as this can contribute to good working relationships. Tell them about what helps you most in supervision, what can cause problems for you and pinpoint any particular learning or other needs you have. Remember this relationship will be a different relationship from the one you had with your practice educator, but it will be similar in many ways. If there is no written contract to direct your relationship, at the very least you will need to determine when you meet, how regularly and for how long – who sets the agenda, who records it, what happens if it is cancelled and how emergency situations are dealt with. Help your manager or supervisor/s by identifying issues you wish to discuss in advance and making available any information they need. Use supervision to seek feedback on your performance and air any unhappiness and/or discontent.

Being supervised by several people, such as a team including senior practitioners, can be tough so find out how they co-ordinate activities. Try and meet middle and senior managers as well as first-line managers as their activities as a management team will impact on your work.

2.2: building effective working relationships with your immediate team

Your new team is the community of practice (Wenger, 1998; Wenger-Traynor et al., 2023) that will have the greatest impact on the effectiveness of your work and your happiness in the job. They are likely to be the greatest source of advice and support too, so good working relationships with them are vital.

Colleagues will want to be respected by you (also see Chapters 7 and 8), so make a point of seeing everyone. Even if people are busy, they usually appreciate being approached and can feel valued by you asking for their input. Start, don't finish, with your administrative and support team. They can have a considerable impact on your work and you will need to establish how to work effectively with them. Ask them directly what they like or don't like. Their personal support and goodwill can make a big difference to you in the longer term.

Find out from your social work colleagues what they are interested in and whether they have any particular specialism or areas of particular interest. Actively use their expertise, for instance, by asking your supervisor/s whose assessments are exemplary – try and get your colleagues to talk with you about what they do and don't do. And try not to forget those informal team arrangements that can assist in sustaining new relationships – they can be as simple as contributing to a tea and coffee or birthday fund.

Key dimension 3: clarifying your role and responsibilities and any procedures you must follow

Being clear about your roles and responsibilities is key to successful practice as a beginning professional and we introduce five sub-themes here that are important to doing so.

3.1: to identify and understand any legal and organisational procedures you must follow

Having up-to-date copies of essential procedures for managing situations where people can be put at risk – such as child/adult protection – is vital for safe working. You may wish to print hard copies of these procedures and put them in your induction file. Discern any discrepancies between what the procedures say and your team actually does. If in doubt, get clarification from your supervisor/s and record it.

Some procedures, for example the timing of assessments, need to be followed as they will affect performance measures that can impact on your team or organisation. As with most procedures, you will be working with others in their implementation, so it may pay to visit and discuss them with, for instance, reviewing and finance officers.

It can really be helpful to shadow people following procedures or sit in on key events such as reviews, case conferences, etc. Written procedures are much more meaningful when you see them being applied and it may pay to create your own flow diagrams for common scenarios, critical events and/or emergencies to capture the essentials. Make sure you know who the experts are, so you can approach them when things come up.

3.2: be clear about your role and responsibilities

Your job description and person specification are a good place to start in determining your role and responsibilities – your supervisor/s should be able to clarify any questions you have. Make sure you are clear about what you can or can't do and what has to be authorised by others. Use your supervisor/s and colleagues to check things out and go out of your way to share what you are doing and brief people fully.

3.3: identifying any informal rules, processes and norms that shape behaviour in the organisation alongside formal procedures and processes

To be 'at home' in your organisation you need to know not only the formal rules and regulations but also the wider culture – *the way things are done around here* – and the unwritten culture. Take notice of the small things, for example, how people answer the phone and how they explain how the system works to people who use services. These hidden informal perspectives intertwine with the formal to make up the rich tapestry of organisational life. Listen, ask and look behind the formal espoused theory, in other words what people say they do, to the theory in use and what they actually do (Argyris and Schön, 1974). However, be slow to jump to conclusions or be over-critical if things don't make sense. You may either have misunderstood or important things may just not be said openly.

3.4: understanding the goals of the organisation and how it is structured

Try to gain a broader picture of what your organisation is trying to achieve by reading business plans and service strategies. Use any corporate induction opportunities you get to speak to senior managers. It is worth remembering that the plans of other organisations may also be important to you, since your practice will in part be dependent on and impacted by their improvement plans and direction. Remember there will be variation between employers – try not to make assumptions based on your placement experience.

3.5: be confident and motivated to do the job

Getting to know your new organisation and the people in it can be traumatic and emotionally draining. It is not uncommon to have periods when you can feel a bit 'down'. You can find yourself doubting your abilities and losing confidence. These are perfectly normal reactions and are a response to the changes you are grappling with; even if you are delighted with your new post and you are perfect for the job you can feel this way. These feelings should dissipate as you settle in.

In accepting the emotional aspects of joining an organisation, it is important to learn how to take care of yourself. Be grateful for the support people offer. Start off with 'comfortable' work you are familiar with, and enjoy transferring established skills. Move out from your comfort zone into areas of special interest over time.

Stress is an occupational hazard and workloads can easily be too high (Gibson et al., 1989; Storey and Billingham, 2001; Mordue, 2023; Maddock, 2024; Ratcliff, 2024).

You should find that you have a protected caseload as discussed in Chapters 2 and 4, but it is important that you take responsibility for managing your workload. You may need to be realistic about what you take on and be assertive saying 'no' when you are at capacity, even if you would like to help out by taking on more. Workload management systems are never that accurate so try and establish an open dialogue with your supervisor/s about your workload. Chapter 6 of this book may also be an important resource for you as it looks at ways of managing yourself, stress and conflict. Use it to guide any difficult conversations you might have with your supervisor/s, e.g. about workload, induction or supervision. Prepare well for this type of conversation; keep to the facts and try to leave your raw emotions at the door. Personal 'out of work' support can be invaluable to discuss experiences and feelings but remember to keep confidentiality. Some organisations have started 'learning sets' made up of newly qualified social workers so that people can meet up to discuss their expectations and learn from experiences.

Key dimension 4: identifying and mobilising resources to support you in your role

It is important to gain and utilise the support available in your work and in this key dimension we consider five processes and practices that will help you in doing so.

4.1: understanding and completing essential human resource management processes and policies

There are essential human resource management processes that have to be completed and processes that you need to know about. Often human resources personnel will find you, but if not, they are usually happy to advise on the following issues:

- signing your contract and terms and conditions
- DBS checks
- hours of work and overtime arrangements
- flexitime and time off in lieu
- holiday entitlement and booking
- pension arrangements
- how you will be paid
- discipline and grievance procedures
- performance-related pay and pay progression
- appraisal
- severance procedures

- the probation period and the ASYE

- equal opportunities policy

- absence and sickness procedures

- paternity and maternity leave.

4.2: be aware of and access welfare and support services

In most organisations welfare and support services can be important to your work–life balance. Again, human resources personnel may be helpful in the following areas:

- counselling

- employer's policies on well-being and stress

- occupational health

- trade union membership

- legal advice

- leisure activities

- staff associations and social clubs

- policies on 'whistle blowing'.

4.3: acquiring the essential tools and equipment you need to do the job

Having your own space and the things that you need to do the job such as a telephone, computer, diary and stationery can be important in supporting your role and ensuring you enjoy a successful induction. Colleagues, especially administration staff, are best placed to advise you on what you will need on an everyday basis. Check out ordering procedures and what is hard to obtain but bear in mind that colleagues will have found ways around unhelpful formal procedures.

Although it can make you feel you belong to personalise your workspace, it may be that more 'flexible' working procedures and environments come with 'hot desks'. Wherever you are placed, work out where the 'heart' of team activity is, and make a point of spending some time in this environment. If you get a choice, think carefully about where you wish to sit and who you would like to sit with in the office, as it can affect your working life.

4.4: be aware and follow everyday operating procedures, including health and safety

A number of crucial procedures will be essential to the everyday operation of your organisation, including health and safety. Check out with supervisor/s and colleagues what these are for your particular organisation. They are likely to include:

- signing in and out of the office

- logging your location and movements

- safe interviewing procedures

- office security

- out-of-hours working and safe working procedures

- use of IT equipment and IT assessments

- transporting people who use services and carers

- fire safety

- first aid.

Find out too about everyday administrative procedures such as travel claims, allowances and receipts, timescales for arranging meetings and computer access. Find out what these are and obtain copies of any forms you are likely to need every day. Hopefully this gives you a useful start, but you will find there is a lot to know. For instance, there will probably even be regulations to cover the gifts you may or may not receive from people who use services and carers.

4.5: access training and development opportunities and set the foundation for continuing professional development

This has already formed the subject of Chapter 4 so only a few brief points will be made here. Your induction may include some initial or core-training workshops; for instance, basic IT training. Find out what the organisation's personal development processes are by asking team members about the best resources and which ones they use regularly. Contact your staff or workforce development department to find out about how to access training, book places and any cancellation procedures. Check out any online training and other services such as library services (including the office library), help with research and so on. Finally, you should find it helpful to share your undergraduate personal development plan or skills analysis with your supervisor or line manager.

ACTIVITY 5.2

Making comparisons

Now you have read what we think induction should be about, find out from your employer all you can about the induction period and think about making a comparison of the two – ask yourself the question, where are the gaps and how can I fill them?

Probation

Where employing organisations have probationary periods, they are often up to twelve months in length – if you are unsure about the policy of your organisation, ask your line manager or human resources manager. Indeed, you will probably have been given this information on starting your role. Many employers have aligned their probation periods with ASYE completion. On the basis of this policy, you will be able to determine your role within it and, as we advocate with the induction process, take responsibility for it. The experience of probationary periods of newly qualified social workers can vary considerably (Bates et al., 2010; Grant, 2017) – the following aim of probation periods might therefore be helpful to you:

To jointly review and appraise with your supervisor the effectiveness of your initial practice and the suitability of the post for you; identify your future learning needs, the support you require and lay the foundation for your future performance appraisal and development planning.

ACTIVITY 5.3

Probation

Find out whether your organisation or prospective organisation has a probationary period, and if so, what is your role within it and how does it link to the ASYE?

Your probationary period is an opportunity for you to decide if the job is the right one for you and for your employer to decide if you are right for them. Ultimately, it is your employer's decision whether you pass or fail your probationary period. In the same way, it is their decision whether you pass or fail your ASYE year. Probation and ASYE are linked though, in that good employers will be underpinning the ASYE year with a structured and supportive probation process. So, in order to remain employed in your first social work post, you will be required to pass both your probationary review period and, for many employers, the ASYE year as well. This serves as a reminder for you, as the newly qualified social worker, to check with any potential employer about their ASYE process and probationary systems, both in terms of the support you will receive and to assure yourself that methods of assessment are accurate, valid, robust and sufficient. It is after all your career – you will want to make sure you have every opportunity to demonstrate your capacity to practise as a social worker, and to complete ASYE and probation in a manner that will be acceptable to all potential social work employers.

Probation has three key dimensions. We will take each in turn and explore them.

Key dimension 1: determining the job is the right one for you

A trial or probationary period works both ways – as we have already stated it can help you decide if the job is right for you, and the employer decide whether they think you are right for the job. Dialogue is important. A good employer will want you to be open about problems in the hope of resolving them. Above all, be realistic. It will probably take up to a year to feel established in your role. However, if you decide this is not the job for you, be clear why not and what you are looking for. Discuss these issues with your supervisor and human resources personnel – there may be transfer options that could be to your benefit and that of your employer.

Key dimension 2: demonstrating you are capable and competent to fulfil your role

The essential starting point in demonstrating your ability to fulfil your role is finding out what 'yardstick' your employer will be using to measure your performance. In England, this will be the Knowledge and Skills Statements for social workers (DfE, 2014; DH, 2015) and the professional capabilities at ASYE-level across the nine domains that make up the framework (BASW, 2018). But there are also likely to be additional organisational requirements as part of any probation period. Employer practices will vary and in the past your contract of employment and job description have been key points of reference. Make a point of asking your employer early so there are no surprises.

As part of your probation period, your supervisor/s will be observing your practice, evaluating your records and reports, and listening and talking to team members and other colleagues. Although this can at times appear impressionistic, good practice is now much better defined and many managers are very good at judging performance. For example, ASYE assessments should be made by practice assessors and supervisors who have been specifically trained and assessed themselves to undertake this role.

It is advisable to make appraisal of your performance part of supervision and indeed a building block of your supervisory relationship. The final part of this chapter should help demystify the process of supervision. Do voice your concerns with your manager and/or supervisor/s if there is anything you are not happy about. If other issues arise, show you can take criticism 'on the chin', but make sure you are clear what the problem is and agree a way forward which should include support and help to develop your practice. These evaluations and the plans that arise from them should all be recorded in writing. If your probationary period is not completed successfully, your employer will follow formal procedures as laid out in their policies and your contract of employment.

Employment law is complex, so if you hit difficulties in your probationary period always seek advice from human resources personnel, a trade union, the Advisory, Conciliation and Arbitration Service (ACAS) or a solicitor. These last comments are not meant to frighten you – we can only offer very broad guidance and, if you need it, you must make sure you take qualified specialist advice.

Key dimension 3: identifying areas for improvement, your learning needs, and any support requirements

Do ask hard questions about support and development opportunities, as it is important that you are able to develop your practice and career. Indeed, our advice is that you ask these questions at your interview for a potential social work post, so that you are clear before accepting any post about the support you will receive and the methods by which you will be assessed as capable, in order to pass your probation period. One of the first things you are likely to do as part of your ASYE period is complete and sign a learning agreement with your employer. This agreement will specify your workload, the frequency of reflective supervision, arrangements for protected development time, and so on. Importantly, it will also contain details of how ASYE reviews are linked to your employer's probation and appraisal processes. Just as you should ask for feedback on your performance if this is not provided, you should also say if you are not getting the help you need to develop your practice or you do not understand what is required of you. Seek advice from human resources personnel or your trade union if this is not resolved.

It does not mean that your performance is unsatisfactory if you have learning needs. On the contrary, it is good practice to work with your supervisor/s to evaluate your practice and improve it. These learning needs will ideally be discussed within the process of supervision – the final section of this chapter.

Supervision

Professional supervision is at the heart of social care. As the Chief Executives of Skills for Care and the former Children's Workforce Development Council put it:

> *High quality supervision is one of the most important drivers in ensuring positive outcomes for people who use social care and children's services. It also has a crucial role to play in the development, retention and motivation of the workforce.*

> (Skills for Care/Children's Workforce Development Council, 2007, p3)

Supervision is defined as:

> *An accountable process which supports, assures and develops the knowledge, skills and values of an individual, group or team. The purpose is to improve the quality of their work to achieve agreed objectives and outcomes. In social care and children's services this should optimise the capacity of people who use services to lead independent and fulfilling lives.*

> (Skills for Care/Children's Workforce Development Council, 2007, p4)

Supervision in a contested profession

Supervision, as highlighted in Chapter 3, is also a focal point where the key components of the service meet and all key activities and relationships are co-ordinated (see Hafford-Letchfield and Engelbrecht, 2020; O'Donoghue and Engelbrecht, 2023). Supervision requires commitment, respect and honesty from all participants if it is to be of benefit to the organisation and individual. Good supervision appears associated with effective job satisfaction, retention and effective professional practice (Carpenter et al., 2012; Ravalier et al., 2023), although this evidence base is limited and is in places contested (Manthorpe et al., 2015).

The Social Work Reform Board identified four purposes for supervision:

- to improve the quality of decision-making and interventions;

- to enable effective line management and organisational accountability;

- to identify and address issues related to caseloads and workload management;

- to help to identify and achieve personal learning, career and development opportunities.

(SWRB, 2012a)

The updated Standards for Employers document includes the expectation that newly qualified social workers should have access to regular, high-quality supervision by a registered social worker, and this should be weekly for the first six weeks and then fortnightly for the first six months and monthly thereafter (LGA, 2014). Alongside Howe and Gray (2012), Skills for Care has also provided useful online guidance for newly qualified social workers here: **www.skillsforcare.org.uk/Topics/Social-work/Social-work.aspx**. The importance of preparation is emphasised here and it is suggested that this should allow workers to share and discuss appropriate topics with their supervisors:

- their reflections on their practice, including what's gone wrong;

- how they have accessed and used support in their work;

- their ability to implement personalised care and to maximise the participation and control that individual adults, families, carers, groups and communities have over their lives;

- how they have used training and development opportunities;

- their learning needs and how these will be met;

- the evidence they are collecting to demonstrate their achievement of ASYE-level capabilities.

(Skills for Care, 2011b)

Our services and profession are by nature contested. The management of service provision necessarily involves battling with dilemmas, ambiguity, conflicting interests, incompatible expectations, value issues and judgement calls where there may not be options that can be rationally chosen as the 'best' (Healy, 2000; Munro, 2011). It is at this crucial point of co-ordination, clarification and decision-making that these conflicts are identified and responded to. The final part of this chapter has begun by exploring the nature of supervision and moves on to why it is important (including the often-overlooked emotional aspects to supervision), threats to its effectiveness and how you can evaluate the process.

ACTIVITY 5.4

Supervision

As a newly qualified social worker it is important that you take control of your own professional supervision. Think back over your previous experiences of being supervised and make some notes on:

- *what you valued most;*
- *what was least helpful;*
- *what you did to ensure that supervision was effective;*
- *what you might have done that undermined the effectiveness of supervision.*

If you can, share your thoughts with your supervisor to help shape your new relationship.

Supervision as a forum for dialogue

Supervision is a crucial forum for dialogue in social care as it is where the professional and the organisation meet. In the past, professional reflection and personal development arguably dominated supervision at the expense of case and performance management and to the detriment of services and professional practice. More recently, it has been argued that case management and performance issues have come to dominate supervision and that professional needs and issues have been marginalised (Jones et al., Manthorpe et al., 2015; Ravalier et al., 2023). The Social Work Reform Board (SWRB, 2010), Munro Report (2011) and others stress the importance of moving away from top-down, target-driven management to enable social workers to learn from their experiences and have more freedom to exercise their professional judgement. However, it can be argued that supervision has never been entirely a professional domain. Supervision is also where managerial and organisational perspectives and needs meet and are resolved. Part of the tension that is endemic to supervision is competition for the space and the agenda that both you and your supervisor must respond to.

Managers and professionals have responsibility to ensure that there is a balance between competing but often mutual needs. The process of supervision must accommodate these needs to be effective. Figure 5.2 gives a personal illustration of your need for supervision.

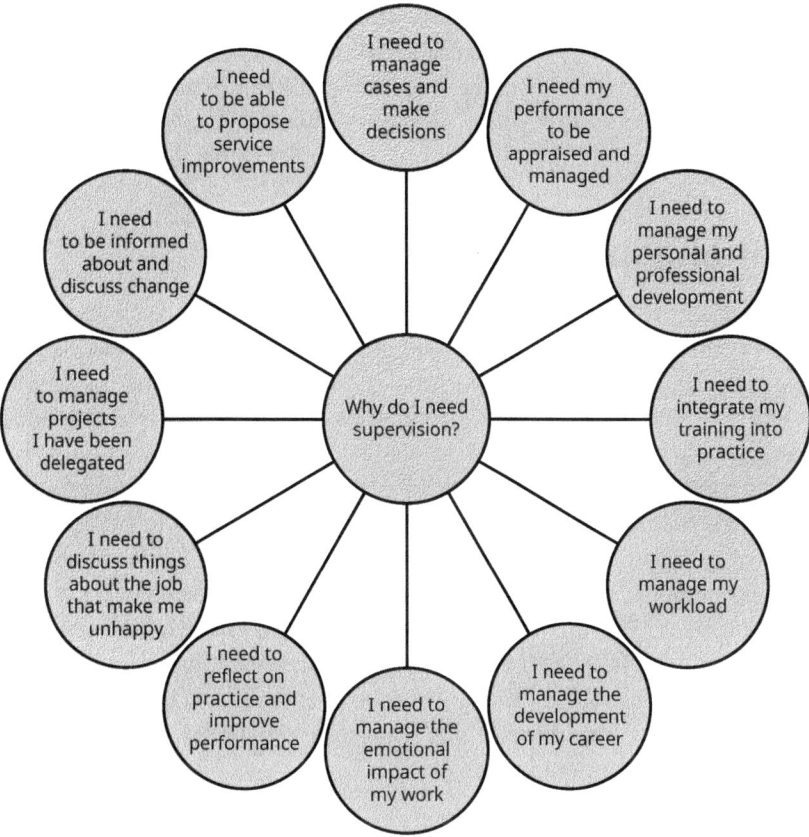

Figure 5.2   Why do I need supervision?

There are also good grounds for approaching the process of supervision critically. If personal reflection and personal development are too easily lost from the agenda, opportunities to discuss social work values and the wider social and political effects of interventions may also be easily mislaid (Phillipson, 2002).

Time for supervision is undoubtedly a problem (Manthorpe et al., 2015). It is very easy to make the shortage of it an excuse for unbalanced supervision. There is a danger that managers who are under pressure will undermine supervision by dominating it – rather than allowing time for exploration and reflection. What should be dealt with, and could be dealt with efficiently in formal supervision, ends up being dealt with 'on the hop' in informal supervision. This often does not allow for proper communication and joint consideration of the issues. Even in assessment or emergency teams where 'on the hop' supervision is unavoidable, formal sessions are still essential.

Supervision needs careful planning, review and plenty of time. To illustrate, one particular need in Figure 5.2 may dominate a supervision session. Future sessions may therefore need a different agenda to compensate. Keep an eye on the range of needs to ensure your supervision is balanced over time.

Supervision is likely to be your biggest training and development opportunity. Sometimes more powerful than activities such as training courses, supervision should allow you the space to ask questions, make sense of things and learn through your practice. With a good supervisor your personal growth and development will be enabled, and as you become more confident you will work in a more independent manner.

Emotional aspects to supervision

Whilst supervision is not counselling or therapy, it is very similar in that it requires sharing and openness, careful listening and challenge, joint problem-solving and joint decision-making. It also reaches for personal growth and to address the emotion that is at the heart of our work. In short, it demands a trusting and enabling supervisory relationship which can be very hard to achieve if in every supervision session you find yourself working with somebody different, as can happen in some teams. If you work with more than one supervisor, your manager/s will need to be active ensuring consistency of provision. You too can contribute to the effectiveness of shared supervision by being sure to communicate as effectively as you can, and by briefing your supervisors properly. There is often opportunity to play one supervisor off against another and take advantage of breakdowns in communication and inconsistencies, so keep a reflective eye on yourself and try and be proactive in making things work. But if communication gets very difficult and issues are not being dealt with effectively, raise these issues with your manager.

Time pressures and a more procedurally driven and outcome-orientated service can mean that the culture of supervision changes to downplay the importance of emotion in our work. Managerialism is often represented as undermining the amount of supervision time devoted to the management of emotion, as well as the learning and development essential to practice. If the emotion of our work is not managed there can be a considerable impact on our effectiveness. We do not learn well if we are frightened, depressed, grieving or frozen; distress, if not responded to, can undermine our practice and our health (Hawkins and Shohet, 2007; McMahon et al., 2022).

It is not just that our work involves traumatic and negative experiences and sharing other people's grief and pain. The change process is also an emotional experience. The more fundamental the change, the more emotion (Holmes and Rahe, 1967). If you are going to be effective in improving the quality of life of carers and people who use services; if you are to respond to service changes effectively; and if you intend to develop your own practice, there will be a lot of emotion about. Chapter 6 should be a help to you here as sometimes we might feel manipulated or frightened by the people we work with. You will need to be able to discuss these issues openly in (and outside of) supervision to ensure you remain purposeful and objective about your work.

Leadership and supervision

As a newly qualified social worker, you will be motivated to do the work you have been employed for. You will have, at least, the basic knowledge and skills to do the job.

An effective manager will recognise that you (like us) have a lot to learn and allow you the space to do so. They may start by giving you lots of supervision time and guidance, gradually reducing this as they gauge the strengths and weaknesses of your practice and as you develop. You will need to play your part by taking more responsibility for your work and for supervision as time goes on. This chapter ends with two activities that you can employ to help you evaluate the development of your supervision.

ACTIVITY 5.5

Evaluating supervision

You can use the following questions to evaluate the development of your supervision practice over time.

- *Is my supervisory relationship changing as my needs change?*
- *Am I working more independently over time and developing my practice, allowing my manager to delegate?*
- *Am I taking more responsibility for supervision, increasing my contribution and exercising more control over the process?*

The Effective Supervision Unit

Until the publication of the Providing Effective Supervision unit (Skills for Care/Children's Workforce Development Council, 2007) there had been no national framework related to the supervision of social workers. Although this document has now been superseded, it links with the Standards for Employers (LGA, 2014) to provide valuable reference points in evaluating your supervision with your supervisor. In particular, parts of the old Providing Effective Supervision unit can still be used as a detailed evaluative tool (see Tables 5.1, 5.2 and 5.3) leading to genuine, shared in-depth exploration of the quality of supervision you are receiving. So, it is worth giving these documents some time and attention.

ACTIVITY 5.6

Supervision audit

This is the final activity of this chapter. Use this audit tool to evaluate the supervision you receive. It has been adapted from the Skills for Care and Children's Workforce Development Council (2007) Providing Effective Supervision unit of competence/capability. There are three tables, each with a different focus. We provide a commentary on each of the performance criteria and space for your own notes.

Table 5.1 Implement supervision systems and processes

Performance criteria	Commentary	Notes
a. Implement supervision in the context of organisational policies, performance management and workforce development.	Locate and familiarise yourself with your organisation's supervision, appraisal, probationary and personal development policies and procedures.	
b. Develop, implement and review written agreements for supervision.	You will have an agreement that specifies supervision arrangements and responsibilities. They can be rudimentary, simply stating frequency, length and who has responsibility for setting them up. More complex contracts cover cancellation procedures, preparation and so on. Others may set ground rules for the relationship and identify such things as areas of interest or for personal development.	
c. Ensure supervision records and agreed decisions are accurate and completed promptly.	Keep a record, at the very least, of decisions made in supervision. Whoever has the responsibility for recording them will need to see they are signed off. Usually it is the supervisor/s' responsibility, but you should have a signed copy for your induction file or at least access to them. Areas of agreement should also be recorded.	
d. Enable workers to reflect on supervision issues and act on outcomes.	Your supervisor/s should encourage and give you space to reflect on your practice and identify your strengths, weaknesses and development needs and review your actions and care plans.	
e. Monitor and review own supervision practice and learning, reflecting on the processes and implement improvements to supervision.	There should be opportunity for you to comment on the quality of the supervision you have received. This could involve an exercise such as this one.	
f. Identify wider issues and raise them appropriately in the organisation and with other stakeholders.	Your manager or supervisor should act as a broker identifying with you practice issues that need to be picked up on in the organisation more widely, so that the quality of services can be improved.	
g. Enable access to specialist supervision, support, advice or consultation as required. Specialist supervision can include peer, therapeutic or clinical supervision.	Specialist supervision can be an excellent way to develop your practice and can also be essential in some roles and situations that demand more support that your manager or usual supervisor/s can provide.	

Table 5.2 Develop, maintain and review effective supervision relationships

Performance criteria	Commentary	Notes
a. Create a positive environment for workers to develop and review their practice.	Supervision should challenge your practice but it should be a positive encounter that you value and where challenge is matched with encouragement and support. You should be encouraged to take responsibility and take control in reviewing and evaluating your practice.	
b. Clarify boundaries and expectations of supervision, including confidentiality.	It pays to review your previous experiences of supervision and what works or doesn't work for you. Good supervision contracts will cover these broader issues as well as clarifying confidentiality and what are (or not) suitable matters for supervision.	
c. Ensure relationships are conducted in an open and accountable way.	Both you and your supervisor/s are accountable for your practice so the relationship must be strong enough for you to share the details of your practice, including problems you are experiencing. Hidden practice can be dangerous practice.	
d. Help workers to identify and overcome blocks to performance, such as work conflicts and other pressures.	Effective practice is not just down to you. Others can influence your effectiveness in a positive fashion, as well as negatively. Chapter 6, in particular the section on dealing with conflict, may be of use here. Your supervisor/s should also be able to help with these broader issues.	
e. Assist workers to understand the emotional impact of their work and seek appropriate specialist support if needed.	It is a tough job – one that can affect us all deeply. The emotion of your work needs to be on the agenda for the sake of your own health, but also because it can impact on your practice. Some people who use services can be manipulative or frightening – openness about their impact on you will help ensure your practice is purposeful and objective.	
f. Ensure the *duty of care* is met for the well-being of workers.	Your employer has responsibility for your health and safety including safe working arrangements outside of the office, stress and workload balance.	
g. Recognise diversity and demonstrate *anti-discriminatory practice* in the supervision relationship.	Supervision should respond to your individual needs and actively seek not to discriminate against you.	

(Continued)

Table 5.2   (Continued)

Performance criteria	Commentary	Notes
h. Give and receive constructive *feedback* on the supervisory relationship and supervision practice.	Both you and your supervisor/s need to reflect on and discuss the quality of your supervision and aim to improve it over time.	
i. Audit and develop own skills and knowledge to supervise workers, including those from other disciplines when required.	Your manager should be seeking to develop their skills as a supervisor. You can help them do this by giving them positive and constructive feedback, identifying areas where supervision can be improved. Having good supervisory practice on the agenda is also useful as the supervision of others will become one of your responsibilities as your career progresses.	

Table 5.3   *Develop, maintain and review practice and performance through supervision*

Performance criteria	Commentary	Notes
a. Ensure workloads are effectively allocated, managed and reviewed.	It is very difficult to come up with a definitive workload management system that determines fair workloads for all, as your work will be too complex and variable to be easily categorised and measured. Good dialogue that regularly addresses what you are being allocated, how, and whether it is manageable, is essential.	
b. Monitor and enable workers' competence to assess, plan, implement and review their work.	Your performance as a case manager should not only be evaluated, but there should be opportunities for you to develop and improve it.	
c. Ensure supervisor and workers are clear about accountability and the limits of their individual and organisational authority and duties.	Induction and supervision are the best places to clarify any areas of confusion that can arise. Job descriptions and procedures are often not definitive discussion works.	
d. Ensure workers understand and demonstrate *anti-discriminatory practice*.	Your qualifying course will have given a lot of attention to this topic, but do not let it drift – make it an explicit feature of your supervision agenda.	
e. Ensure work *with people who use services* is outcomes-focused and that their views are taken account of in service design and delivery.	Work with individuals needs to be achieving outcomes agreed with them. Supervision also needs to address the broader development of services and service quality and people who use services can be involved in this.	

Performance criteria	Commentary	Notes
f. Identify risks to users of services and workers and take appropriate action.	Risks need to be clearly identified, methodically assessed and actions agreed to manage them effectively. Any assessment and agreed plans should be recorded.	
g. Obtain and give timely feedback on workers' practice, including feedback from people who use services.	Both you and your supervisor have a responsibility to evaluate your practice and improve it. Actively seeking feedback on your performance (especially from people who use services and carers) and discussing and acting on it is a joint responsibility.	
h. Identify learning needs and integrate them within development plans.	It is important that you are clear about what areas of your practice you want to develop. Make sure your learning objectives and development plans are focused on these needs.	
i. Create opportunities for learning and development.	You should be offered and take opportunity to make use of a range of on and off the job development opportunities. Their effectiveness in meeting your needs should be evaluated.	
j. Assess and review performance, challenge poor practice and ensure improvements in standards.	Supervision should encompass appraisal. Your performance should be evaluated jointly against agreed standards on the basis of readily identified evidence. The evaluation and agreed improvement plans should be recorded together with any differences of opinion.	
k. Enable multidisciplinary, integrated and collaborative working as appropriate.	This is essential to service quality and demands regular review and evaluation. Chapter 10 of this book will no doubt help here as multidisciplinary working is an essential element of practice. Many quality problems originate here, and many quality improvements lie with more effective multi-agency and collaborative working.	

Summary

Your period of induction will be crucial in determining your role and responsibilities and the rules, procedures, expectations and goals of the organisation you intend to, or have just joined. In this chapter, we have reviewed some of the central elements that are necessary in doing so and have integrated our discussion with supervision.

High-quality reflective supervision is at the heart of social care and will be crucial to the success of your future practice. So, we have spent some time considering what makes good supervision and how you can ensure that you are receiving what you need. You are important to this process. Indeed, it is one of the key aspects of learning that will help you throughout your career. We would also urge you to evaluate the quality of your induction period and supervision processes and keep on doing it in your future roles as well as a newly qualified social worker.

Further reading

Hafford-Letchfield, T., & Engelbrecht, L. (2020). *Contemporary practices in social work supervision: Time for new paradigms?* Routledge.

This timely research-based book explores the centrality of supervision in social work and encourages social workers to challenge themselves within the context of supervision.

Howe, K., & Gray, I. (2012). *Effective supervision in social work.* Sage/Learning Matters.

Written by two experienced authors, this worthwhile book represents the development of their thinking about supervision over the past 20 years, in particular around the relational and organisation contexts of supervision.

Local Government Association. (2014). *What you should expect as a social worker.* https://www.local.gov.uk/workforce/-/journal_content/56/10180/3511605/ARTICLE

This is the sister document to Standards for Employers (LGA, 2014) and provides a short and helpful, four-page summary of what you should expect from your employer, including standards of induction.

O'Donoghue, K., & Engelbrecht, L. (Eds.). (2023). *The Routledge international handbook of social work supervision.* Routledge.

This comprehensive edited collection includes perspectives on supervision from around the world. It focuses on the research evidence and the importance of relationships within the supervisory context. The international flavour will support you as part of a wider global profession and guard against insularity.

Social Care Institute for Excellence. (2020). *Effective supervision: A practical guide for adult social care managers and supervisors.* SCIE. https://www.skillsforcare.org.uk/resources/documents/Support-for-leaders-and-managers/Managing-people/Supervision/Effective-supervision-guide.pdf

This is a useful online guide containing practical help to develop supervisory practices in the adult social care workplace.

Chapter 6

Looking to our Future - Building your community of practice and contributing to service quality and development

Ivan Gray and Jonathan Parker

Introduction

Throughout each chapter of this book, we encourage you to look to your future by making the best of your post-qualifying programmes and consolidation of learning as NQSWs. In doing this you will also improve service quality through improving your own practice. In this chapter, we ask you specifically to look beyond this and take every opportunity to contribute to the development of your community of practice, which we explain shortly, and to service quality and development.

Whilst you are likely to have more immediate concerns, like having more time for yourself or with your family after a demanding qualifying programme, it is good to ask you at this early point in your career to find some time to look to the future of social work and our services. From the outset of your journey, it is important to explore how you might contribute to service quality and development.

Are we having a laugh? So, here you are embattled and struggling against the odds, maybe finding organisational survival a problem and certainly wondering why government has not taken the care it should have in caring for you and the people you care for. We are certainly asking a lot, and we have already asked for more than you need to do in order to successfully complete your ASYE and other programmes. However, accepting that you need to take care of yourself, the future really does depend on you although you will not be alone in this endeavour. There is also some payback in being this ambitious. You are probably in social work to 'make a difference' in a positive way, and this thinking about the development of social work is one way for you to maximise your effectiveness and your impact.

As a newly qualified social worker you may sometimes feel alone in your role. In reality, of course, you are always part of a bigger team, including all the people in your organisation that support your work and the network of interrelated services with whom you work. This is even the case for people practising as independent social workers or when you are the only social worker in the team.

The quality of your individual practice, and the way people who use services experience it, will always be affected by this broader context in which your work is set. This impact can be experienced as positive or negative. So, for example, if you set up a care planning meeting and the administrative team get the invitations out too late and key people do not attend, the quality of your practice is diminished, and ultimately, those who use services lose out. If you put together a care package with people who use services but their day-care provision is poor, your assessment work and the rest of the plan may be undermined.

Where services do not work together, people who use services may experience an inadequate and fragmented service that not only does not respond to their needs but can even confuse or damage them. On the other hand, good systems, relationships and service provision can greatly enhance your practice. For instance, an effective family support service or a specialist assessment can much enhance the outcomes of your work. Volunteers and supportive local leisure facilities can greatly improve a care package and ready access to training and developmental activities can improve the quality of your practice.

Individual practice is often integrated within organisational practices. We are perhaps best seen as members of a *Community of Practice* (Wenger, 1998, 2015; Wenger-Traynor et al., 2023), in which our individual perspectives, aspirations and actions form part of these wider systems and relationships. In social work, these are underpinned in England by our explicit and shared value base that holistic practice is influenced by all professional capabilities (BASW, 2018) and the new skills statements (DfE, 2018; DH, 2015). For social workers in Northern Ireland, Wales and Scotland, the expectations and requirements are set out in Chapter 2.

Whatever standards and requirements are set for you, influencing the broader context in which your practice is set remains central to high-quality professional practice. It starts with helping the different systems communicate and work together (BASW, 2018). However, you need to reach beyond these systems relationships to make a more direct contribution to developing service quality.

On placement it is often hard to be able to contribute to developing service quality, especially over the long term, and it is not unusual to find that social work students tend to focus on developing their own practice and take, as given, the broader context in which it occurs. So, as a newly qualified social worker, contributing to service quality and development is likely to be identified as a key area for personal development and for this reason it is the subject of this chapter. Before exploring this important area of work, it is worth making a few observations.

Learning cultures and 'collective leadership'

Chapter 4 has already explored how important it is to services that you continue to develop professionally throughout your career. Your effectiveness as a practitioner is dependent on your effectiveness as a learner and it is fundamental to you as a newly qualified social worker and beyond. Yet your practice will always be dependent on the resources, systems, procedures and relationships of the organisation in which you work, and the network of provision in which it operates. Personal expertise is not enough, so that beyond your continuing professional development lies the issue as to whether organisations are continually 'learning'. Do they seek continually to improve the quality of the services they provide or do they simply repeat past mistakes and failings? The likely importance of developing a learning culture has been recognised in the literature (Senge, 1990, 2006; West et al., 2014; Halmaghi and Elida-Tomita, 2023).

Yet the biggest block to developing a learning culture is perhaps the power relationships that stop people contributing to problem-solving and decision-making. This has led to the development of the concept of 'collective leadership', often referred to in the literature as 'distributed leadership' (Watson, 2002; Mehra et al., 2006; Gray et al., 2010; Gray et al., 2013; West et al., 2014; Harris et al., 2022) where responsibility for the leadership and management of services is distributed as widely as possible within the organisation, mobilising the full expertise and the abilities of all staff to innovate and lead. In effect, in an organisation practising collective leadership, everyone is a leader or manager, including the newly qualified social worker. Regardless, every one of your actions will indeed shape the existing and emerging culture of the organisation (West et al., 2014; Harris et al., 2022) – this can be a sobering thought.

Collective leadership is more readily practised in organisations employing social workers because they will have developed expertise and responsibility for the effective leadership and management of their cases, so it is not as hard to reach beyond this and engage them in the broader endeavour of effective leadership and the management of services. This perspective, of collective leadership, determines the aim of this chapter – to *start* the process, if it has not started already, of you developing your leadership and management skills (see BASW, 2018) and in doing so can contribute to the development of a learning culture.

But will I be allowed to get involved?

Perhaps a big question you may ask is: will my agency or organisation allow me to be involved in service changes and development? Your contribution to the development of service quality may not be fully facilitated by your organisation. A criticism of current service provision is that we suffer from 'managerialism' (Jones et al., 2011; Albano et al., 2020) which is viewed as the imposition of centrally determined agendas that do not allow for the involvement of staff in service development and improvement. Other commentators (e.g. Munro, 2011) have also picked up on this and the need to develop a more creative and flexible approach to service provision that enables social workers to learn from their experiences and have more freedom to exercise their professional judgement (Williams et al., 2012; Gray et al., 2013; Parker, 2025).

It might be the case that you will find all your contributions encouraged, welcomed and implemented and you are already part of an organisation with a culture of learning.

Most of us though will be part of a work in progress, so that contributing fully to service quality and development is aspirational. This schism between managerialism and collective leadership constitutes a polarity that needs bridging (Johnson, 1996; Albano et al., 2020). Managers need to offer social workers more scope to contribute, and professionals also need to reach out and embrace some managerial perspectives and issues so that they can contribute to service developments. You may find this challenging as it requires grappling with the acknowledged resource constraints and demanding policy initiatives, such as the personalisation agenda (DH, 2007; Gardner, 2011), that may require significant changes in your practice. One key piece of sound advice is to ensure good alignment between your organisation's strategic objectives and your own.

Whatever your circumstances, empowered or struggling against the system, it may not be possible to promote our social work values that commit us to providing services that are as responsive as possible to the needs of people who use services, without addressing the issue of service quality and improvement. If we sometimes find our circumstances to be daunting, and the impact we might have limited, it is encouraging to remember that small changes can make a big difference. Tom Peters, the 'managing for excellence' champion, once suggested that some of the biggest service improvements can be small ones (Peters, 1989). He uses the example of a significant service improvement resulting from a team moving a filing cabinet, having worked around it for the last two years. He suggests it was a massive step forward – not in the least because the team had at last felt empowered enough to do it.

It is also worth remembering that as an agent of service improvement, a social worker is particularly well positioned. Apart from people who use services and their carers (who are the closest to the issues), you are well placed to identify and respond to

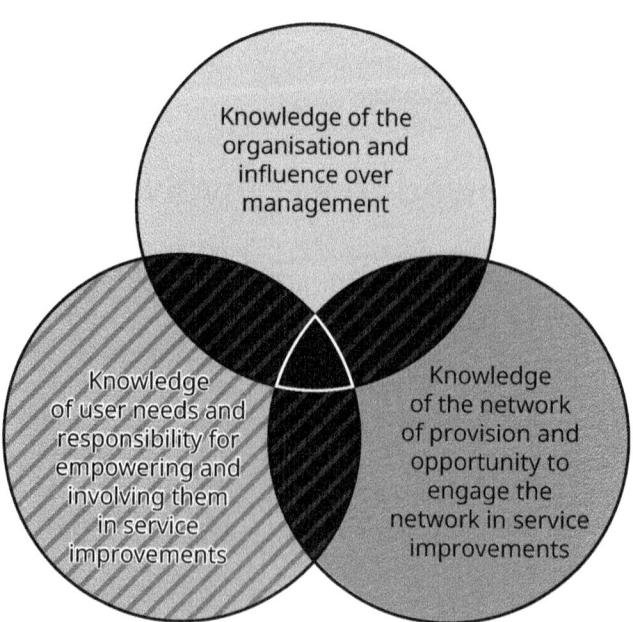

Figure 6.1   The role of the social worker as broker for service improvements

problems. You will also be gaining understanding of your organisation, how the system works (or not) and how to influence teams, managers and other groups that make up the service. You are a crucial 'broker' between management, the wider organisation, networks of service provision and those that use them. You not only negotiate and secure an individual's care package; you also have the potential to broker available services and their quality (see Figure 6.1).

Herein lies an important point: if collective leadership suggests that leadership should be diffused as much as possible within an organisation, it raises the question as to whether it should be distributed to people who use services. This was the thrust of the personalisation agenda, allowing users to lead and manage their own services (DH, 2007; Gardner, 2011) and has driven the peer/partnership approach (Mahesh et al., 2024). As a social worker you will play a key role in engaging both people who use services and carers in service improvements through identifying problems, designing improvements and implementing solutions. For example, this can be achieved by evaluating the effectiveness of services they receive or working with representatives of people who use services, using their expertise to bring about service improvements (see Angela's Case Study 6.1). To ensure this involvement is genuine will require you to challenge, question and change your practice and seek to change the way your organisation does things.

CASE STUDY 6.1

Angela's involvement in service development

Involving the public, users of services and carers, in health and social care development initiatives has been increasingly promoted in government policies in the UK and is high on the agenda of regulatory bodies (Mahesh et al., 2024).

My own experience of involvement has developed over many years, from being a silent voice at a formal strategy meeting, to participation as one of many stakeholders, and now to an expert in my own field. As a user of mental health services, I wanted to do something positive to 'make a difference'. Initially, I was thrust into an alien environment which excluded me through its structures and jargon. The professionals did not know what to do with me. I sat at a meeting and then left. To continue, I had to question my purpose and function.

Through a user forum, I began to accept invitations to speak about my experiences. I spoke to others so that I could offer a balanced perspective of how people experienced services. I came to conclude that often what people were offered was 'service-led' rather than 'needs-led'. I wanted to communicate that the voice of the 'consumer' was key. Receiving a service appropriate to individual need made sense and was surely more cost effective? My aim was not to be critical, but to simply report 'how it is' and offer constructive input on how it could be better – for both the practitioner and person using services. The practicalities of being involved proved to be a challenge. These included:

- *being required to attend meetings at 9am which involved a long journey by public transport;*

(Continued)

(Continued)

- *having no prior discussion/training to be able to participate from an informed perspective;*

- *waiting months to receive any payment for expenses;*

- *finding myself sat next to my own psychiatrist at a service review!*

It is only by voicing these difficulties that change can occur. It is not always easy when fluctuating mental health can bring periods of acute anxiety and withdrawal. In spite of this, I have worked hard to gain respect and credibility in my involvement activities and have begun to engage in meaningful dialogue with all stakeholders. I am encouraged when I have tangible evidence that I have been heard and taken seriously.

The gains of involvement are rarely financial, so what motivates me? I want services to be of a high quality and to provide good outcomes for those who use them. I want to use my years in the system in a positive way; to give something back. Through this, my confidence and sense of self-worth have significantly increased.

I started out as the token user of services – wheeled in and out at the appropriate time and my involvement was meaningless. This has developed into what I would describe as inclusive and productive partnership working.

So, what are your options: how can you get involved in developing services?

There are a number of options open to you as a newly qualified social worker to become involved in the development of your organisation and service. What you need to beware of is being used either because more senior team members no longer have the capacity to develop and drive change or as a 'straw man' used to show up an inadequacy of the service.

- In your everyday work you can seek, with your team, to make immediate improvements in working practices when dealing with individual cases or systems that affect service quality.

- You can take responsibility for championing a particular aspect of a service, developing particular expertise and sharing this with your team.

- You can identify, in your everyday work and in supervision, quality issues and solutions to them that would enhance services or even new ways of working – and then get these on the team agenda.

- You can be a member of a project team or working party designing or implementing a service development that has been delegated to you.

- You can contribute to team development planning or business planning initiatives to generate improvement plans.

- You can review and evaluate a case with colleagues to learn from what went well and what went wrong, in order to improve the service (SCIE, 2012).

All the above options are dependent on how effective you are as a problem-solver. Taking a problem-solving approach to your work is the key to contributing to service improvements, to the development of your team and the wider organisation. So, what is effective problem-solving?

A problem-solving approach

In his seminal work concerning organisations, Charles Handy (1993) describes managers as 'organisational GPs' – they diagnose and then prescribe treatment plans that deal with organisational disorders. They investigate problems with service quality and formulate and implement solutions. In a collective leadership approach everyone seeks to improve service quality and contribute to organisational problem-solving, but how can we maximise our effectiveness as problem-solvers?

- Determine parameters of the problem and define it

- Collect information and analyse the problem

- Prioritise and set objectives for improvement

- Plan for improvement

- Implement plan of action

- Monitor, review and evaluate

This cycle of activities is a logical and rational approach that brings order and control to any process. Central to the management of any task, the problem-solving process appears in many guises. It can also be called the decision-making process or the planning process – there are many variants. In social care we might re-badge it as the case planning or assessment process, while in other professions it appears as the teaching or the nursing process. The challenge is not to develop a completely new set of knowledge and skills but rather transfer knowledge and skills you already use as a case manager and apply them to services more generally. This process can be applied to just about any activity area to improve service quality; for instance, slightly re-framed it becomes the 'team development planning' or, if you like, the 'business planning process'.

- Determine purpose of the team and define it

- Analyse performance and team/organisational environment

- Prioritise and set objectives for the team

- Outline team development plan

- Implement team development plan

- Monitor, review and evaluate plan

An important aspect of problem-solving is that the process is 'iterative'; there is a feedback loop that allows progress to be reviewed and changes made to problem definition and analysis. Sometimes this process is presented in a linear fashion (see Figure 6.2).

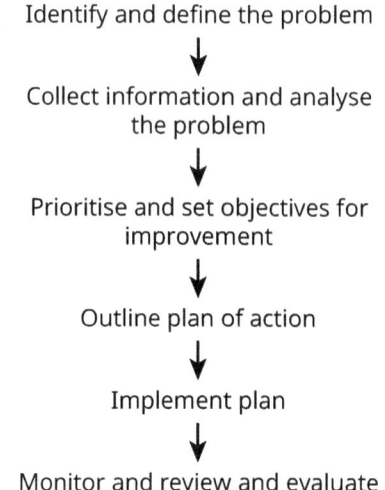

Identify and define the problem
↓
Collect information and analyse the problem
↓
Prioritise and set objectives for improvement
↓
Outline plan of action
↓
Implement plan
↓
Monitor and review and evaluate

Figure 6.2   A linear representation of the problem-solving process

Although the lack of a feedback loop in this linear representation is a disadvantage, it does have its uses. It offers a logical structure to a written report and could shape any recommendations you might make if you are leading or contributing to a working party exploring a quality issue. This way of working may be quite familiar to you as a newly qualified social worker, and similar to the processes you are involved in when working with cases. Transferability of learning and skills is something that you will be become quite adept at (see Case Study 6.2).

CASE STUDY 6.2

James and the day centre

James had been discussing the services provided at a day centre attached to his office with members of that centre. They were requesting more overt involvement and a users' forum. James discussed with centre members what that forum would be like and took his ideas to his next supervision with his manager. James agreed to consider what happens in other day centres and to use his research skills from his degree to search for information on similar projects, and to take a view from those who used the day centre on the best way forward. After discussing a range of options he took a plan back to his manager and set up a forum in which all who wished to could be involved and have a say in addressing issues of concern, feedback on services offered and present ideas for future activities and projects to develop. James's manager supported him by acting as a facilitator and conduit for people using the day centre to develop the service. When his manager suggested to him that he was involved in project management and developing the service, James said he simply thought he was working with those using the day centre to enable them to make choices. He had not thought that the two could be the same.

This problem-solving process can also be used more proactively, such as the basis for project management. Rather than identifying a problem with the delivery of an existing service, it can be used to introduce new service developments.

- Agree project brief with stakeholders

- Research and evaluate design options and change strategy

- Agree project design and objectives

- Formulate project implementation plan

- Implement project plan

- Monitor, review and evaluate project

The problem-solving process, like most models, is necessarily a simplification. Reality and application can be more complex and more problematic. Hamm (1988) describes the different levels of problem-solving as a cognitive continuum.

Accepting that you may get involved in problem-solving at all levels, let us explore each of the problem-solving stages in turn and then discuss some of the broader issues.

Individual judgement: You apply problem-solving process to a case or situation using your professional knowledge and expertise to determine a response.

Peer-aided judgement: Your assessment is agreed by your supervisor or your report and proposals become the basis for a care plan as the result of a multidisciplinary planning meeting.

Systems-aided judgement: You follow a process determined by experts and organisational/professional experience that helps you problem-solve (e.g. child protection and risk assessments, and flow charts used by advisors at a single access point).

Quasi-experimental: Pilot projects and action learning groups where a group methodically analyses a service issue and adjusts activity on the basis of findings.

Scientific research: Problem-solving where there is a clear systematic research methodology, structured information collection, verifiable analysis, and the presentation and dissemination of findings and/or outcomes.

Problem identification and definition

Applying the problem-solving process can take up a lot of resources. Therefore, direct your activity towards priorities. A useful rule for thinking about this is Pareto's 80:20 rule (NHS online library, 2020). This suggests that 80 per cent of breakdowns in service quality lie with 20 per cent of the problems. Try to identify these *key* problems, rather than those that will actually have little impact on overall quality. Quality assurance systems can help identify and quantify service quality problems; business plans can generate priorities for improvement; and risk analysis can also be used to determine priority problems. Many organisations have also developed complex risk assessment processes that can help identify where services might break down (Bostock et al., 2005; see also Munro, 2011).

The clearer the problem definition the more focus can be given to problem analysis, objective setting and planning. The greatest clarity comes from being able to identify the problem. Performance measures may help as they quantify organisational and agency priorities; however, because they are often set top-down, they may not represent what professionals would consider to be the key performance and quality outcomes. Sometimes teams have set local performance measures that capture what they consider to be the important dimensions.

Collecting information

It has been suggested that in war and in management, the easier information is to come by, the less useful it is. A problem needs researching thoroughly, including identifying and agreeing on what constitutes evidence-based practice and sometimes interviewing stakeholders. Information collection and exploration in social work and social care can be as complicated as full-blown social research and, as such, it is time-consuming and expensive.

Often, we will operate with insufficient information, having to make judgements on the basis of what is available at the time. This can prove more costly in the long run, but in a crisis we often have little choice. In general, however, planned and methodical information collection impacts positively and directly on the effectiveness of problem-solving. It is worth remembering that the crucial information you may need to solve a problem could lie in the experiences of those stakeholders who are involved in the problem. Engage them in problem-solving and you immediately improve the quality of your information collection.

Analysis

Problems vary in their nature and demand different approaches to analysis. So, for instance, it may be possible to accurately measure and use statistical analysis to identify the causes of some problems. Yet, many problems faced by social work practitioners and managers cannot be analysed in this way and demand qualitative approaches. A combination of approaches is often necessary. To illustrate: if you want to improve the percentage of assessments completed within a timescale set by a performance measure, you may wish to interview a small number of staff to identify possible causes for delays. Then you might carry out a survey across the service so that you can target the dominant causes. Analysis can embrace a number of activities and can be very multifaceted, especially in complex social situations. Some options are shown in the box below.

BOX 6.1

Options for analysis

- *Applying social science – social science provides us with a range of different explanations for human behaviour. Each can cast a different light on an issue and also suggest a different response (Cunningham et al., 2023).*

- *Applying social work methodologies – different social science approaches have generated different social work methodologies and interventions. These can readily be mobilised to help you analyse management problems and interventions (see Teater, 2024).*

- *Applying models of good practice – sometimes there are models of good practice that can be used to compare current practices against – e.g. see* **www.skillsforcare.org.uk/ Learning-development/The-ASYE-child-and-family/Case-studies.aspx.**

- *Using standards and benchmarks – it is increasingly the case that desirable behaviour is defined by the production of detailed standards. An example of this is the national management standards from the Management Standards Centre (MSC, 2015). These can be used to judge not only individual performance but the general performance of a particular activity.*

- *Analysing the change environment – analysis needs not only to address the problem but the capacity of individuals, work teams and organisations to implement change and how the change might be managed effectively and successfully (e.g. see SCIE, 2015).*

- *Systems analysis – if organisations or services are viewed as interacting social systems, then analysis should approach problems as multidimensional and caused by the interaction of several systems, all of which may need to be addressed. The impact of an intervention in one part of the system might be explored on the system as a whole. Otherwise a solution in one area may create a problem elsewhere (Fish et al., 2008).*

- *Action learning and appreciative enquiry – it is possible to work with a team helping you analyse a problem and identify possible causes or build on strengths and capabilities to bring improvement (Hart and Bond, 1995; Bryman, 2015). Working with the multidisciplinary team reviewing a case to both identify what has gone well as well as what might be improved on, as recommended by Munro, is an example of this (Munro, 2011; SCIE, 2012).*

Setting objectives

A common approach to objective setting and planning is that they should be SMART.

- S – specific;

- M – measurable;

- A – achievable;

- R – realistic;

- T – timely.

(See Parker (2025) for an application to social work planning.)

This is a popular formulation which was and still is contrasted with a tendency in social care to be inexact, or to focus on the 'art' rather than the 'science' of social work. As a mnemonic it has value but should not be used slavishly, as 'process' as well as 'outcome' objectives do matter, particularly in a value-orientated activity like social care. To demonstrate, an objective such as: *To ensure that stakeholders are committed and motivated in implementing the change* is not 'SMART', but it might be crucial in determining the success of the service improvement. One could argue that it could be made measurable, but this might be an unnecessary effort that does not do justice to the qualitative nature of the objective. It certainly will not be hard to reach for evidence that stakeholders are engaged and motivated.

It is important to remember that objectives serve two crucial purposes. They structure both planning and evaluation. Each objective should have a plan of action consisting of the actual steps that will be taken to achieve it, and monitoring may focus on the implementation of this plan of action. Evaluation should involve a review of each objective. Objectives can have different priorities. Some may need to be identified as 'success criteria' and can be separated out, as such, to provide the crucial measures against which a problem-solving activity or project can be evaluated.

Plan of action

As we noted previously, it should be possible to link each element of a plan of action to an objective or objectives. A simple plan identifies what will be done, who will do it and when they will do it by. However, there are more complicated planning tools such as bar and Gantt charts (e.g. see **www.businessballs.com/project.htm**) that can assist with planning more complex implementations and facilitate monitoring (also see Walker et al., 2008 for a review of useful management tools in practice education). There are also opportunities here to identify creative ways of achieving objectives, rather than relying on standardised responses. Involving your team and other stakeholders in planning can often generate creative options and build commitment.

Risk analysis can be used to identify and gauge the possible causes of breakdown in an improvement project. Sometimes, when a risk is judged to be considerable a contingency plan can be developed that can be quickly put in place when a problem is identified. When broad, alternative options for achieving an objective are identified, techniques such as a decision-making matrix can be used to try and make an informed judgement about the best way forward.

It is good practice to include an objective that encompasses the monitoring and evaluation of any implementation. This should be planned for in advance to avoid the tendency to leave evaluation to the last minute and to do it badly, thereby excluding any huge gains that can be made from learning from mistakes. As a newly qualified worker, the more time spent on planning, the better. It will help you to identify success and see where things do not always work as planned. In this way, you can monitor your progress and development.

Monitoring and evaluation

It is all too common *not* to monitor and/or evaluate. This can have a number of unfortunate outcomes, including the stalling of any implementation. It is essential to determine who will monitor, and how. Early identification of difficulties in implementation can often lead to timely resolution. Disruption or re-thinking should be planned into the work.

Monitoring can be aided by establishing milestones. These are key dates along the 'journey' of implementation that pinpoint when crucial activities will have been completed. This gives a welcome structure to monitoring, and a project or development team can use these 'way marks' to meet and consider progress and respond to problems.

Evaluation is a review of a project's effectiveness. It should explore each of the objectives in turn, as well as asking whether the problem as a whole has been responded to or whether the aim of the project has been achieved. Any evaluation can raise insights to inform other developments within an organisation. In other words, it is as essential as the problem-solving process is to the functioning of learning organisations. As implementation or work on the problem or project is likely to be ongoing it can allow for re-analysis and the iterative setting of new objectives and a new plan. In effect, it allows us to learn from experience and continuously improve services. Activity 6.1 considers how you monitor and evaluate your own work.

Going beyond objectives and performance measurement: evaluating service outcomes

It can be argued that while it is important we try and measure activities, perhaps by target setting, success criteria and performance measurement, a potentially negative impact may be that the real purpose of changes and improvements are lost. This has led to services attempting to reach beyond measurable outputs to 'service outcomes'. This can be at an individual, community or societal level and demands thinking further than whether a child's needs assessment was carried out on time and according to the relevant performance criteria to evaluating the impact of the assessment in respect of meeting their needs and improving their long-term quality of their life. The next stage beyond this would be to ask if the range of services provided were having a wider social impact in enhancing the quality of life of a community.

Evaluating service outcomes is much harder than identifying if project objectives have been achieved or measuring outputs (e.g. how many assessments were provided). Going back to the different levels of problem-solving, determining service outcomes can involve us in complex, long-term and expensive social research. Yet it is important that we try and reach beyond the numbers to the features of a service that really determine its quality.

ACTIVITY 6.1

How do you monitor and evaluate your own work?

Think about your own work as a newly qualified social worker. Write down some of the ways you monitor and evaluate your work. Consider what you have learned when you evaluate your work and what you have learned when you have not evaluated your work.

(Continued)

(Continued)

Remember, effective evaluations:

- *are planned;*
- *evidenced;*
- *explore the overall aim of the intervention, each objective and any success criteria;*
- *involve key stakeholders;*
- *are the basis for personal and organisational learning and development;*
- *try and evaluate service outcomes.*

If you are interested in learning more about service evaluation and the political and par-ticipatory functions it can have, try reading Ovretveit (2014), Everitt and Hardiker (1996), Rossi et al. (2004), Unrau et al. (2007) and/or Parker (2025). In respect of evaluating your own work, which can then be applied to your organisation's services, consider the work of Ashencaen Crabtree et al. (2012, 2015) and Parker et al. (2012, 2014) in exploring the learn-ing and practice of cultural competences and reflective development of social work students on placement in unfamiliar places.

Some issues arising from the problem-solving process

The problem-solving process is not, of course, a panacea. It will not solve all problems you may face in contributing to the development of services and improving service quality, although it is an essential tool and method. Thinking critically, some of the issues with it are:

- *It oversimplifies*: it can be argued that the basic model oversimplifies reality and that in practice actual problem-solving is very different. For instance, things don't happen stage by stage. Information comes in all the time leading to changes in analysis, plans and objectives – in an altogether much more fluid process.

We argue that it is important to use a simple model to help order our thinking and actions, and of course we accept that all models by their nature simplify to provide structure. Accepting that the actual process of assessment is more complicated, with a practitioner moving flexibly around the cycle, does not mean that formal analysis, objectives and agreed plans are not necessary.

- *It's too positivistic and too individualistic*: the approach can be seen as assuming a knowable objective reality that can be analysed and changed rationally. An alternative interpretation often cited in social care is that meaning is created by people, so that the process of negotiating the definition of a problem, agreeing objectives and a plan of action are more important than 'scientific' analysis.

This may be the case in public services, where there could be several stakeholders with different problem definitions, analyses and objectives that have to be recognised and reconciled. However, the importance of mobilising groups and communities as problem-solvers could be seen as the pathway to effectiveness in any organisation. Senge's (1990) formulation of a learning organisation emphasises the importance of group problem-solving as does total quality management and theories of Communities of Practice (Wenger, 1998, 2015; Wenger-Traynor et al., 2023). Case planning meetings, reviews and case conferences can all be seen as exercises in group problem-solving. For instance, a good chairperson is likely to consciously try and follow the problem-solving process, encouraging people to share information and analyse it rather than jumping straight to a possible plan of action.

- *Need for criticality and creativity*: A problem for professionals wanting to contribute to the leadership and management of their service by improving service quality is how this is shown (see BASW, 2018). Argyris and Schön (1978) suggest the need for a double feedback loop to achieve critical problem-solving (see Figure 6.3). That is to say, the culture of an organisation influences the problem-solving process so that everyday identification of problems and responses to them are standardised and based on hidden assumptions that define culture – *the way we do things around here.* A double feedback loop challenges these value assumptions and power relationships, e.g. who defines the problem; how it is defined; how causes are identified; how objectives are prioritised; which systems are not challenged; which plans are eventually adopted; and whether carers and people who use the services have been consulted and involved. Although limited resources can restrict options considered in the plan of action, the feedback loop can also be used to challenge the efficacy of the process itself, e.g. was the definition of the problem clear enough; were enough sources of information used; and to what extent was the analysis critical?

We have already discussed some of the other options for developing creative problem-solving involving people, particularly with service users and the multidisciplinary team, learning from successes as well as problems. Another option is researching and learning from what others have done. This can involve identifying evidence-based practice, e.g. SCIE's (2015) latest organisational change resource (see **www.scie.org.uk/publications/elearning/organisational-change-in-social-care/**) but can also involve learning from other disciplines. For instance, NHS Improving Quality (see **www.nhsiq.nhs.uk/**) and the Institute for Healthcare Improvement (see **http://ihi.org**) in the USA have an excellent range of quality and service improvement tools on their websites that you will find very helpful.

- *Learning styles and problem-solving*: According to your learning style (see **www.talentlens.co.uk/develop/peter-honey-learning-style-series**), you might be seen to emphasise different parts of the problem-solving process to the detriment of others. For instance, a theorist might enjoy the analysis, a reflector review and evaluation, a pragmatist the planning and an activist the implementation. Effective problem-solving, and therefore effective leadership and management, may demand a balanced style. This critical self-awareness can be seen as an extension of the double feedback loop and encompass questioning how your personal history and value base might influence your approach.

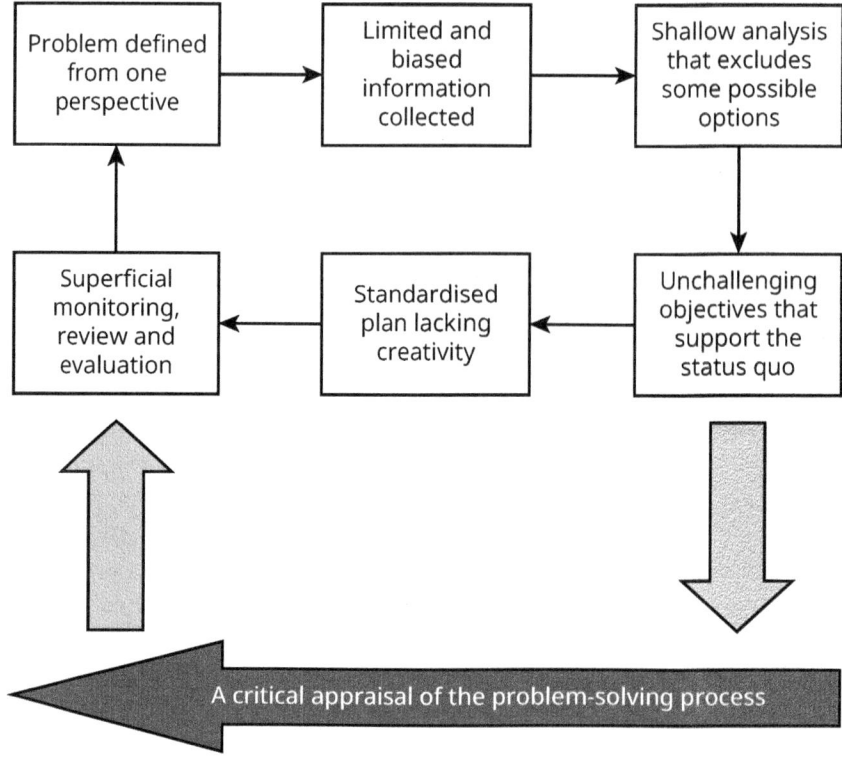

Figure 6.3   A double feedback loop

Applying the problem-solving process to your team or unit

Team development involves developing the ability of the team to respond to whatever it might be faced with and to improve its systems, processes and relationships. Or if you like, it is about building the capacity of your team. It is worth noting that team development planning is often now called business planning and is about determining the objectives the team seeks to achieve.

The problem-solving process can underpin any methodical approach to managing an activity. What often varies is the analysis. So, if we explore team development or business planning, and refer again to 'analyse performance and the team/organisational environment', this will probably be your biggest challenge as a newly qualified social worker. The factors you can draw on in this analysis are outlined in Figure 6.2.

There are a number of things to note in how we have represented Figure 6.4.

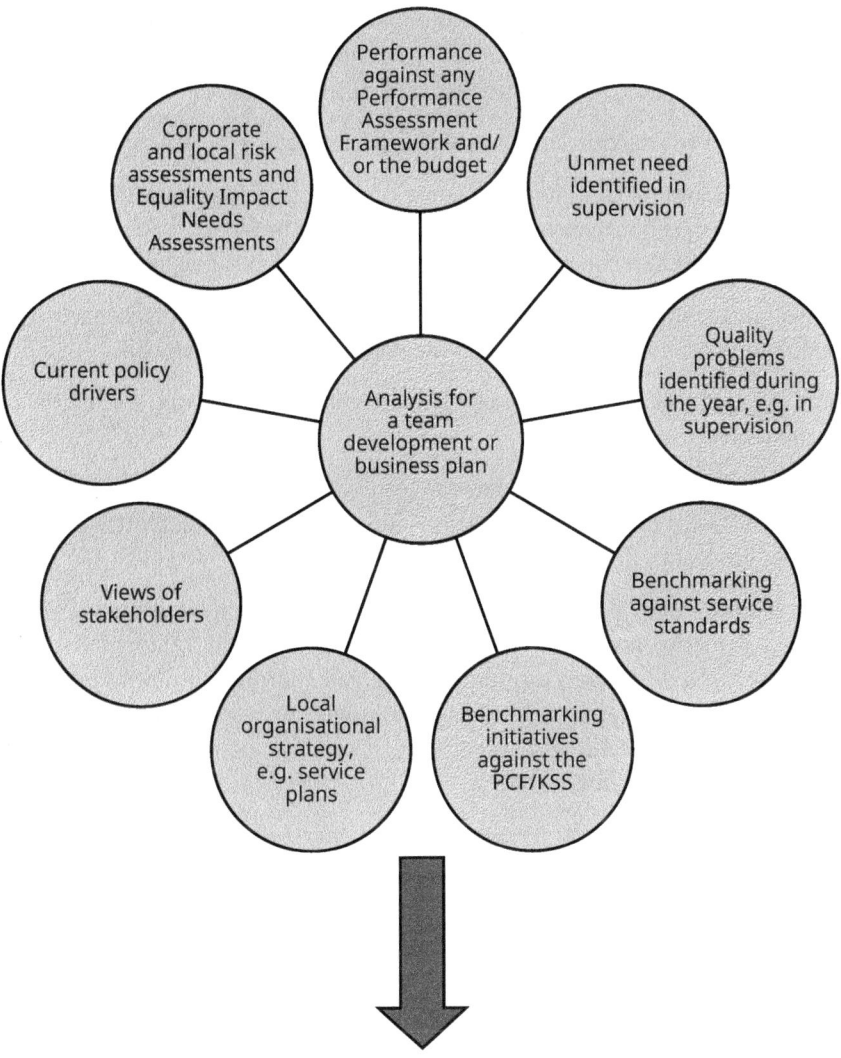

Figure 6.4   *Analysis for a team development or business plan*

- We have emphasised the involvement of all stakeholders. Each has a part to play in the service, either as contributors or beneficiaries. Not only are they the best source of information but are crucial in agreeing and implementing any future plans. People who use services are the most important stakeholders.

- Making judgements about previous organisational performance involves collecting information. Some information is readily available as performance measures but others will need collecting as they arise, e.g. out of supervision.

- As a team you will need to keep abreast of national policy initiatives.

- Your manager will play an important role of feeding you organisational information to which you may not have ready access. There may be local organisational strategies and service plans that you need to incorporate into any business planning.

- You will probably need to carry out some benchmarking activity such as reviewing team performance against the service standards for your area of work.

- Some 'good practice models' are worth considering (see following section on learning organisations).

- We suggest that the different factors feed what is often called a 'SWOT' analysis to identify key objectives that, as in Figure 6.3, are translated into the detail that becomes the team's development or business plan.

- If you and your team are not ready or able to get involved in a full team development/ business planning process then try and identify a simple team service improvement which you all agree is a priority and can all contribute to (see Case Study 6.3). Sometimes, once you start reviewing some aspects of service provision and thinking about options that might better meet need, it can become part of how a team works and can develop over time.

CASE STUDY 6.3

A carer's support group

Karla was concerned that her new team never really looked at the gaps in locally available services, but based care plans on what was assumed to be there. She believed there could be a much wider range of services and that some big gaps could be filled. In supervision, she began to identify what she thought were unmet needs and talking about projects she had become involved in on placement as a student, or knew colleagues had been involved in. Her team manager started exploring this in supervision with others, and after discussion in a team meeting it was suggested that a carers' support group would be valuable. Karla and others pointed out that it was important to be sure what carers wanted and she started working with a colleague to talk to carers about what might be developed locally to offer them more support.

Learning organisations

As we move towards the end of this chapter, it is important to address an issue we raised earlier. Another approach to contributing to service quality is to develop your team and organisation via continual learning, i.e. one that mobilises its resources to continually learn and develop itself. Developing a 'Learning Organisation' (Senge,

2006) is what many organisations in the public, private and independent sectors strive for, and leadership and management learning and development programmes are often designed to direct the efforts of leaders and managers towards building one. For instance, the Social Care Institute for Excellence aims with its strength-based leadership approach to develop leaders that change organisational culture (SCIE, 2022).

Unfortunately, changing established organisational culture is not easy and top-down management and unresponsive hierarchies are both persistent and pervasive. Certainly, changing organisational culture and contributing to the development of a learning organisation may seem well beyond your reach as a NQSW, or so it might seem at first glance. But there is a good argument for the importance of 'bottom-up' initiatives to change organisational culture and improve services. An approach that recognises this is a community of practice approach that focuses on mobilising the energy and expertise of work teams to deliver and improve services.

Joining and Contributing to your Community of Practice - the Key to Developing a Learning Culture in Social Work

Social work is a profession that is seemingly forever in tumult, and we all need a perspective and stance that helps us navigate our way through them. Such an approach needs to help you in caring for and looking after yourself and it also needs to enable you to tend to those around you. So, it needs to be about what human beings do best in the world, which is organising ourselves to look after each other and to work together.

A good option for you to consider as you build and develop your practice is a community of practice approach. It is a leadership model for professionals that shapes how they lead themselves and how they lead others. Whilst some of your effectiveness as a practitioner depends on your individual skills, understanding and values, your spirit and your motivation, a lot lies with the network or the community you belong to. We are at heart social creatures and do not stand alone. Our actions are social actions so your working community can enhance your work or if it malfunctions impede it. So, recognising, drawing on and developing your community of practice is essential to your effectiveness and your health and wellbeing. How you join it will make a big difference to your future career and your future happiness, that is why in the previous chapter we gave careful attention to your induction. This chapter is about how you continue to lead it.

Your social work course was a community of practice where your learning was dependent on your colleagues. The ASYE was designed to help bridge the gap between this community and the team and the organisation you are joining and the network of suppliers and co-providers that support it. Your new community of practice. Fundamentally, social work is about community and groupwork. In essence, social work is concerned with mobilising communities to work with you in helping themselves. Sometimes, of course, parts of your communities will work against you, it is not all about harmony, it is also about conflict and some of this is not healthy conflict. What is essential is that you see yourself as a social worker needing to attend to and improve the health of these communities that are your world as a practitioner.

Developing communities of practice

Wenger (1998) suggests organisations are designs which construct their own discourses to justify themselves. Social work could be seen as locked into professional and managerial cultures, design initiatives and discourses. Yet it is possible to identify several learning cultures in social work (Gray et al., 2008).

- A professional learning culture

- A managed learning culture

- A humanistic learning culture

- A democratic learning culture

Social work perhaps needs a diverse learning culture that embraces the features of all four cultures as detailed in Tables 6.1 and 6.2 below.

Table 6.1   Contending learning and development cultures and types of learning organisation

Professional learning culture (as strived for by professional bodies)	Managed learning culture (as strived for by human resource management)
Professional college sets practice standards and practitioners have a long-term relationship with their college	Standards are quality standards determined by managers
Professionals manage their own learning and development	Learning and development is the responsibility of line managers
Competence determined by experienced professionals using personal judgement	Competence determined by appraisal or assessment against published standards
Learning and development driven by personal career and practice agendas. Strong emphasis on professional value base	Learning and development driven by business need and business case. Strong emphasis on cost effectiveness
Learning and development evaluated in terms of professional growth and development	Learning and development evaluated according to business outcomes and impact on the service
Supervision is focused on personal development	Supervision is focused on case and service management
Sanctions are removal of professional accreditation and judgement is made by peers	Sanctions are managerial, i.e. progression, reward or use of capability procedures
Dialogue with a fellow professional, critical reflection and professional education are crucial vehicles for personal development	A range of training and development methods are used according to learning need and cost efficiency considerations
Professionals are expected to contribute to professional development as a duty	Professional trainers and consultants are employed, relationships are commercial

Table 6.2   Social work learning cultures (Gray et al., 2008)

Humanistic learning culture (as strived for by therapeutic communities)	Democratic learning culture (as strived for by total quality management)
Individuals are liberated by reflecting on their actions and the consequences of their actions for others and making choices. The community both challenges behaviour and supports individuals	Organisational and social expertise and creativity can be increased if the power relations that exclude some from problem solving and decision making are addressed
Learning and development are natural human activities. Group influence and experiences can be mobilised to bring personal change	Learning and development are natural human activities but power relationships in society seek to use them to control
Competence is competence in life and is about self-actualisation	If groups are liberated they can make a contribution to social competence, that is to the capability of society or an organisation to learn and develop
Learning and development is driven by social and personal needs that are inseparable	Learning and development should be directed towards the social good
Learning and development is evaluated in terms of personal growth and development and social responsibility	Learning and development is evaluated in terms of the contribution it makes to social outcomes
Supervision focuses on personal life experience and emotional responses to situations	Supervision is by peers through group problem solving and decision making. The focus is on group working experiences and social or organisational outcomes
Dialogue and reflection are crucial activities facilitated by a counsellor or mentor or by friends and colleagues	Group discussion and analysis are crucial activities facilitated by peers
Engagement in learning and development must be a matter of personal choice	Engagement in learning and development is a social duty, but voluntarism is espoused

Our services have to be managed, so much of the organisational activities that make up social work are most readily located in professional and managerial learning cultures. This needs balancing by consideration of the more communal, humanitarian and democratic learning cultures. Key features of these two balancing cultures are outlined below in Figure 6.5 and they can be seen to demand of professionals a range of groupwork skills (Gray et al., 2008).

It is important that the behaviours that support these features receive as much consideration as those that define professional and managerial learning cultures. The points below identify some of the behaviours that will support a more diverse learning culture and a community of practice.

Shared resources and expertise:

- What are your areas of expertise?

- How do you share your expertise with colleagues?

- What are the areas of expertise held by your colleagues?

- Do you make use of your colleague's expertise?

- Do you have shared team resources, e.g. books, papers, electronic resources?

- Do you coach and advise colleagues when they need help?

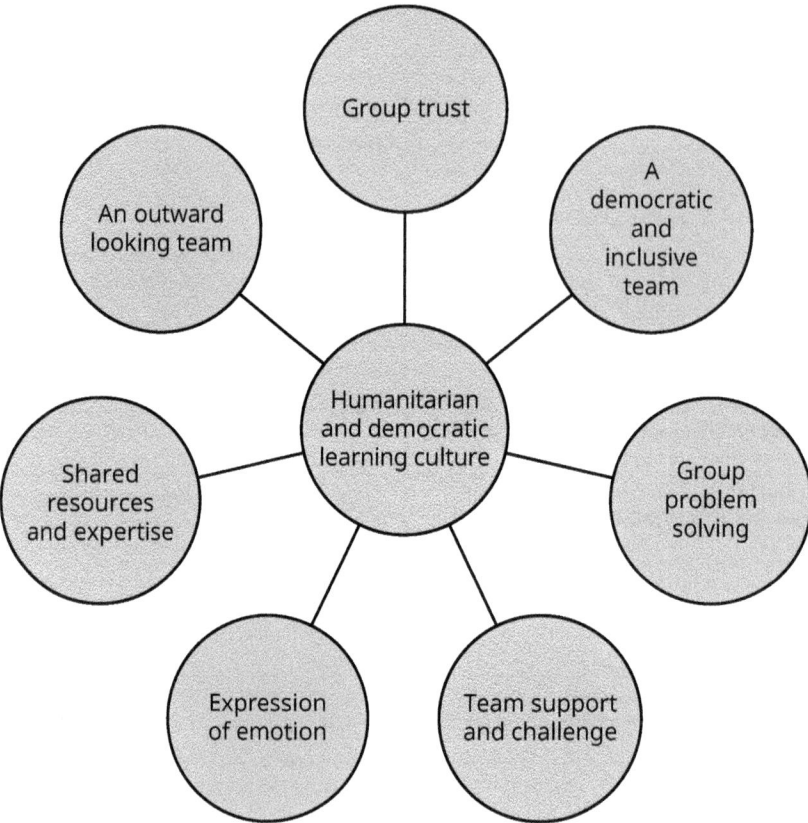

Figure 6.5   Features of a humanitarian and democratic learning culture

Group problem-solving:

- Do you share practice problems with colleagues?

- Do you listen to their thoughts and suggestions?

- Do you listen and share your perspectives when colleagues share their practice?

- Do you contribute to more formal group problem-solving and learning situations, e.g. team meetings, group supervision?

- Do you share information about new policy and practices with the team?

Democratic and inclusive

- Do you have a shared team development/improvement plan?

- Do you identify common quality problems in delivering services?

- Are you active in working collaboratively to improve services?

- Do you contribute to team decision-making and the introduction of new policies and practices?
- Do you ensure all colleagues are included in team activities?

Expression of emotion:

- Do you reflect on the feelings generated by your practice?
- Do you share your feelings with colleagues?
- Do you share feelings and emotional experiences from your personal life?
- Do you listen and accept colleagues' expression of feelings and emotional responses?

Outward looking:

- Do you involve people who use services in improving the service?
- Do you welcome colleagues from other teams into your team and share resources?
- Do you collaborate with other teams in developing and improving the service?
- Do you identify and share the expertise and resources of other teams?

Support and challenge

- Do you challenge behaviours, perspectives and practices that you see as unhelpful or inappropriate?
- Do you give colleagues balanced feedback?
- Do you identify team members who might be excluded or marginalised and help draw them into the team?
- Do you welcome and help introduce new members into the team?
- Do you try and resolve conflict and find common ground and ways forward?

Group trust

- Are you honest and open in the team?
- Do you demonstrate that you value colleagues and their views?
- Do you take opportunity to praise colleagues and give them positive feedback?
- Do you share personal information with colleagues?
- Do you share your values and viewpoints?
- Do you initiate and contribute to team social events?
- Do you support colleagues grappling with difficult situations and seek support yourself?

ACTIVITY 6.2

Developing your community of practice

Reflect on the questions above.

Have you been aware in the past of the importance of your community of practice and have you attempted to improve the contribution you make to it?

Can you see a way of involving your fellow NQSWs in developing your community of practice?

Can you share this audit with your supervisor, and might it be included in your ASYE portfolio?

Summary

Social work needs a diverse learning culture that fully embraces humanitarian and democratic learning cultures as well as professional and managerial. This means, that whilst the standards and protocols that shape practice should be welcomed and mobilised by professionals and managers in order to improve organisational practices and service provision, similar efforts need to be directed towards developing the community of practice as a crucial source of learning and as an essential foundation for the improvement of services (Gray et al., 2010). This humanitarian and democratic learning culture is concordant with social work's value base, and its development is dependent on its established skills set. So, social work through the commitment and the expertise of its professionals is much better placed to maximise service improvement compared with other organisations and professions. A community of practice approach also serves to maximise the support an individual receives from their organisation enhancing their sense of belonging and their wellbeing as well as their ability to make a social difference. It also is the best source for individual learning and development and both individual practice and team working benefits from the synergy that it provides.

We hope the perspectives we have presented in this chapter will help you build on your professional skills and increase your influence over service quality and development by being able to contribute more to the leadership and management of services. We know that some of you will find that your organisation does not encourage you to play a full part in this, but you will always be able to make some improvements and may find some ways forward by which you can help them change features of their culture that are unhelpful and move towards achieving the features of a collective leadership culture, one where continual learning is welcomed. Whatever your experience, we hope you share with us the perspective that service development and quality improvement cannot, and should not, be separated out from professional practice. This means that leadership and management skills are part of professional capability and skills development, and that they should feature strongly in your continuing professional development. The essence of empowerment and collective leadership is, perhaps, best seen as not just professional involvement and leadership but also the involvement of people who use services and carers in the leadership and development of services. At the very least this should involve opportunity to play a part in leading their own care plan, but their potential and the potential of our services will only be fully reached when they are enabled to contribute to building service quality and determining the future of services more generally. A community of practice approach will maximise the support an individual receives from their organisation enhancing their sense of belonging and their wellbeing as well as their ability to make a social difference. It also is the best source for individual learning and development. Both leadership of the service, individual practice and team working all benefit from the synergy that it provides.

Further reading

Dudley, J. R. (2020). *Social work evaluation: Enhancing what we do* (3rd ed.). Oxford University Press.

Although this is a North American text it presents a comprehensive and rigorously constructed array of models and techniques for improving and enhancing social work practice.

Ovretveit, J. (2014). *Evaluating improvement and implementation for health*. Oxford University Press.

If you are looking for a book outside the social work zone to expand your horizons and knowledge in terms of evaluation, then try this text.

Parker, J. (2025). *Social work practice: Assessment, planning, intervention and review* (7th ed.). Sage/ Learning Matters.

This book considers the process of social work as a whole in the UK. As such, there is a significant focus on evaluation of practice from a range of perspectives each of which contributes to the enhancement of service quality.

Williams, S., Rutter, L., & Gray, I. (2012). *Promoting individual and organisational learning in social work*. Sage/Learning Matters.

Offers help in leading and enabling others and contributing to the development of communities of practice and learning organisations.

Chapter 7

Research and NQSW: Developing yourself as research-minded and critically reflective practitioner

Richard Williams and Louise Oliver

Introduction

Social workers in England are mandated to be evidence-informed by Social Work England's Professional Standards and the British Association of Social Work Professional Capabilities Framework. This is done via the identification and exploration of multiple sources of evidence to inform decision-making. This chapter will focus upon developing practice via the application of findings from research. We will argue that, throughout a social worker's career, the need to be an evidence-informed practitioner, to be critically reflective and demonstrate criticality of thought, necessitates being research-minded.

Throughout this chapter, we have an underpinning theme and that is that 'there is no such thing as perfect research'. As practitioners, as academics, and as the authors of this chapter, both of us (Louise and Richard) hold this to be true. Consequently, this chapter explores research and how to determine its quality and, therefore, the validity of the findings of that research. After all, we work with people often at some of the most difficult points in their lives and they have the right to expect us to be the best-informed practitioners we can be. Hence the key question is, how valid is the information we are using to support our practice, or, to put it simply, is the research any good?

Learning from research means going beyond research that simply agrees with our beliefs. It means striving for new knowledge that will add to everything we do. This is key to our development as practitioners. We can reflect upon changes in practice during the 21st century. For instance, The Adoption and Children Act 2002 extended the definition of significant harm to include 'impairment suffered from hearing or seeing the ill-treatment of another'. This recognises that witnessing domestic violence can have a serious impact on children's wellbeing and development. But why did it take until 2002 to integrate this into law? The reason was the lack of evidence from research to support this crucial change in policy. Domestic violence was viewed differently by agencies in the 1970s compared to how it is responded to now. The Domestic Violence and Matrimonial Proceedings Act 1976 provided legal protections to women who had experienced domestic violence. There was a long way to go before the impact upon the child(ren) was given the credibility it deserves – and then the evidence from research came as forward-thinking practitioners asked the right question i.e., what is the impact upon the child? This has led to the Domestic Abuse Act 2021. Another example is that the Children and Young Persons Act 2008 amended section 23C of the Children 1989 Act by requiring local authorities to pay a bursary to certain care leavers who undertake a course of higher education acknowledging that it cost more for a care experienced person to attend university, e.g. to fund accommodation during the holidays. It was findings from research that supported the changes in policy and practice.

Background and context

We currently live in a world with access to a vast amount of accessible information, in what some now call a post-truth era. Finding credible evidence from research can be a challenge. The use of the internet and Artificial Intelligence (AI) gives us access to information in different ways. We can read research papers (some will be open access, some via subscription or paid for papers), published reports, podcasts, videos and more, all based upon research data. AI will even summarise papers and reports without having to read them. It will also, however, generate false references and summaries. There is so much information available, including misinformation, that looking for well-balanced information can sometimes feel like searching for the proverbial needle in the haystack. The danger of this post-truth world is that it can give rise to further inequalities and social injustices, exacerbating instability for many (Burke et al., 2022, p.1). This is why being research-minded is so important, to challenge social injustice, to strive for equality, purposefully seeking out truth, authenticity and making change, both in your own practice but also in the world we live. To be able to do this, we need to be able to discern what information is reliable, valid and authentic – we need to be research-minded.

What is research-mindedness and why is it important in social work?

The word 'critical' comes from the Greek word *kritikós* which means 'able to judge', 'discerning' or 'for judging'. This root highlights that critical thinking involves the ability to analyse, interpret and make reasoned judgements rather than simply accepting information at face value and research-mindedness is just that. It is about having the ability to think critically and weigh up the evidence before applying it to support the development of social work practice, it is not being negative. As can be seen in Figure 7.1, social workers who are research-minded are curious, critically reflective and have the capacity for critical thinking (McBeath and Austin, 2014; Liedgren, 2020).

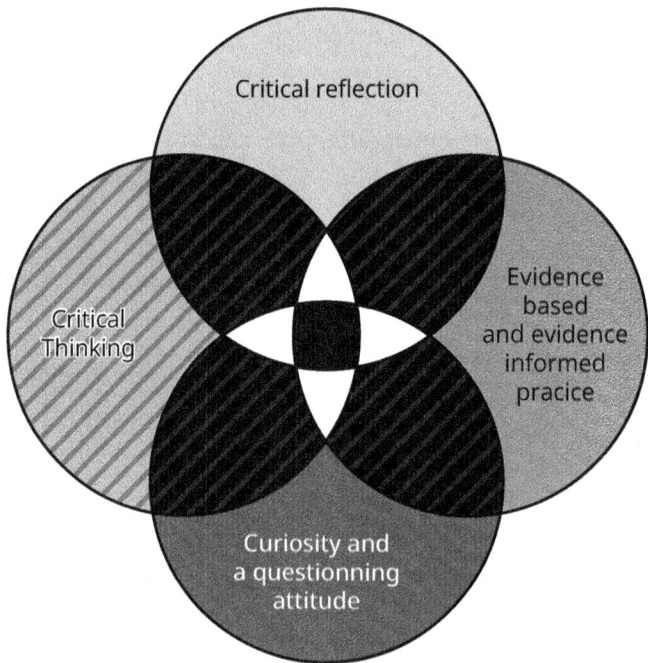

Figure 7.1   Attributes that support research-mindedness

Those who are research-minded have the willingness and integrity to change and make change, which is based on the authenticity and credibility of the evidence. This is not just about reading research, weighing up the evidence and applying it. Being research-minded is about consciously choosing to explore further, to be a truth seeker, to ask to question everything and not accept the status quo. To question policy, practices and decisions, and not do something just because that is the way it has always been done.

Social workers are influenced by the world they live in and, in turn, their decision-making can be influenced by societal norms which are built upon privilege, power, oppression and discrimination, including that held by social workers themselves. Foucault (1977, 1991) theorised that certain institutions, and we can include social work here, can exert subtle yet powerful governed conditions upon other people and their behaviours, with the potential for severe consequences, including their right to a private and family life (see the Human Rights Act 1998 Article 8).

To question the ways things are understood and, in turn, done, can take courage, not just in terms of questioning colleagues or people in higher positions of authority but also in terms of the willingness to question the world we live in and how we perceive it. As Dewey (2005) stated, 'reflective thinking, in short, means judgement suspended during further inquiry; and suspense is likely to be somewhat painful' (Dewey, 2005, p.13). There is a disquiet when challenging our thinking, questioning our acceptance of the world we live in and having feelings we wish we did not feel (Harvey and Oliver, 2025). Once these notions and ideas begin to be exposed, then we have the power to make change (Fook and Gardner, 2007).

As part of a decision to make change, there is a need to guard against taking things at face value, and to critically reflect as well as purposefully engage in critical thinking. This entails accessing information and to have the integrity to continue exploring the research when our initial ideas are supported and when our thinking is challenged by the evidence we find. By working through this information, we can appraise the research to discern whether the evidence is valid, rather than simply seeking something that agrees with our position. We try to set aside bias, and critically appraise the information being presented, in order to question and challenge our understanding. Critical thinking was once described as 'a liberating force' (Facione,1990); it encourages us to question meaning, carefully consider the use of language and critique concepts which uphold the status quo.

When bringing together these key concepts of curiosity, critical reflection, critical thinking and practice, it leads to something called *praxis* (Freire, 1970), which is a conscious decision to make change and is an important aspect of social justice. For example, if I assume I am right, if someone disagrees with me, I place them, presumably, as being wrong. It does not allow that interaction, it does not allow that development, it does not allow that opportunity for debate. Gaining knowledge is about the willingness to question and remain mindful of the evidence in front of us, to sustain praxis.

ACTIVITY 7.1

Being comfortable with difference

When engaging in social media: purposefully follow someone who you would not normally. This does not have to be someone with opposing views (we do not mean giving voice to those who promote oppressive or discriminatory views) but someone with a different lens on the world to your own. This will stretch your world view and, in turn, potentially challenge your own status quo.

Reflect on how this feels and whether you need to question and reflect on your usual way of looking at the world.

What's the difference between being research-minded and practice being evidence-based or evidence-informed?

We are starting this discussion with an example: Richard's best friend, who was a professor in the School of Medicine in Southampton University, as well as a professor in Bournemouth University, was diagnosed with a cardiac amyloidosis which is a life limiting condition. He was part of a large-scale control trial at a hospital in England. The control trial had three groups: 1) a group that had the specific drug that they were trialling; 2) a placebo; and 3) a group that had no medication whatsoever. In this controlled trail, the researchers were looking at the outcomes of each group and therefore, later on, basing their practice on the outcomes. He later found out that he was on the trial drug which gave him a few extra years to his life. They were able to base their findings and their interventions based on the results of that trial, therefore generating evidence-based practice.

Social work research, however, tends to take a different form. Social work research does not tend to have large-scale random control trials. They do of course exist, such as clinical-based practice, but they are a rare event because of the ethical challenges of having no treatment control groups. Often, therefore, we need to become mindful of the findings of the research associated with social work. We tend not to base our intervention on the research alone, but we learn from the research, we are mindful of what researchers have found and the strengths and limitations of their research. We use our own practice experiences to critically explore the research and our understanding of the situation/intervention under investigation. We also draw upon the experiences of others, especially those the intervention/situation impacts. Hughes (2019) notes that engaging with the voice of service users deepens our knowledge and understanding. It also facilitates a change in our perceptions and thinking regarding practice by developing a critical understanding of professional social work through the lens of those who access social services. This is generating evidence-informed practice.

The difference therefore between evidence-based practice, evidence-informed practice and being research-minded, merits consideration. Evidence-based practice tends to take a positivist approach to scientific inquiry, such as using large-scale quantitative studies to develop interventions. Whilst evidence-informed practice is built upon different sources, from research (including qualitative studies), learning from people with lived experience (service users/clients/customers/patients), our own experiences and practice wisdom (Alla and Joss, 2021). Being research-minded, we would argue, is an ethos of practice development and a commitment to critically explore and question practices. It therefore retains close ties to evidence-informed practice and evidence-based practice.

ACTIVITY 7.2

Exploring the use of research

Find a colleague or a friend and ask them where they get their information from and think about what you can learn about how others engage with information. Use this to reflect upon your own engagement with information. Is there anything you might seek to change? Write this down and use your thinking next time you engage with research.

How do you know you are reading good quality research to sustain being research-minded?

Take a step back – when we engage with others in a research-minded way, we are engaging in a debate about the research, and the research informs the arguments within the debate. This then becomes an evidence-based/informed discussion, the evidence being the research that has been undertaken, the validity, the authenticity, or the generalisability of the research that we are using and by bringing these criteria to the debate, we demonstrate critical thinking.

When we appraise the quality of research, the questions we ask and the tools we use change depending on the type of research. This then encourages a critical appraisal of the research, exploring the quality of its method and therefore the validity of the findings found by the research. We know that this takes time, which is scarce for many social workers including yourselves as newly qualified practitioners, but there are ways we can work more effectively with our time. It is about being methodical in our approach to finding the papers we want to read.

1. Start off by choosing from the body of literature, see if it is peer reviewed. Peer review means that experts in the field under investigation have made a judgement on the quality of the research and how the research has been presented in the paper and therefore whether it is of a good enough quality to publish. This adds an element of quality control, although it does not offer a guarantee. The Critical Appraisal Skills Programme (CASP, 2025) identify publication bias. In fact, research bias is something that merits careful consideration. The Critical Appraisal Skills Programme (CASP, 2025) define research bias as:

    …an important concept to understand when it comes to evaluating the quality of research. Bias is a systematic mistake in the planning, execution, or analysis of a study that results in inaccurate conclusions. It can manifest at any point in the research process and exert a notable influence on the dependability and accuracy of the results.

    We will also want to consider the background and the experience of the author(s). Who funded the research? Then we can think about potential bias that can seep into research without being made transparent within the research paper and bring this into our critical thinking.

2. Further tips on quickly finding relevant papers might be to consider when research was published (but also the date the research data was gathered). When seeking up-to-date research, it is clearly preferable to read recently published papers. For example, this becomes relevant when wanting to learn more about Intimate Partner Violence, in which our understanding is constantly evolving. The way we conduct research in this area has adapted and therefore our practice has changed with it. Reading older texts would give an overview of this evolution, which can be useful, but to understand how to make change, reading up-to-date research is crucial.

3. Next, choose titles of papers which appear to be most relevant, and discard papers which are not. Having whittled this down, it helps to read the abstract and think

about the following question: Does the abstract indicate findings that are interesting and that you want to learn more about? If you really want to go further, then have a look at the method. It is worth thinking about the research question and whether the method used is a good fit to answer the research question.

4. Once you have decided the paper is relevant you then read the whole article, be prepared to ask questions about the validity of the findings that you are looking at. To iterate the key theme of this chapter, there is no such thing as perfect research, which encourages us to always appreciate that the strengths and limitations of research need to be considered. Indeed, published papers will often have a *limitations* section, although this should not be taken at face value.

In terms of types of research, there are different markers for quality. Quantitative research uses numerical data and statistical analysis to make sense of the data. It is designed to quantify variables and for the results to be generalisable; that is to say, whether the findings can be applied to other settings. Therefore, large numbers of participants are required to offer consistency in results (CASP, 2025). Quantitative research can be used to develop interventions, understand trends in large populations and, due to its reliability and generalisability to populations, as well as the ability to conduct comparisons of data, is considered to be factual. Quantitative studies do not, however, gain the depth of information attained by qualitative research.

Qualitative research uses narrative data, using such methods as interviews, focus groups and open-ended questions in questionnaires. It also tends to have smaller sample sizes to allow for depth and richness of information gathered. The value of the data is highlighted by Jones (2003) who discussed the value of qualitative research methods, such as biographic research and notes:

> *What may have been lost in not using a method with the potential for larger numbers of subjects, so producing large data sets, was more than compensated for by the method's capacity for deep and meaningful case studies. These are rich with potential for the discovery of new material and for the generation of further hypotheses, for effecting change in social policy and ultimately validating and illuminating participants' lives. (Jones, 2003, p.63)*

Qualitative research, however, cannot be considered generalisable in the same way that large-scale studies can.

Mixed methods combine both quantitative and qualitative methods, therefore having the potential to combine the best of both methods. Qualitative research can make the research connectable so that people will stop and listen to it and the beauty of the large participant numbers in quantitative research is that it has the potential to contribute something which is robust in research terms. The key, therefore, is to use the most effective method for the research. We are now going to present a few examples of the appraisal of quantitative research to demonstrate this further.

When choosing an individual piece of research to highlight what we mean in terms of evidence-informed practice, we will draw upon one particular study. Richard had conducted research funded by the Home Office which allowed access to data which facilitated comparing outcomes of care experienced children with children permanently excluded from school. It was argued that the two groups had sufficient common characteristics to justify the outcomes being compared. Access was granted to the data of 100% sample of each group within a particular geographical region representing two and a half million population size. This, arguably, gave the findings potential generalisability to a wider population. The research was able to explore the participants' outcomes five years later when they were young adults. So, Richard and the research team were able to explore the data based on participants' criminality, being victims of crime and death by suicide.

It is important to acknowledge, Richard and the team knew nothing about any individual, therefore were unable to give any indication as to the reasons why anybody was permanently excluded or why anybody was care experienced, why they had become involved with social services. The research did identify the rate at which the young adults who had previously been a child in care of the local authority became victims of a of a sex crime and it was significantly higher than the rate experienced by young adults who had been permanently excluded. This did not indicate that anybody who had been care experienced was going to be a victim of a sex crime. But it was, argued, as information to inform practice.

What follows are three versions of presenting the application of the above findings from research to (social work) practice. We apply a range of factors to consider when appraising the quality of research and thus the validity and applicability of findings.

Firstly, there is an uncritical approach to research and its application to practice: when planning for looked after children to leave care, risk assessments undertaken by social workers need to carefully consider the planned placement to safeguard these young people from risk of sexual assault and being attacked by a relative. This is not achieved if attention has not been paid to prior research evidence (Pritchard and Williams, 2009).

Secondly, there is a beginning critical approach that attempts to defend the application of the findings to practice: Pritchard and Williams (2009) compared the outcomes of a cohort of 438 former looked after adolescent males, as young adults, with a similarly socially disadvantaged cohort of 215 young men who had previously been excluded from school. Former care experienced children were ten times more likely to be victims of sexual assault and ten times more likely to be attacked by a relative. The probability of this occurring by chance was calculated to be less than one in ten thousand ($p < 0.0001$). Statistical significance links to generalisability (Boddy, 2016; Miller, 2023), and generalisability is enhanced when the sample size is large (Andrade, 2020), so these findings have a validity that merits their application to leaving care placement risk assessments.

Finally, the critical approach is developed furthest and introduces a balance that includes counter arguments: Pritchard and Williams (2009) compared the outcomes of a cohort of 438 former looked after adolescent males, as young adults, with a similarly socially disadvantaged cohort of 215 young men who had previously been excluded from school. The sample were 100% of those who fitted the criteria from the Wessex region and the data was gathered from police and health agencies.

Jay and Hersen (2011) suggest that research found to be applicable to one group may not always be applied to another group, the issue being the generalisability of findings. However, as Lindsey and Schlonsky (2008) argue, there is a clear need for practitioners in child welfare to use evidence effectively in their work with families. This highlights the need to develop critical appraisal skills and, at its core are the questions, is the research any good and are the findings valid?

A relatively simple contribution was made by Pawson et al. (2003) who argued that it is the source from which knowledge comes that is of greatest significance. In this instance, Pritchard and Williams are experienced researchers and the large sample size, the sample selection and the reliability of the data source enhanced the quality of the research and therefore the findings. It is their judgement, therefore, that these findings have a validity that merits their application to leaving care placement risk assessments and, overall, meets the challenge in social work to address the gap between research and practice.

It would be so much easier if published research was allocated a mark and a summarising comment. Perhaps, 90%, very good, findings can be generalised to the whole of UK, or, 40%, satisfactory, would benefit from higher participation rates, not generalisable. Instead, we must make our own judgements, and we do this on behalf of the people we support in our practice.

Numbers can be misleading, they can persuade us to make judgements and to set aside our critical approach – our willingness to question. For instance, a study of child homicide assailants over a 10-year period (Pritchard et al., 2013) found that mothers with a mental health diagnosis (MHD) killed 34% of the children, fathers with a MHD killed 17% of the children and Violent-Multi-Criminal-Child-Sex-Abusers (VMCCSA) killed 22% of the children.

Who are the people most likely to kill children?

- Mothers with a mental health diagnosis

- Fathers with a mental health diagnosis

- Violent-Multi-Criminal-Child-Sex-Abusers

The answer is obvious, but only if one asks an additional question, at what rate do these groups kill children?

- Fathers with a mental health diagnosis killed at a rate of 30 per million (pm)

- Mothers with a mental health diagnosis killed at a rate of 91 pm

- Men with VMCCSA records killed at a rate of 5,102 pm

Therefore, the men with VMCCSA records are a significantly higher risk to children.

ACTIVITY 7.3

Using CASP

Choose a published, peer-reviewed paper presenting primary research or a paper which is a systematic literature review and use the relevant CASP checklist to appraise the research. Available at: https://casp-uk.net/casp-tools-checklists/.

Keep this checklist handy when you are updating your knowledge.

How does being research-minded develop you as a social worker throughout your career?

Barnett and Coate (2005) explore how to build strong foundations to learning and they considered the value of three interrelating building blocks. They are *knowing, acting* and *being*. With knowing, they argue that this is a dynamic and changing state, which grows by interacting with different sources of information, and as someone works through the information, at times, wrestling with the information, it shapes their understanding and therefore shapes the way they act. Acting is about the skills which are used within practice, they are learnt through education and practice learning. Social work has its own professional conduct, expected behaviours and language, and as someone learns them and critically reflects on them, their capabilities develop, as does their way of being. Being is about developing a sense of self, confidence and autonomy in practice. Therefore, 'to acquire durable capacities for flourishing in a world that is, to a significant degree, unknowable' (Barnett and Coate, 2005, p.63).

Being research-minded supports us to further develop our knowledge, understanding, skills and, in turn, our identities as social workers. A core global definition of social work (IFSW and IASSW, 2014) is:

Social work is a practice-based profession and an academic discipline that promotes social change and development, social cohesion, and the empowerment and liberation of people. Principles of social justice, human rights, collective responsibility and respect for diversities are central to social work. Underpinned by theories of social work, social sciences, humanities and indigenous knowledges, social work engages people and structures to address life challenges and enhance wellbeing.

The definition is clear about a social worker's role being one of promoting social change, to support justice and challenge oppression and discrimination, all of which is underpinned through theories and research, which help us explore, challenge (debate) and question the world we live in. To achieve this successfully, is to be research-minded.

In practical terms, it might be that when in practice, something catches us by surprise or makes us feel uncomfortable or does not fit within our world view, which Schön (1983) would describe as being a reflective practitioner. From this, we may begin to think about this in more depth, become curious, devise questions that need to be asked. We can start by engaging with others about this – colleagues, supervisors, managers, those with lived experience of the issue. Then we start to read around the subject, trying to find answers to our questions. We appraise the information we have gathered and through critical thinking and reflection, we develop a new understanding, a new knowledge and whether it is our own practice or systemic practice, we become contributors to change. We are engaging in continuing professional development. Making a further practice suggestion, to be able to access research, most local authorities purchase access to one of the key subscription services that provide core online resources, including research – the two most widely used ones are Research in Practice and Community Care Inform – and of course there are also search engines, such as Google scholar, to access open access research.

ACTIVITY 7.4

Reflecting on the ways you apply research

Reflect (either in writing/talking/art/music) on a time when you have applied research to your practice and reflect upon your application and how you shared with your colleagues, and what you did and what you learnt. Keep this throughout your time as an NQSW and review it frequently.

Personal qualities of being research-minded in practice

- Apply theories
- Willingness to challenge your own and others' thinking
- Independence of thought
- Self-aware/self-reflective
- Compassionate and caring practitioner
- To want to make a difference to others' lives
- Social justice activist
- Truth seeker
- Amplifier of seldom-heard voices
- Information gatherer (from multiple sources)

Summary

In this chapter, we wanted to invite you to take time and to make the effort to think critically, question and become a better informed, wiser, more capable practitioner. We have presented a range of tools to employ in your practice and emphasised the value in being research-minded. We do not know where you are on your personal journey with research-mindedness; however, if you are at the start, we hope you find this chapter a helpful step on the path to becoming research-minded. If you sustain research-mindedness in your practice, then please role-model this way of being to others. For those who are somewhere in-between, we hope this chapter has helped enhance your truth seeking.

Further reading

The critical appraisal skills programme (CASP). (2025). CASP Checklists. https://casp-uk.net/casp-tools-checklists/

These are free downloadable checklists which offer a guided approach to critically appraising different types of studies.

McBeath, B. & Austin, M. J. (2014). The Organizational Context of Research-Minded Practitioners: Challenges and Opportunities. *Research on Social Work Practice*, 25(4), 446–459. https://doi.org/10.1177/1049731514536233

Chapter 8
The NQSW Perspective

Andrew Morris

Introduction

The transition from student to professional is a defining period in any career, and for newly qualified social workers (NQSWs), this journey is particularly transformative. This chapter aims to shed light on the experiences of NQSWs as they navigate the first year of social work, offering insights into the challenges and triumphs encountered during this pivotal time. By reflecting on their journeys, four NQSWs who have contributed to this chapter provide valuable lessons and perspectives that can guide future practitioners and enrich the social work profession. Topics include:

- The perspective of a neurodivergent practitioner

- The NQSW role after qualifying from the apprenticeship route into social work

- The transition from classroom to full-time practice

- Taking the first steps as a NQSW

The chapter concludes with a reflection on my early experiences as a NQSW, highlighting the profound nature of the transition into professional practice. Firstly, we need to recognise the significant shift and the challenges that come with this new role.

Acknowledging the challenges and transitions

The first year of social work is an exciting yet challenging time. You'll face new responsibilities, expectations, and experiences that can be thrilling and overwhelming. Transitioning from academic learning to frontline practice exposes the gaps between theoretical knowledge and the realities of social work. You'll need to adapt quickly to the dynamic and unpredictable nature of the profession, developing the skills and resilience required to navigate complex cases and make informed decisions.

One of the primary challenges you'll encounter is bridging the gap between theory and practice. Despite the comprehensive education provided by social work programmes, the realities of frontline practice often demand a different set of skills and a deeper understanding of the nuanced aspects of the profession. You'll find yourself applying theoretical knowledge in real-world situations, honing your judgement and decision-making abilities through hands-on experience.

Key themes: professional identity, workplace culture, emotional resilience, and self-care

Throughout this chapter, you'll see that several key themes emerge from the reflections of your peers. These themes include professional identity, workplace culture, emotional resilience, and self-care.

Professional Identity: Developing your professional identity is a central aspect of your journey as a NQSW. This process involves integrating your personal values with professional principles, establishing a sense of purpose, and building confidence in your abilities. Many NQSWs reflect on how their experiences shape their understanding of what it means to be a social worker, and how they navigate the expectations of the profession while staying true to themselves.

Workplace Culture: The culture of your workplace will significantly influence your experiences. Supportive team environments, effective supervision, and opportunities for professional development are crucial factors that contribute to a positive and nurturing workplace culture. Conversely, challenges such as high caseloads, administrative burdens, and inconsistent support can hinder your growth and development. Reflecting on these aspects will help you identify areas for improvement and advocate for a more supportive work environment.

Emotional Wellbeing: Social work is an emotionally demanding profession and developing emotional resilience is essential. Reflecting on your experiences will help you recognise the emotional impact of your work and develop strategies to cope with stress and prevent burnout. Building emotional resilience involves seeking support from colleagues, engaging in reflective practice, and cultivating a positive work–life balance.

Self-Care: Self-care is a critical component of sustaining a long and fulfilling career in social work. Prioritising your well-being and maintaining healthy boundaries is essential. Reflecting on self-care practices will help you identify effective strategies for managing stress and maintaining your physical, emotional, and mental health. This focus on self-care will not only enhance your professional performance but also contribute to your overall quality of life.

Using reflective pieces from NQSWs

This chapter features reflective pieces written by NQSW practitioners, offering an authentic and insightful glimpse into their journeys. These reflections provide a rich source of learning and inspiration, as your peers candidly share their experiences, challenges, and growth. By examining these reflective pieces, you'll gain a deeper understanding of the complexities of the NQSW journey and the strategies employed to overcome obstacles and achieve professional development.

The reflections highlight a range of experiences, from the exhilaration of successfully navigating a complex case to the frustration of dealing with administrative inefficiencies.

They reveal the resilience and determination of NQSWs as they adapt to their new roles and responsibilities. These reflections also underscore the importance of support systems, including supervision, mentorship, and peer networks, in helping NQSWs thrive in their first year of practice.

Overall, this chapter is a testament to the strength and dedication of NQSWs like you as you embark on your professional journeys. By reflecting on their experiences, your peers offer valuable insights and lessons that can inform and inspire you. Through the themes of professional identity, workplace culture, emotional resilience, and self-care, this chapter provides a comprehensive exploration of the NQSW experience, highlighting the opportunities for growth and the importance of ongoing support and development.

Remember, you're not alone on this journey. The reflections and advice shared in this chapter are here to support you as you navigate your first year in social work. Embrace the challenges, celebrate your achievements, and continue to grow personally and professionally. Welcome to the world of social work – you're about to make a difference in your communities!

Reflecting on my newly qualified social work journey as a neurodivergent practitioner

Completing my NQSW in May 2024 marked the end of a significant chapter in my social work journey. Prior to this, I had completed my BA in Social Work while undertaking an apprenticeship. The transition from academic learning to frontline practice was both challenging and eye-opening, revealing the gaps between theoretical knowledge and the realities of social work practice.

Bridging the gap between theory and practice

While my degree provided a foundation of knowledge, it did not fully prepare me for the complexities of real-world social work. The structured learning in university felt detached from the dynamic and unpredictable nature of frontline work. Within weeks of being allocated complex cases, I realised that the real learning – the kind that makes a capable practitioner – only happens through experience.

I thrive in high-pressure situations where decisions need to be made in the moment. Too much time to overthink can lead to self-doubt and hesitation. Each case I encountered required me to seek out relevant knowledge, driving me to learn in a way that was meaningful and applicable to the person I was supporting.

Developing core skills: mental capacity assessments

One area where I faced a steep learning curve was assessing mental capacity. While I understood the legislation and had the skills to build rapport, I lacked confidence in conducting the assessments themselves. Knowing what to say, how to frame questions, and what to listen for were aspects I had to learn on my own. Many of my initial inquiries were met with vague answers, pushing me to research independently, seek feedback from colleagues, and critically reflect on my assessments. This iterative process helped me refine my approach and develop confidence in my professional judgment.

Challenges with reflection and neurodivergence

Critical reflection was another area where I struggled. Traditional models of reflection often left me feeling overwhelmed. Questions like 'What could you have done differently?' or 'What went well?' triggered anxiety rather than clarity. My neurodivergence means I am highly observant, often noticing subtle shifts in body language, which makes me a responsive practitioner. However, translating my observations and reasoning into structured written reflections was difficult.

Fortunately, my practice educator was incredibly supportive. She helped me break down my reflections by prompting me to articulate the thought processes behind my decisions. While this was time-consuming at first, it eventually unlocked my ability to reflect more effectively in writing. I found that I could express my insights fluently in conversation, but when writing, I needed to be more deliberate in capturing my reasoning.

Practical barriers: paperwork and workplace support

One of the most frustrating aspects of being a newly qualified social worker was the inefficiency of the paperwork. The back-and-forth nature of document sharing often resulted in multiple drafts, creating confusion and consuming valuable time near deadlines. A more user-friendly system – such as a structured booklet – would have significantly reduced this administrative burden.

Additionally, I encountered challenges in securing reasonable adjustments and hands-on support from my employer. Despite engaging with Access to Work, I found the support inconsistent. Losing access to proofreaders, which had been a critical learning support during my degree, further compounded my difficulties.

Key recommendations for improvement

1. Streamlining Paperwork – Reducing duplication and improving document management would enhance efficiency.

2. Tailored Support for Apprenticeship Graduates – Those transitioning from apprenticeships may benefit from a shorter newly qualified worker programme, while those from traditional university settings might need an extended adjustment period.

3. Defined Caseload Limits – Clearer guidelines for protected caseloads would prevent overburdening new practitioners and mitigate burnout.

Advice for fellow newly qualified neurodivergent practitioners

1. Be Your Own Advocate – Identify challenges and explore potential solutions. Engage with Access to Work, occupational health, and assistive technologies like AI-powered tools, albeit cautiously.

2. Find Your Support Network – A 'tribe' of peers, mentors, or colleagues can provide invaluable encouragement and guidance.

3. Understand Your Neurodivergent Needs – Whether it's using fidget tools, noise-cancelling devices, or structured routines, embrace strategies that support your focus and well-being.

4. Stay Organised – Completing paperwork promptly reduces stress, even though I still struggle with this myself!

5. Use Supervisions Effectively – Come prepared with a model of reflection that works for you.

6. Engage in Critical Analysis – Compare two opposing theories when asked to provide critical analysis to structure your argument more effectively.

7. Prioritise Self-Care – Flexible working arrangements, part-time schedules, and setting boundaries are all valid choices to maintain well-being.

8. Keep a Journal – Regular journaling, despite task avoidance tendencies, proved beneficial when compiling reflections.

9. Join a Union – The support and advocacy provided by unions are well worth the investment.

Creating change: Neurodiversity in the workplace

Navigating my newly qualified year as a neurodivergent practitioner was often isolating. While my fellow students were supportive, they did not share my lived experience. A turning point came when I attended a British Association of Social Workers (BASW) training session for neurodivergent professionals. Recognising a similar corporate background on Teams, I reached out to a colleague, and from there, we established a Neurodiversity Café within our organisation. This initiative has since expanded across the workplace, fostering a more inclusive and understanding environment.

Final thoughts

My newly qualified journey was a whirlwind of learning, adaptation, and self-discovery. While it was far from smooth, the experience strengthened my resilience and professional confidence. If I could go back in time, I would remind my past self – and any neurodivergent practitioner embarking on this path – to embrace their unique ways of learning, seek out supportive networks, and advocate unapologetically for their needs. The system is not yet fully inclusive, but change is happening, and we are part of that progress.

(Annabelle Penhaligon – NQSW Practitioner)

Reflections on the NQSW role after qualifying through the apprenticeships route

I have now completed my newly qualified journey. My pathway to social work has been working in the role of Case Co-ordinator in Adult Social Care for several years in the Local authority (LA). Then completing an Apprenticeship sponsored by the LA with study through the Open University.

Personal and professional growth after qualifying

Due to my previous experience working in an adult social care team and working throughout my Apprenticeship, I feel this gave me a brilliant preparation for working as a qualified professional. I feel I have been very fortunate to be working in a team where I was well known by the team manager, who was already aware of my strengths and weaknesses and who I had a good working relationship with. The downside of having an established presence in the team was keeping on top of all the tasks needed to be evidenced during my newly qualified year, as taking time out to do this could feel like you weren't contributing fully to the team. After spending three years studying, my inclination was to want to be a fully functioning team member. However, this was my perception and was never conveyed to me by other team members or Team Manager. This harks back to my tendency for perfectionism, something I have previously reflected on during my study days as it can be a factor in imposter syndrome.

The value of structured professional development to aid the transition from student to social worker

I would say that one of the issues I had with completing the newly qualified social work tasks was that it did feel, at times, like it was an extra module following on from my degree. This is not necessarily a bad thing, but it was tiring at times. I felt like I was repeating myself and that I was in a never-ending process! I can see the benefit to both employer and employee of the NQSW programme as it consolidates your training in a supportive environment, and it does give you time to adjust from being first and foremost a student to being a professional with all the accompanying responsibilities and accountability. In addition, it sets the stage for taking personal responsibility and the importance of continuous professional development throughout your career. A positive aspect of the programme was that I set agreed goals in my Personal Development Plan with my Team Manager who then allocated casework to support these goals. I was also encouraged to attend in-house training opportunities to develop my skills. I feel I particularly benefitted from a Mental Capacity Assessment 'Train the Trainer' course which encouraged leadership development and facilitated a deeper dive into the law and issues surrounding this subject which can present so many dilemmas to social workers, families and others involved in supporting adults.

The importance of support and adaptability

One of the most positive aspects of the NQSW programme was reaching the six-month milestone and final assessments of progressive development. My NQSW Supervisor had obviously taken a lot of time and care to complete these and it was really good to see how my practice was viewed from their perspective. I feel this really helped me to appreciate the progress I had made since the start of my journey and gave me a lot of confidence. On the downside, I had to change from my initial NQSW assessor a few months in, as due to sickness and work pressures, the NQSW conditions for supervision and meetings were at high risk of not being met. This felt like a really awkward time as I had to bring this to the attention of the Practice Education and Development Team and basically say that my needs were not being met. Fortunately, I was supported really well around this, and the Practice Education and Development Team assigned a NQSW Supervisor to ensure my Supervision structure and NQSW meetings were maintained. I think it's really important for NQSW Supervisors to be supported in the workplace to be able to provide the level of time and commitment needed for the role, as undertaking the role alongside a really demanding practice role is incredibly difficult to juggle.

Challenges in the NQSW role

One of the things I found quite challenging during my NQSW when completing reflections was having to demonstrate and link to the knowledge and skill statement and the Professional Capabilities Framework, as this could make things a bit confusing and cumbersome. It would be preferable if there could be one framework to demonstrate evidence of professional capability. I also think the timescale could be pared down to say nine months, but not sure what my rationale for this is, other than it is quite onerous on top of three years of study and working full time.

Advice for fellow NQSWs

The advice I would give to someone undertaking the NQSW is probably the same as I would give to someone starting on their social work training: Be as organised as possible with the necessary tasks ahead – for example, I make a table of what tasks need to be completed and by what time and tick them off as I go – this gives a sense of achievement when a task is completed, you can see an end goal, plus you are less likely to overlook something and can make sure the review meetings are booked in advance.

(Catherine Blamey – NQSW Practitioner)

Reflections on the transition from classroom to full-time practice

My NQSW journey has been a transformative one. It came with excitement of a real change that would positively impact the lives of vulnerable adults and support their families.

Initially, when I first entered the profession as a newly qualified social worker, I had great expectations of myself, I envisioned myself as a hero, an advocate for social justice and someone who would impact positive change in the lives of vulnerable adults and their families.

In advocating for this family, I applied the knowledge obtained during my university studies and placement to make a difference in the lives of my clients.

Professional and personal challenges

The social work profession requires that I become emotionally resilient especially in dealing with complex cases or when faced with bureaucratic constraints. As I settled into my new role, I realised quickly that theory and practice were not always in perfect harmony. The difficulties were the complexities of human behaviour and the diverse needs of clients. I realised that social work was more complex and challenging than I had anticipated. I started to question if I was equipped to handle the demanding needs of the profession. I became apprehensive about the thought of balancing my learning requirements with complex and challenging cases. However, these challenges also contributed to my professional growth and learning. It also helped me to prioritise my cases and learn from my mistakes.

When I began the programme, I quickly confronted the reality of my fears – I often felt overwhelmed by the demands of complex cases, ongoing training, and the challenge of managing tight deadlines. I reflected deeply on the emotional toll of handling sensitive and emotionally charged cases, meeting assessment deadlines, participating in NQSW learning activities (workshops, paperwork, and action learning), and navigating organisational procedures and policies. Securing adequate guidance and support to complete the programme felt critical yet daunting. At times, the emotional weight of the work became overwhelming, and I found myself tearful, particularly when faced with the struggles and hardships of vulnerable adults and their families or during the aftermath of a client's death.

It became challenging towards the end of my nine-month review following the death of my father. During this period, I experienced severe pain, and this impacted my ability to focus on my work. It was indeed a very challenging period for me, but I remained resilient and determined to complete my NQSW programme.

The importance of support, shared learning, and self-care in overcoming personal challenges and enhancing professional practice

My supervisors (case and reflective) were very supportive. They provided me the opportunity to express my feelings and the impact of my bereavement on my practice and offered support.

In dealing with my grief, and helping me in processing the reality of it, I did a grief and loss presentation during a NQSW workshop for my NQSW colleagues.

I shared my experiences on this concept (grief and loss) with them to enable them to support their clients in a more effective way towards their recovery. I felt sharing this information with my colleagues would help reduce the anxiety and uncertainty that come with loss. During my bereavement, I realised that building a good rapport with clients and their families during a bereavement process could promote a therapeutic relationship.

I also learned the importance of self-care seeking support and engaging in regular supervision and that looking after my well-being was relevant and would increase my productivity and longevity in this profession.

Personal and professional growth

During my practice, I also encountered ethical dilemmas that tested my professional integrity. I recalled a situation where a 99-year-old woman with a medical health issue was supported by her 73-year-old daughter. I offered support to them, but they declined support. Even though, the risks were immense and were shared with them. They refused support because they felt they could not afford the care cost. Despite my efforts in trying to make them understand that contributing towards their cost is 'means tested'. The problem was balancing the autonomy of the clients with my concerns for their wellbeing and safety. It was difficult for me to balance between respecting the clients' wishes and feelings and overseeing their wellbeing and safety, as the clients were deemed to have the capacity to make their own decisions. However, my training availed me the opportunity to gain new knowledge and skills which has enhanced my social work skills and helped me manage my cases.

The critical role of self-awareness in fostering growth

In this profession, I have witnessed the strengths and resilience of the people that I support which is very inspiring, but on the other hand, it has exposed significant levels of poverty, social isolation, and social injustice.

One of the most important lessons I learned as a newly qualified social worker was the importance of self-awareness and reflection. Taking time to reflect on my practice allowed me the opportunity to evaluate my interventions and explore areas of improvement. It also provided me the opportunity to gain awareness of my values and biases which helped me in providing more inclusive support to my clients. Putting myself in their shoes to understand what they might be feeling and become more culturally sensitive and respectful of clients' beliefs and religion. When I encountered a situation where my patience, empathy, and problem-solving skills were tested, I reflected on my experience and gained a deeper understanding of my strengths and limitations which helped me enhance my professional practice. In addition, I consulted and sought guidance from my supervisors, manager, and other colleagues.

The importance of cultural competence, advocacy and empowerment

My interactions with people of diverse cultural backgrounds have helped me become more culturally competent and anti-discriminatory in my approach. The driving force of my role is advocating for clients. I advocated for clients during multi-disciplinary meetings and challenge panel discussions. I ensured that my clients got the best possible outcomes. Working within my scope to challenge all oppressive practices by empowering clients to showcase their strengths and become more independent adopting a strength-based approach.

Diversity enriched my practice and made me culturally sensitive in supporting my clients to meet their desired outcomes irrespective of their background.

I worked with a diverse group of vulnerable adults with support needs, and this helped me to expand my social work scope, roles, and responsibilities by learning on the job. Working with these groups and using the right communication methods to ensure that they are involved in matters regarding their care was essential to improving my knowledge on the job.

The value of interdisciplinary work to improve outcomes

Social work is a multidisciplinary field, and I have also worked with other professionals, including pharmacists, doctors, nurses, mental health teams and occupational therapists. Spending time with these colleagues has helped expand my knowledge in working holistically to support my clients. More so, in pooling our expertise and resources, we created an integrated social and health care system that is accessible to the most vulnerable adults in the community. This integration has benefited both the team I work with and the clients we support by reducing bureaucratic processes, unnecessary delays, duplication of services, safeguarding concerns, and increases in death rates.

How to support the next generation of NQSW

During my NQSW time, I would have liked to have more shadowing experiences, a clear pathway post-NQSW, and a buddy support system. Additionally, after the NQSW programme, it would have been helpful to have a gradual increase in casework. This would help social workers fully adapt to their new role as a social worker.

Final thoughts on my NQSW journey

My experience as a newly qualified social worker has been a transformative journey of self-discovery and professional development/growth. I benefited from regular supervision, reduced/protected caseloads, workshops, protected learning time, training, a safe learning space, action learning and support from colleagues/peers during my NQSW programme.

I experienced different opportunities each day and used them to make a positive difference in the lives of the people that I support. It also helped me to identify areas that I need to improve and highlight the need for continuous learning and adaptation.

For me, the main reward of working in this profession is the appreciation that radiates on the faces of these vulnerable adults accessing support and the positive feedback they provide makes me love the profession.

Finally, social work to me as a profession is a lifelong learning process, and I am committed to the profession and the job satisfaction that comes with it despite its challenges. However, my dedication and passion for this profession have made me become a fully trained social worker.

(Chidinma Nwaiwu – NQSW Practitioner)

Taking my first steps as a newly qualified social worker

In my first social work position, having a NQSW role has been imperative for my learning and development as I find my feet as a professional. During University, I did not have any Local Authority experience, mainly because I was so interested in Forensic Social Work, which is where my final year placement took place [in a Low Secure Unit with male patients]. I felt it was what I wanted to do; however, I was advised to start in a Local Authority and gain experience there. Now I believe this was the best advice I could have received, as I love my position in the Local Authority and how diverse the work is. I believe I really have found my passion and am no longer looking to work in a forensic setting.

The value of structured support and continuous learning for new social workers

Not all social work positions have a NQSW programme requirement; however, having this has allowed me the time and space to learn the role and everything that comes with it. University is great for theory, but I did not feel prepared for the practical side of social work. Therefore, having that extra support in place along with a smaller caseload and less complex work has allowed me to learn at my own pace. The majority of us may train for three years at university, but this is a job where you are continuously learning and developing your practice.

The importance of support networks and structured supervision

During my NQSW programme, I have had support from my line manager as well as other senior managers within the organisation. I have also had support from the practice and education team, including my NQSW assessor. I was also buddied up with a more experienced social worker in my team and still ask questions. As part of this support, I had fortnightly supervision sessions with my line manager in the first six months, changing to monthly after this point. I also had supervision sessions with my NQSW assessor approximately every six weeks.

Overcoming imposter syndrome

In my NQSW year, what I have enjoyed most is being able to see my own development and also having this recognised by other professionals. Imposter syndrome was mentioned a lot at university, and I remember thinking; well we are students of course we are going to doubt ourselves! However, when I started working as a qualified social worker, it hit me – I questioned my knowledge and ability because there was so much I didn't yet know. As I gained more and more knowledge and confidence, and colleagues provided me with positive as well as constructive feedback, I started noticing how far I had come. I think at the start of my career, I felt there was this huge mountain to climb, but now I have accepted that I will always be learning in this job, and it is perfectly ok to ask questions as even the most experienced social workers do not know everything.

Balancing professional growth with casework and reflection

If I could change something about the NQSW programme, I think I would just try to have it more structured to fit in around casework. It can be very easy to want to focus more on casework than the work required for NQSW, even though they do go hand in hand. However, in my particular circumstance, the support around me has been amazing in helping me to stay on track as much as possible. I used to think that a two-year NQSW would be beneficial, but actually, when I arrived at the 12-month point, I changed my opinion. The idea of being outside of the NQSW role and being on your own can be frightening, but you are not suddenly on your own. Support is still there; you just have more knowledge and confidence so are able to do more with a lot less input from others. Other than that, in my experience some of the paperwork for NQSW has been hard to get my head around, but if I was ever unsure of anything my NQSW assessor would clarify it for me.

Advice to new social workers

If I could offer any advice to NQSWs just starting their NQSW journey, it would be to try and remain calm and remember that you were offered that position for a reason. Yes, there may be a lot you do not yet know, but your NQSW role is the perfect opportunity to learn and ask those questions. You might be bringing knowledge to the team that other people do not have, in my experience, everyone brings something different and together you support each other. I would advise anyone just starting out to ask questions – there is no such thing as a silly question! Also, remember how far you have come to get to where you are. Believe in yourself and enjoy the learning process. Don't forget to seek feedback often, from professionals and service users, as feedback will help you to pinpoint areas that need development. Finally, and most importantly, take care of yourself! Being a social worker is a tough job and if you don't take care of your own wellbeing, it will be much, much harder! You wouldn't let your phone run out of battery, don't let it happen to you either. Your self-care is a priority!

(Jodie Chalk – NQSW Practitioner)

Reflections from an experienced social worker

Many, many years to when I was a newly qualified social worker, the term NQSW wasn't even a thing. You qualified and you were a social worker, and it was a little scary.

My final practice learning placement was in a non statutory setting working with people who were alcohol dependent and street homeless. It was interesting, but it wasn't what I saw myself doing when I finished my degree. I didn't have much of a preference as to which client group I worked with, so I applied to all the social work jobs I could find. My daughter was still very young and my wife was pregnant with our son, so I needed to get back to full-time employment ASAP. I took the first job that was offered, which was working in an older person's CMHT. It was a great team, and I found myself working with some fantastic colleagues. I learned so much this first year.

You'll make mistakes – and it's okay

The local authority was changing homecare providers. We were no longer using one agency and moving to another one. I had an older gentleman who had homecare from the old agency, and it needed to be changed. I wrote a letter to the service user [it was a long time ago and he preferred this type of communication], to advise of the change. A few days later I had a call from his daughter. She was not happy about not being consulted about the change. In hindsight, I should have spoken with her and her father to advise them of the change and allow them to switch to direct payments to keep the old care agency. They chose to use direct payments, and we got everything sorted out. It felt like a very obvious thing to do, and I gave myself a hard time for not thinking about it. This inevitably led me to question my career choices – I was a qualified social worker and shouldn't be making silly mistakes like that! When I spoke to my manager about it in supervision, she helped me reflect on the situation and learn from it. Talking it through with her helped me process my own negative self-talk, as well as find strategies to manage similar situations in the future. This was useful, but the most useful thing I took away from that session was that we all make mistakes – they are part of learning, and they do not define our competence as a social worker.

Use supervision wisely

Annabelle, Chidinma, Catherine, and Jodie all talked about supervision as the cornerstone of your professional growth and development. Some may view it as a formality – just another box to tick each week. With a busy schedule, both you and your supervisor might feel the pressure to rush through sessions to get back to pressing tasks. However, this mindset can lead to missed opportunities for meaningful reflection and growth.

Supervision should be seen as a priority, a dedicated space for you to reflect, learn, and evolve. It's a time to explore problems, work through dilemmas, and gain new insights to enhance your practice. In our current work environment, where remote work and solitary visits are common, supervision becomes even more crucial for connecting with your team and yourself.

To make the most of your supervision sessions, preparation is key. Jot down notes about any service users or families, reflections, or concerns before your session. Be open and honest with your supervisor to build a trusting relationship. The more you invest in these sessions, the more you will gain from them. Supportive relationships are vital for all practitioners.

When you see supervision as a valuable opportunity rather than a formality, you unlock its full potential. Imagine entering each session with a sense of purpose, armed with questions, reflections, and a willingness to learn. Your supervisor is there not only to oversee your work but to mentor and guide you. They can provide a fresh perspective on cases that might be troubling you, help you navigate complex situations, and support your professional development.

Incorporating feedback from supervision into your practice is another essential step. After your sessions, take time to reflect on the discussions and plan how you will implement the advice and strategies shared. This proactive approach ensures that supervision becomes an integral part of your ongoing growth rather than a disconnected activity.

Consider also the benefits of peer supervision. While traditional supervision involves a hierarchical relationship, peer supervision allows you to learn from colleagues at a similar level. This can be particularly valuable as it offers different perspectives and fosters a sense of camaraderie. Engaging in peer supervision can enhance your reflective practice and provide additional support.

In essence, supervision is a multifaceted tool that, when used wisely, can significantly enhance your professional journey. It's an opportunity to pause, reflect, and recalibrate, ensuring that you are providing the best possible support to those you serve while also taking care of your own development and well-being.

Build a strong support network

I echo Jodie and Catherine's views – having a robust support network is essential for your emotional well-being. Identify people you connect with and bring them into your support network. Some colleagues might offer empathy and a listening ear, while others provide technical or policy expertise. Building a diverse team around you will give you a range of perspectives and support.

This support network isn't limited to the workplace. Partners, friends, and family can also provide valuable support, as long as confidentiality is maintained. Since the advent of remote working, it's easy to feel isolated. If you find yourself struggling, reach out to your support network. Suggest meeting for coffee or lunch to maintain personal connections and prevent feelings of isolation.

A strong support network serves as a safety net, catching you when the pressures of the job become overwhelming. Having trusted individuals to confide in can alleviate the emotional burden and provide practical advice. It's important to actively nurture these relationships by staying in touch regularly, offering support in return, and expressing gratitude for their presence in your life.

Engaging in professional groups or associations can also expand your support network. These groups often provide opportunities for continued learning, networking, and sharing experiences with peers outside your immediate workplace. Attending conferences, workshops, or webinars can introduce you to new contacts who can offer additional support and insights.

In a remote working environment, it's crucial to be proactive in maintaining connections. Virtual coffee breaks, video calls, and online group chats can help bridge the gap created by physical distance. Make an effort to check in on colleagues and be responsive when they reach out to you. Building a strong virtual support network can provide a sense of community and belonging, even when working apart.

A well-rounded support network enhances resilience, providing emotional sustenance and practical assistance. By cultivating these connections, you'll find strength in solidarity and feel more equipped to handle the challenges of your role. Remember, seeking support is a sign of strength, not weakness. It demonstrates self-awareness and a commitment to maintaining your well-being.

Your boundaries will keep you safe

Learning to say no without feeling guilty is crucial. Recognise your limits to avoid drowning in tasks. Social work is unpredictable, with crises and unexpected events, but knowing when to say no is key to managing your workload effectively. Remember, as a newly qualified social worker, you're still learning. Comparing yourself to more experienced colleagues can be detrimental.

Taking on too much can lead to mental overload, affecting your sleep and overall well-being. If you find yourself in this state, talk to your supervisor or support network. Develop self-care strategies that work for you and use them consistently. As social workers, we often give great advice but struggle to follow it ourselves.

Establishing boundaries is not only about saying no but also about setting clear expectations with your clients, colleagues, and supervisors. Communicate your availability, workload capacity, and personal limits to ensure that you are not overextended. This transparency helps others understand your constraints and fosters a collaborative working environment.

Practising self-compassion is another important aspect of maintaining boundaries. Recognise that it's okay to prioritise your well-being and that doing so ultimately benefits your clients as well. Overworking can lead to burnout, which negatively impacts your ability to provide effective support. By setting boundaries, you create a sustainable work–life balance that allows you to thrive in your role.

It's also essential to regularly reassess your boundaries and adjust them as needed. As you gain experience and confidence, you may find that you can take on additional responsibilities or handle more complex cases. However, always be mindful of your limits and be prepared to re-evaluate your boundaries if you start to feel overwhelmed.

In the end, maintaining healthy boundaries is about ensuring that you can continue to provide high-quality support to your clients while also taking care of yourself. It's a delicate balance, but one that is essential for long-term success and well-being in the social work profession.

Imposter syndrome is normal for NQSWs (and beyond!)

This is not uncommon, as Jodie said above. You've worked hard to become a qualified social worker, completing your units and placements. At the end of your training, you felt on top of the world. But starting work can make you feel like you're at the bottom again. Surrounded by seemingly confident professionals, you might doubt your abilities and feel like an imposter.

It's important to remember that everyone doubts themselves at times. Social work involves managing highly emotional situations, uncertainty, and limited resources. Even the most resilient individuals experience doubt. Imposter syndrome is normal and will diminish as you gain experience and confidence in your role.

Acknowledging imposter syndrome and talking about it openly with your peers and supervisors can help normalise these feelings. Many experienced social workers have gone through similar experiences and can offer reassurance and advice. Understanding that these feelings are a common part of professional growth can alleviate some of the pressure you may feel.

One way to combat imposter syndrome is to focus on your accomplishments and the positive impact you have made. Keep a journal of successes, client feedback, and personal achievements. Reflecting on these moments can boost your confidence and remind you of your capabilities.

Seeking mentorship from more experienced colleagues can also provide valuable support. A mentor can offer guidance, share their own experiences with imposter syndrome, and help you navigate the challenges of your role. Building a relationship with a mentor can provide a sense of security and boost your confidence as you continue to develop your skills.

Remember, imposter syndrome is not a reflection of your abilities but rather a sign that you are pushing yourself to grow and develop. Embrace the journey, learn from your experiences, and allow yourself to acknowledge your progress. With time and experience, your confidence will grow, and those feelings of doubt will diminish.

Develop your own style

There is no one-size-fits-all approach to social work. Observe your colleagues and you'll notice a variety of styles. Some are assertive and direct, while others are warm and empathetic. There are also those who adhere strictly to policies and procedures, maintaining professionalism and organisation.

Each style has its strengths and areas for development. As you gain experience, you'll develop your own style that suits you best. Be authentic, do your best, and incorporate techniques you admire in others. The more strategies you develop, the more effective you'll become as a social worker.

Take the time to reflect on your values, strengths, and areas for improvement. Understanding your own preferences and tendencies will help you develop a style that feels authentic and effective. It's important to stay true to yourself while also being open to learning from others.

Observing colleagues can provide valuable insights into different approaches and techniques. Pay attention to how they interact with clients, handle challenging situations, and navigate the complexities of the job. Adapt the strategies that resonate with you and incorporate them into your practice.

Continuously seeking feedback from supervisors, peers, and clients can also help you refine your style. Constructive feedback provides opportunities for growth and improvement. Embrace feedback as a tool for development rather than a critique of your abilities.

Flexibility is another key aspect of developing your own style. Different situations and clients may require different approaches. Being adaptable and willing to adjust your methods based on the needs of each case will enhance your effectiveness as a social worker.

Ultimately, your unique style will emerge from a combination of your values, experiences, and ongoing learning. Embrace the journey of discovering and refining your approach to social work. With time, you'll find a style that feels natural and allows you to grow. It may be a long journey, but it will be worth it. Below is a summary of some of the challenges you may face, along with learning opportunities you may also uncover.

(Andrew Morris – Experienced Social worker and lecturer in social work)

As we begin to draw this chapter to a close, it's important to take a moment to reflect on the journey that newly qualified social workers (NQSWs) embark upon during their first year in the profession. This chapter has been dedicated to sharing the reflections and experiences of NQSWs, offering valuable insights into the challenges they face and the opportunities for growth that arise along the way. Through these reflections, we hope to provide you with a deeper understanding of what it means to transition from student to professional and to inspire you as you navigate your own path.

Challenges and transitions

The first year of social work is marked by a series of significant challenges and transitions. NQSWs often find themselves in a whirlwind of new responsibilities and expectations, as they move from the structured environment of academic learning to the dynamic and unpredictable world of frontline practice. This transition can be both exhilarating and overwhelming, as the realities of social work reveal the gaps between theoretical knowledge and practical application.

Among the primary challenges faced by NQSWs is the need to bridge the gap between theory and practice. Despite the comprehensive education provided by social work programmes, the complexities of real-world practice require a different set of skills and a deeper understanding of the profession. NQSWs must quickly adapt to their new roles, developing the judgment and decision-making abilities necessary to navigate complex cases and support their clients effectively.

Opportunities for growth

Amidst these challenges, the first year of social work also presents numerous opportunities for growth and professional development. The experiences shared by NQSWs in this chapter highlight several key themes, including the development of professional identity, the influence of workplace culture, the importance of emotional resilience, and the necessity of self-care.

Professional Identity: Developing a strong professional identity is a central aspect of the NQSW journey. This process involves integrating personal values with professional principles, establishing a sense of purpose, and building confidence in one's abilities. Many NQSWs reflect on how their experiences shape their understanding of what it means to be a social worker and how they navigate the expectations of the profession while staying true to themselves. This journey of self-discovery and professional growth is both challenging and rewarding, as NQSWs learn to define and embrace their roles within the social work field.

Workplace Culture: The culture of the workplace plays a significant role in shaping the experiences of NQSWs. A supportive team environment, effective supervision, and opportunities for professional development contribute to a positive and nurturing workplace culture. Conversely, challenges such as high caseloads, administrative burdens, and inconsistent support can hinder the growth and development of NQSWs. Reflecting on these aspects helps NQSWs identify areas for improvement and advocate for a more supportive work environment. By fostering a culture of collaboration and support, social work organisations can create an environment where NQSWs can thrive.

Emotional Resilience: Social work is an emotionally demanding profession, and developing emotional resilience is essential for sustaining a long and fulfilling career.

Reflecting on their experiences allows NQSWs to recognise the emotional impact of their work and develop strategies to cope with stress and prevent burnout. Building emotional resilience involves seeking support from colleagues, engaging in reflective practice, and cultivating a positive work–life balance. By prioritising emotional well-being, NQSWs can maintain their passion for social work and continue to provide high-quality support to their clients.

Self-Care: Self-care is a critical component of professional sustainability. NQSWs emphasise the importance of prioritising their well-being and maintaining healthy boundaries. Reflecting on self-care practices helps NQSWs identify effective strategies for managing stress and maintaining their physical, emotional, and mental health. This focus on self-care not only enhances professional performance but also contributes to overall quality of life. By incorporating self-care into their daily routines, NQSWs can ensure they remain resilient and effective in their roles.

Looking ahead

As you move forward in your career, it's important to remember that you are not alone on this journey. The reflections and advice shared by your peers in this chapter are here to support and guide you as you navigate your first year as a newly qualified social worker. Embrace the challenges, celebrate your achievements, and continue to grow both personally and professionally.

The first year of social work is a time of significant growth and transformation. By reflecting on your experiences and learning from the insights of others, you can develop the skills, resilience, and confidence needed to succeed in this rewarding profession. Remember to stay true to your values, seek support when needed, and prioritise your well-being. Welcome to the world of social work – you're about to make a difference!

Before we end this chapter, we would encourage you to undertake the following Activity 8.1.

ACTIVITY 8.1

My story as a social worker

Having studied the narratives of those contributing to this chapter, we now ask you to begin thinking about and writing your social work story in the light of what you have just read. We have left this until the end of the chapter to give you time to digest people's own experiences and narratives. This is an ongoing task and not something that can be completed but it is something that you can keep coming back to, advancing on, reflecting on and seeing just how much you have learned and developed over time.

Summary

In closing, this chapter serves as a testament to the strength and dedication of NQSWs. By sharing their experiences, your peers offer valuable insights and lessons that can inform and inspire you. Through the themes of professional identity, workplace culture, emotional resilience, and self-care, this chapter has aimed to provide you with a comprehensive exploration of the NQSW experience. As you embark on your journey, take these reflections to heart and let them guide you towards a fulfilling and impactful career in social work. There is no selected further reading for this chapter.

Best of luck with everything – you're going to be amazing.

Further reading

As well as reading this book we would draw your attention to your specific country requirements and expectations and peruse the reading suggested in Chapter 2. Alongside this, the following will be useful.

Novell, R. J. (2013). *Starting social work: Reflections of a newly qualified social worker.* Routledge.

Whilst this is quite an old book it offers a firsthand account by a newly qualified social work whose experiences may well resonate with you. The book is optimistic and passionate which can be valuable when you are starting out.

Chapter 9

Workforce Development and Training Perspectives

Jonathan Parker

Introduction

One of our experienced and established social work colleagues informed us, as we were writing this chapter, that her work as a workforce development coordinator responsible for NQSWs was taken in addition to her role as a full-time case progression officer. As if that wasn't enough, she also told us that the local authority, struggling with under-resourcing as it was, had also asked her to take on a full caseload of difficult care proceedings and 'edge of care' work on a temporary basis. The temporary basis turned out to be nine months before some relief in workload was offered. It is in this context, often, that newly qualified social workers are supported in their first few years of practice. Whilst this is a difficult and somewhat unjust situation it does mean that you will need to develop understanding and a partnership working relationship with those who are responsible for your mentorship and support as a newly qualified practitioner.

Very few people studying and striving to become social workers are naïve enough to believe the job will be easy. However, some of the experiences that people have would not be expected in a respectful working environment in social work. As we have mentioned at the outset to the book, many of us were faced with large paper-based case files on qualification and expected, to a large extent, simply to 'get on with it'. We hoped that things had changed, and of course every workplace is different, and things are not all bad, but austerity measures and continued underfunding of local authorities, trusts and boards have left their mark. What is encouraging and apparent, however, is the level of energy and commitment of those responsible for building the next generation of social workers to ensuring an adequate, even exemplary level of assessment, support and continued learning.

In this chapter, we will look at the expectations, concerns and wishes of workforce development leads and others involved in the enhancement of the social work workforce. The core focus will be on the place of developing, supporting and assessing newly qualified social workers in contemporary practice. We will explore some of the problems identified by these more experienced social workers and the solutions they suggest, promote or have utilised. Case studies will be used to exemplify key themes. While this chapter will relate to practice in England in the main, it applies to all four countries wherever possible as many of the issues translate across borders.

It is important that you are exposed to the views of more experienced social workers as you begin your own journey. The wisdom and perspectives expressed can be used to guide you, to raise questions and to explore the best possible ways forward. Much of the material for the chapter was gathered by asking our colleagues for their views and to look positively towards solutions for the complex and important area of workforce development, recruitment and retention. The guiding questions we used to gather this information create the structure of our chapter.

What do workforce leads see as the most significant challenges faced by newly qualified social workers (NQSWs) in their first year of practice?

The exigencies of practice have a tremendous impact as social workers progress and become subsumed within the social services system. This happens to the extent that some team managers and those in senior positions no longer understand the need for the support and assessment and development of new social workers. In one English authority it was noted that managers sometimes did not understand the ASYE Programme, neither did they have a full appreciation of their role in the programme or the expectations of the NQSW themselves.

There are also potential issues that affect NQSWs themselves. As we mention in Chapter 10, it is sometimes the case that social workers in practice begin to believe they no longer need to have a deep and critical appreciation of social work knowledge and theory. So, workforce development coordinators we spoke to saw it as a challenge for NQSWs to continue to take their learning into everyday practice and to expand upon it.

One workforce development lead questioned whether the learning undertaken during qualifying education prepares new social workers adequately for the demands of the job. She found that emotional resilience was not always present within new social workers and worried that this can lead to early burn out. She reflected that the aspirations new social workers bring to the job do not always meet the realities of the emotional, physical and cognitive demands.

What kind of support is in place for NQSWs where workforce leads practice?

In one authority, NQSWs are assigned a Practice Development Advisor (PDA) for the first two years of employment. The support offered by the PDA consists of monthly mentoring, reflective peer groups so new social workers can learn from and support one another, bespoke workshops and training. NQSWs within that authority are also given protected caseloads for two years, a full and guided induction, quarterly review meetings and 12 study days per year.

In terms of support, one local authority stated that whilst they don't have an official Academy, there is still a lot of support in place for NQSWs which follows the Skills for Care ASYE programme. The workforce development team of that authority run a forum relating to the ASYE on a monthly basis. Alongside this there is a protected caseload for newly qualified staff, and protected time to complete their portfolio. Like many authorities they operate a buddy system within teams to provide support, mentoring, and to offer shadowing and observation of visits. The workforce development team have an 'open door' policy to ensure support is available at all times. NQSWs are included in a 'training by role matrix', which lists the mandatory training all new starters are expected to undertake which is tailored towards their development and ASYE to ensure that covers all aspects of training needed in that first year.

In one local authority, NQSWs can book in further consultations with Workforce Development (WFD) to discuss any case issues or learning. Reflective supervision sessions are available and specific training sessions can be created if there is nothing more formal coming up or available. This can be individual or group in nature to address whatever needs are identified. There is ongoing support and oversight from Team Managers (TM) with regards to the ASYE portfolio. In one area, NQSWs don't hold child protection or court proceedings for the first year. This can be reviewed person by person and they may be added as a case worker if this is in line with their abilities. What is important in this is that you as a NQSW must not feel pushed into work beyond what can legitimately be expected in your first year.

The workforce development team in one authority hold meetings with NQSWs and their managers at key points throughout the year, when they start, next at months 3, 6, and 9 and then final meeting at month 12. The meetings are designed to ensure that new social workers are meeting standards. If there are any concerns the introductory and supported time can be extended for another three months. An innovative approach that you might find or even suggest in your local authority is a regular teaching day in which all staff can share and get to know one another's work. As one respondent said, *'We hold Teaching Tuesday events every week, this is not just for ASYEs but it is something that I found really useful when I started at (local authority), as each week we invite different teams, or services within Bury to speak just for an hour so it's always clear what services are available for families in the local area and how we can make referrals etc. which helps NQSWs quickly understand what is out there and how to access.'*

Another local authority that focused on new practitioners in adult social care stated that 'we offer an extensive ASYE programme for NQSWs'. This included building on the understanding and application of theories for practice. Importantly, the development of 'Hot Topic' sessions to discuss these issues also provided opportunities for NQSWs to foster relationships with peers and to inculcate an approach of learning together just as the PDA did in the previous local authority. A common element to respondents was the provision of supervision and mentorship.

What do workforce development leads believe are the most effective strategies for supporting NQSWs as they transition from education to practice?

Workforce development leads are committed to the idea of protection of the new social worker, described as containment, which given its association with Winnicottian psychodynamic thinking, offers an image of emotional supportive development. Other supportive architecture that helps NQSWs include developing a clear structured programme of support recognised by others, which in turn requires good links with team managers, and a commitment to good reflective supervision. One respondent amplified this by stating that shadowing and buddying experiences often started in qualifying practice were important in entrenching positive and supported development. They acknowledged that the efficacy of this depended to a large extent on the experiences that NQSWs may have had on their qualifying courses or in prior employment. This builds on long traditions of at least recognising that supervision and buddying up with new practitioners is key to both keeping them within the practice and allowing a person to develop for themselves. Encouraging and supporting sessions that are led by NQSWs themselves in particular areas of interest and development can also give a holistic exposure to practice which is key to survival and ongoing development.

One person we spoke to acknowledged the difficulties of providing support to you as newly qualified workers, something many of you will no doubt have experienced. She said, 'I think it's actually very basic but often hard to fulfil the promise (we make to NQSWs) due to pressures within the LA, but lower caseloads, protected time, supportive and stable environment gives them a safe space and opportunity to reflect'. The same respondent also spoke about the individual learning and developmental needs of each NQSW. She recognised the need to consider each new worker's previous placements and learning outcomes so that a tailored professional development plan could be developed and implemented at the pace required by that individual. This was considered to be especially important if the NQSW's placements had not been with that local authority. If you have taken a position in a different local authority to those you undertook your placements in you will recognise that each area and, indeed, each team can be very different in terms of their practices, culture and 'feel'. So, this is something to ensure your supporters are aware of; even more so if, as the respondent recognised, staffing needs require a 'bums on seats' approach.

Providing what is promised, despite the difficulties in doing so, was considered most important. For one authority this started with attendance at careers fairs and creating open and honest relationships with university partnerships. Doing what is promised helps you as NQSWs feel valued and is part of the support needed as a new social worker.

How are programmes and structured courses and schemes for newly qualified practitioners evaluated? How do workforce development leads and local authorities ensure they meet the needs of new social workers?

One way of evaluating the success or otherwise of the ASYE programme is to seek feedback from the NQSWs at six months, 12 months and at the end of the programme. This is in addition to completing collaborative audits and 360 feedback with attention to the requirements of Skills for Care. The lead in one authority stressed that they actively listen to feedback given making sure that actions stem from the comments made. Often, the feedback is reviewed on specific Team Days for the programme and adjustments to it are made accordingly. In another, a triangulated approach to evaluation included detailed feedback from those social workers and others with whom the NQSWs had worked and practised, a formal Skills for Care assessment and a final evaluation and assessment conducted by the principal social worker responsible for the ASYE in that authority.

One local authority informed us that they base success of their ASYE programme on the number of students who remain with them after completing it, telling us that they like being in Bury. The commitment to evaluating the utility and success of another NQSW support programme was by holding weekly audits of ASYE caseloads to ensure the local authority is keeping within its guidance. The audit is overseen by the assistant director as a further layer of evaluation. Supervision is also seen as a valuable element of quality assurance. This is where it is important, as a NQSW, to be honest in your comments about your own experiences and whenever invited to feedback we would encourage you to do so. Feedback and discussion through supervision is key to local authority workforce development teams being able to adapt, challenge and develop their support programmes. Final elements of quality assurance and evaluation are undertaken in one authority by the principal social worker at a final review meeting held also with Skills for Care.

How are the views of the social worker's fellow colleagues, managers and service users included in the evaluation?

Following on from the previous question, we asked how the inclusion of the views, perceptions and comments of other colleagues are collected and used to enhanced supportive training and development. One of our colleagues explained that in her authority team managers are part of NQSWs' formal reviews and the audit process. Also, direct feedback is invited from service users within the audits and portfolios, and feedback is requested from peers after Direct Observations of NQSW practice are made. For another, the views and perceptions are collected throughout the year and addressed as they come in. This allows for any issues or concerns to be addressed as soon as they arise rather than waiting for formal points of feedback which could allow those concerns to become entrenched and more difficult to deal with.

One former workforce development lead told us that this question sparked off a good deal of discussion and reflection in the team recognising that this was not the strongest area of practice and needed development. Whilst feedback is gathered according to the Skills for Care guidance there was an identified need to gather the views and perspectives of colleagues more rigorously if they were going to use it to inform practice. Again, this is perhaps something that you as a NQSW can assist with by reflecting on your experiences openly and honestly with team managers and workforce development leads.

What have workforce development leads observed about the impact of supervision on the professional growth and well-being of NQSWs?

We know from history, from other areas of practice in the social and helping professions, and you will no doubt know from experience, that supervision continues to represent a 'hot potato' in qualified practice, with the need recognised but being 'more honour'd in the breach than the observance' as Shakespeare's Hamlet put it. Workforce development leads that we spoke to, however, indicated that it is absolutely crucial to developing best practice and to supporting new colleagues in the social work profession. One also pointed out that the variation and inconsistency around supervision exerts a significant impact on NQSWs' professional growth and ability. Another workforce lead commented that supervision is vital because it supports both professional and personal development for NQSWs who are learning to navigate the social work profession. The comments are interesting as they reflect clear beliefs but do not say why or how the processes of supervision help you as NQSWs. So, the task for you as new practitioners is to determine what works for you in terms of supervision and support and to learn to communicate this to those responsible for your support and development. Becoming a social worker is relational and cannot be done to you or done by you in isolation from peers and, indeed, context and those people you work with.

The centrality of supervision is something that you will have been introduced to from early in your student days. It is recognised as being imperative for your professional development but also for your personal well-being. One of the workforce leads contributing to our discussion believes that regular and consistent supervision leads to NQSWs feeling more supported and settling into their new roles more quickly. Moreover, they were seen as being quicker in becoming more autonomous in decision making and having the confidence to find and implement their own solutions.

Supervision is not always what it should be, however, and our respondent acknowledged that some new social workers do not receive good quality supervision. She said that it was noticeable that these unfortunate social workers are often less adaptive, experience higher stress and are less resilient. Her solution was to focus on supervision, and to offer from the workforce development team, the opportunity to reflect and guidance away from thinking like a student to practising as a qualified and independently thinking social worker.

What role do peer networks or mentoring schemes play in the success of NQSWs, and how might these be facilitated within local authority and agency social work?

We have already seen that Peer Reflective Groups were one way of ensuring both bonding between new social workers and of developing a social work mentality. In one authority, the cohort of NQSWs in their second year of practice were teamed to 'buddy up' those in their first year as NQSWs. If there is an inadequate audit of progression and support the local authority held a reflective discussion to address any concerns arising. The local authority also has initiated regular reflective practice groups to encourage progression through peer mentorship. Another local authority has developed something similar through a set of 'Hot Topic' sessions in which coordination by the principal social workers and ASYE coordinator facilitates and allows the NQSW group to develop and support one another. The focus on semi-directed or supported peer learning ensures that the work of the local authority and the direction of social work services are added to the developmental mix which is, of course, central to the work. Whether these groups should be formal or informal is often debated as is whether they should be peer-led or profession-led. It is worth you thinking what you would prefer and to make these views known.

What are the common pitfalls or barriers that hinder the development or retention of NQSWs and how might these be addressed?

For one respondent, it was the high caseloads, the complexity of the work, staff turnover in general within the teams including change of managers that created a turbulent and unsettling environment. The local authority has attempted to address this through providing protected caseloads and developing a new role of Consultant Social Workers who are responsible for managing a hub of NQSWs and helping them to negotiate through this context.

For another respondent, it was the constant change in management, and peers, which, in turn, led to feelings of instability. This was exacerbated when NQSWs were left without a named manager, even for a short period of time. Concomitantly, this was perceived to have a negative impact on oversight of their case work and led to feeling unsafe in their decision making. This workforce lead and social worker indicated that one of the common pitfalls she has seen is local authorities not adhering to their agreed caseload reduction for new workers and allowing them to carry cases that should be undertaken only when the NQSW is stable and securely supported in their role such as pre-proceedings/care proceedings.

Developing a culture that pushes the importance of training is something that one of our discussants is trying to prioritise. Her local authority is working on giving permission to NQSWs to decide their own training and learning needs and the order in which they meet them.

One of our respondents believed that employers and WFD were not setting firm work–life balance boundaries for NQSWs. She thought this could be modelled by other staff within the team and by managers, so it becomes embedded into work culture. Importantly, for NQSWs, she stated that, 'it should not be accepted that they have to work from home and work weekends. This is not sustainable and should not set a precedent that they feel they have to continue to be "good enough". The burn-out from this will come far too quickly if this is how their journey starts'.

Promoting and modelling a balanced approach to work and life outside work is important. Whilst it is important that you take responsibility for your own learning, it is also key that you are supported in doing so and that others take responsibility for modelling this prosocial behaviour to you.

How are the workload and supportive expectations for NQSWs balanced to promote their confidence and competence without overwhelming them?

Many of the suggestions made by workforce development leads previously also obtain in respect of the question of balance: social workers must be able to practise in challenging, complex and often frenetic environments. However, we also know that a professional qualification can never, nor in many ways should it be expected to, prepare you to practise in such situations. NQSWs need a supportive, protected learning environment in which the skills, knowledge and values of practice can be learned, honed and practised. One lead responding to our questions said that her local authority takes a graded, staged approach to childcare social work practice that offers NQSWs a protected caseload which gradually increases every three months. In the first six months of qualified practice, social workers undertake no child protection work and no court work and proceedings before nine months. These timings are further safeguarded by holding reviews which have to be passed before the NQSW can undertake this work. In an adult social care team, new social workers are encouraged to develop their own development plans so that it is owned by the new practitioner and, hopefully, invested in as a result. The creation of learning and development plans is again something that is co-developed in the relationship between supervisor/ mentor and the NQSW. What is important here is that it allows you as the NQSW to identify your needs and to plan, in concert with experienced practitioners, for your own career development.

What feedback have workforce leads received from NQSWs about what they value most in the support they receive from their local authority?

We wanted to explore with our workforce development leads what feedback they had received from your peer NQSWs. One person we spoke to said that, overwhelmingly for her, the feedback is that they appreciate the support gained from their Practice Development Advisors (PDA). In this authority, a named PDA is assigned to every new social worker so there is consistency and a known source of support. Alongside the support given from experienced and qualified social workers, the peer support that NQSWs receive through the Practice Reflective Groups and workshops were also reported on favourably. The chance to observe others in practice, especially in developing a sense of the process of the work, was found to be helpful. NQSWs reported that this worked best when colleagues and mentors were seen to be supportive and concerned.

Are there any changes that workforce development leads would implement to improve the support offered to NQSWs? What might these be and why are they important?

One person we spoke to suggested a simple but very clear change that she wished to see in giving support to new social workers. This was a wish to see consistency in social work managers and the support they provide and understanding of NQSW needs they have.

One of the workforce development leads we spoke to told us that throughout the year NQSWs' case complexity increases according to their individual development and is reviewed at various check-in points through the ASYE programme and within supervision. In her local authority, not carrying child protection cases, or court proceeding is the norm, but this is reviewed case by case and person by person. The focus on and tailoring to each individual's needs is a positive model and we hope that local authorities will develop this across the board. The discussant reinforced this emphasis, saying, 'it is about knowing the individual qualities of each of our NQSWs; understanding their learning style, their strengths, experiences and their areas for development, whilst ensuring that they are both working to their strengths but challenged'.

It is noted throughout, but again, supervision was noted as key to developing confidence and competence by one of our respondents. This was considered to be further aided by training and the opportunity to shadow and observe more experienced social workers in the team. She believed that moving to a two-year programme would help to embed this developmental approach and to ensure its success.

Looking ahead, what should the future of workforce development for NQSWs in local authorities focus on?

We asked workforce development leads and experienced social workers to reflect prospectively and to consider what might best grow the social workers of the future. The importance of having structured and focused training, support and development for NQSWs was acknowledged with one local authority seeing that the process should be much longer and more measured. They called for a five-year structured development plan to embed social work skills, knowledge and practice. Alongside this, another suggested that the development of learning and supportive academies in each local authority would be beneficial.

In adult social care, workforce development leads were concerned that NQSWs should be supported to become confident and competent in acting in complex legal situations and Court of Protection cases as these are increasingly common. Developing competence and confidence in court room skills has been a core element of child protection social work for many years. That this is changing to cover adult social care as well demands the inculcation of skills that can only be learned fully and embedded in practice settings.

Workforce development is well embedded in many local authorities, but, for one lead we spoke to, the future focus should be on health and wellbeing. They considered the formal support given in supervision, and through team meetings, or regular teaching days was important in keeping staff but thought there was more to it. Their vision was to 'home grow' the next managers and principal social workers and that this demanded a development in the culture of the local authority. Introducing the idea of a work family through health and wellbeing activities, sports days, team building, yoga classes, quiet rooms, team lunches, 'foodie Fridays' and such would be a start to this process.

Summary

You have read what workforce development leads and other social workers with some responsibility for your development as newly qualified social workers see as important or in need of development. It is now for you to identify what you think. We end this chapter with an activity to identify and delineate what you believe would or will help you in your professional journey.

ACTIVITY 9.1

What do workforce development leads need to know?

First of all, think of the questions we asked workforce development leads and others. Did we miss anything out and if you were in a position to interview these people about NQSW support and experiences what would you seek to ask? Write down your additional questions and keep these as you begin to explore support options in your professional development.

Further reading

Barbee, A. P., & Paul, M. (2020). Workforce development of social workers pre-and post-employment. In E. J. Mullen (Ed.), *Oxford bibliographies in social work*. Oxford University Press. https://doi.org/10.1093/OBO/9780195389678-0285

There is very little work directly relating to social work workforce development. This chapter from the United States offers an insight that, whilst particular to its location, provides a useful insight into many of the areas of practice that need continual development.

Parker, J., & Doel, M. (Eds.). (2014). *Professional social work*. Sage/Learning Matters.

Whilst this edited collection is over 10 years old it contains many of the thoughts that our workforce development coordinators expressed and offers a range of chapters dealing with important areas of development for practitioners at a range of stages of career.

Chapter 10

Professionalism in Social Work: Contributing to future quality and development as a Newly Qualified Social Worker

Jonathan Parker

Introduction

George Bernard Shaw's 1905 play *Major Barbara* introduced the oft-quoted suggestion that all professions are 'conspiracies against the laity'. Whilst we may not agree fully with this assessment it is clear that some professions and professionals have, in the past, acted to safeguard their own positions and vested interests against those outside of that profession, often members of the general public. It may also be the case that this has been so within social work at times. Of course, the rather provocative and 'playful' quotation from Shaw was designed to cause consternation but it begs the question of what we mean by the term 'profession', which as we will see has numerous definitions. That being said, however we define profession, professional and professionalism, and what we actually mean by the terms, they represent concepts that are complex, contested and often misunderstood. In this chapter, we are going to explore with you some of the core meanings of the terminology and what these can mean for today's social workers, especially yourself as a newly qualified social worker, before moving into a discussion of the following:

- the fundamentals of professionalism in social work

- professional identity as a social worker and where the personal meets the professional

- professional social work practice and organisation

- being a social work professional in the modern era

- understanding the centrality of continuing professional development as a social worker today

Our central aim, throughout this chapter, is that we are hoping to ignite your interest and inspire you to look further into what being a professional social worker means for you as you begin your journey and to explore how your professionalism may contribute to the further development and quality of the service.

What does profession and professional mean and why does it matter?

The Latin root of the two terms profession and professional stems from the word *professio,* which concerns the making of a declaration or taking a vow when undertaking holy orders. The history of the terms are long and contested. They have both positive and negative connotations, especially when it comes to social work. If we want to understand their meaning it is helpful to start with your own understandings and we invite you now to complete the following activity.

ACTIVITY 10.1

How do you describe 'profession'?

How do you understand the term profession? What does it mean to you and how would you describe it to someone else? Write down your thoughts and compare them with the following discussion. If you choose to amend your own thoughts after reading the chapter, think why this is and what it might mean for your practice as a beginning social worker. (If you are part of a group of newly qualified social workers it can be worthwhile sharing and discussing your thoughts.)

Comment

You may have asked yourself whether being a professional is simply another way of describing a career choice, or whether it only refer to specific traditional careers such as law, medicine, religious leadership. If it's the latter, then how might they be defined and what does your thinking mean for you as a beginning social worker? Perhaps for you it relates to a pejorative description of a closed, back-covering domain, where the rules are formulated by the profession and any challenge to them dealt with from within. This certainly has characterised some earlier critical definitions which were based on the functions that professions performed in order to keep society stable. It is also something that underpinned Shaw's scathing quotation. On the other hand, you may have written that a profession is a highly ethical and regulated career that demands a high level of specific educational attainment and registration with a body who also require strict adherence to a code of practice, ethics or set of values. Hopefully, the latter understanding is one that drives your wish to be a professional social worker.

The sociology of the professions has an interesting history, with a critical approach gaining traction in the 1970s with Johnson's (1972) examination of a profession as representing an institutionalised means of controlling an occupation which heralded a conceptual indissolubility of 'power' and control with it. This critique stemmed from an earlier twentieth-century dominance of functionalist and trait approaches with analysis from Weberian and Marxian perspectives. Your social science learning during your education and training will come in useful here.

Functionalist understandings of professions emphasised the distinctiveness that professions claimed, locating them in their rationalising tendencies within society, and stemming from an acritical acceptance of Durkheim's focus on professional ethics that helped maintain and stabilise social traditions and social order. Not all functionalist thinkers accepted the benign concept of professions as arbiters and guardians of social stability, however, which allowed a critique centred around bureaucratic eu-function and dysfunction or how societies function well or otherwise for people.

Rather than focus solely on the functions of professions in society, others developed 'trait'-based approaches that attempted to delineate the central characteristics, elements, and attributes distinguishing a profession. However, Johnson (1972) considered trait-based models to be autopoietic (self-creating), bolstering professional power by using the definitions offered by the professions themselves. It is easy to imagine how this understanding might create a self-justifying operation that works against rather than on behalf of and for individuals coming into contact with that profession. This is important when we consider social work.

Functionalist and trait-based approaches were later amplified by interactionist sociologists who examined the processes occupations went through in order to become professions. Macdonald (1995) understood that these action-focused models do not ask what a profession is, but how it operates (the processes) and what the profession did to get to its current position. It asks how a profession assumes and preserves its privileged position, recognising also that the actions of a profession constructs the social reality in which it operates.

Witz (1992), a neo-Weberian herself in approach, recognised that the strategies employed by professions to retain power-in-society represented strategies of social closure and 'occupational imperialism' (Larkin, 1983). What she added to the debate, however, is particularly pertinent to our current consideration of social work and professionalism. She highlighted the relationship between gender, power and the professions, locating the 'professional project' – its becoming and its maintenance – within the patriarchal structure of society. This, in itself, necessitates a critique of social and occupational closure which would privilege males in a profession such as social work, numerically at least, favouring women, although this critique itself requires caution (Parker and Ashencaen Crabtree, 2014). It is also, perhaps, a profession that could be understood as controlling the lives and social position of women. This has been seen in the child protection and safeguarding practices of social workers in which mothers have borne the brunt of social work intervention often negatively and is something that we must continue to critique.

The sociology of the professions is important for our general understanding, but we need to apply this to social work in particular. It is fair to say that functionalist approaches to professions and professionalism have tended to be less negative than Shaw's cynical or perhaps satirical statement might suggest. Also, despite Johnson's concerns cited above, social work as a profession has long been considered to hold the following attributes or traits (Greenwood, 1957):

- possessing a systematic body of knowledge

- holding authority as a profession

- regulating and controlling members of the profession

- having a professional code of ethics

- possessing a culture of values, norms and symbols

Greenwood was writing about social work and social workers when he identified these traits and, clearly, many of these characteristics hold for social work today in many ways and across many countries. However, we struggle in respect of a systematic body of knowledge given that we have borrowed understandings from many different disciplines although our focus on the person in his or her environment and the centrality of relationships begins to mark us out. We may also question whether or not we are members of a distinct social work profession or local authority/third sector employees in the UK. But what of making a declaration or vow? Perhaps when certain careers were considered vocations rather than just jobs (i.e., something you were called to do), this had more immediacy. Think back to Chapter 1 and Activity 1.2 where you were asked to reflect on what brought you into social work. However, social work is more than just a job and in subscribing to the values, codes of ethics and so on, social work can still be seen in this light if we remove some of the more arcane trappings associated with past vocations.

So, what about 'professional'? The term professional can be used as an adjective simply to describe someone who acts in a way that is of high quality or good at whatever it is they are doing. A professional can also be used as an adjectival noun describing a person working within one of the professions. In whatever ways professions and professionals are defined, having the right qualifications, skills, knowledge set and values and having been initiated into that profession and being a member of the professional body are elements that are central to it. However, it can also be much more than that. In more popular terms it has become a means of discriminating between good and bad practices. The processes of being a professional are important and these link to the concept of professionalism in contemporary practice. An example may help here.

CASE STUDY 10.1

Giulia

Imagine you are working with a daughter, Giulia, supporting her older mother, Maria, who is living with dementia. Maria has been walking out frequently often for hours at a time day and night until found. Giulia is at the 'end of (her) tether' and you recognise her need for support. You listen carefully, give her your work contact details, when you are available and what she can expect when she calls you. You also provide out-of-hours contacts, team her up with support groups and plan with her a package of support. This sounds quite professional, both in terms of good, ethical practice and also as someone who is part of a skilled and educated profession. However, consider now the social worker who, like you, empathises deeply with Giulia, and recognising, again, her need for support, gives her his personal mobile phone number in case she cannot contact anyone else and is worried about her mother. This is not showing professionalism but overstepping professional boundaries.

Let's apply your understanding of professional and unprofessional in the following activity.

ACTIVITY 10.2

Writing professionally or personally?

Imagine sending an email, Instagram or WhatsApp message to a family member about meeting up for a meal. Ask yourself how you might write it, what you would say and how you would say it, and how would you sign off.

Now imagine you are writing to arrange a meeting with a service user. How and why might this be different to the message sent to your family member? Note down what is *professional* about the second email or message and what might be *unprofessional* in such a situation. Whilst you are completing this activity, think about how you use social media in different ways or AI help to write messages in both your professional and personal life. Write down the similarities and identify the boundaries in each setting.

Comment

Why does this matter to 'helping' professions and professionals such as social workers? At one level, it might seem as though discussion of the meanings of these words is an arcane and unnecessary distraction from what it is we are hoping to achieve in our role as social workers in walking alongside people who are placed in vulnerable positions. However, it is important for the following reasons:

- it helps to distinguish between good and bad practice
- it helps maintain public confidence by setting clear expectations
- it helps to maintain the profession's reputation, and those of the professionals within it
- it helps to ensure that people receive the best possible care and support

---

Distinguishing between professionalism and unprofessionalism in social work requires deep critical reflection and honesty. Fostering these qualities will help you decide between different actions in difficult and unclear situations.

What is professional social work?

Is it a specific thing? Does it distinguish itself from 'amateur' social work? Is it something unpaid, or done by 'street-wise grannies' as the former Secretary of State Virginia

Bottomley suggested in the 1990s? Does it refer to qualifications, membership of a group with codes of ethics, practice and self-regulation? Is it always a good thing?

What does the research say? A (very) brief overview

The terms profession, professional and professionalism remain popular in usage within the social work literature. A quick search of library databases, using the search term 'profession* AND social work' and limited just to the UK came up with 2,502 hits between 1961 and 2025. The terms themselves can be used in a cavalier fashion; sometimes being used as a descriptor of an activity or role without any particular meaning attached, and sometimes relating to what is expected in terms of good practice. Discussion of the academic meaning of a profession is included only as background although we think we have to keep in mind the potential negative connotations when, as a profession, social work is challenged as a closed shop that regulates and protects itself when things go wrong. Social work is still a profession blamed for the consequences of structural inadequacies and there is a need to counter this by reframing professionalism within a relational and restorative context. This requires an agile and flexible response written in to practice through situational ethics, which means if the best outcome requires something different to the formal, procedural norm then professional judgement should be exercised and respected. Practice wisdom and intuitive professional judgement is something that develops with experience and reflection. Of course, being professional also demands that we can justify our actions and therefore need to record what they were and why we did what we did.

The concepts remain complex, debated and open to interpretation in the literature. For instance, Jones (2024) poses the on-going question whether there is a global social work profession and whether the range of diverse national social work frameworks can be considered as a coherent professional activity. This focuses on the more distanced entity of the profession but still makes us think how one can be a professional within it (see Rogowski, 2020). This has been a common theme for many years. As the neo-liberal and managerialist agenda was taking hold of public services in the 1980s and 1990s, Aldridge (1996) argued that social workers needed to claim distinctive knowledge and skills as a profession, something that often still today eludes us. One core element of managerialism was regulation as a means of enhancing accountability and ensuring continual improvement. However, Simpson et al. (2020) critique the idea that increased external regulation has enhanced social work professional identity suggesting rather that it has upset the power balance in favour of the regulator against professional autonomy and identity. By default, this upsets the power imbalance in favour of the profession against those with whom we work as social workers. So, we still need to think deeply about what our professionalism means.

The power balance can also be seen when social workers become bound within a professional imaginary and fail to see the impact of poverty on families, seeing personal inadequacies as explanations of abuse rather than structural factors (Innes-Turnill, 2023). This is echoed by the critique of potential epistemic injustice if one accepts uncritically social work as a profession (Maglajlic and Ioakimidis, 2022). So, in this research we can see that the self-regulating and protective aspect of the professions can still remain; something we must guard against, and something that our focus on critical self-reflection can help to do.

In the light of increased managerialism and neo-liberal ideologies, McDonald et al. (2008) argued for the importance of clear policy and practice knowledge for practitioners if they were to maintain their professionalism. This was important within the context of growing interprofessional practice and learning (Marsh, 2006; Quinney and Hafford-Letchfield, 2012). The importance of continuing professional development in maintaining a professional approach to practice in an increasingly complex world is also highlighted (Higham, 1999, 2014; Postle et al., 2002). So, professionalism can guard against external regulation and political control but can also be used to protect against criticism from those we work with. It is a double-edged sword.

Stone et al. (2020) see the development of professionalism in explicitly following codes of practice using research ethics as an example. The 'virtuous' social worker who follows the rules is the professional one. Dominelli and Holloway (2008) add to the debate by arguing for a distinct social work professional code of ethics for research, making the case for a discrete profession in the traditional sense. However, this does not always work in practice as we saw in Munro's important contribution to social work reform after the death of Baby Peter Connelly (Munro, 2011). Despite this, we must not simply dismiss the importance of following processes and procedures designed to enhance professional practice, but we must see this as a first and essentially technical step towards a more rounded approach that holistically includes emotion, relationship and humanity as well as simple rule following. (See our later discussion of Fletcher's situation ethics.)

Skoura-Kirk et al. (2021) consider professionalism in terms of procedural competencies such as relational practice and communication and meta-competencies such as linking theory to practice and critical reflection. They argue that these skills can be developed through role-play simulation during qualifying education. Guthrie (2023) offers a competency perspective from her own experience as a social worker with autism, suggesting that reflecting on perceptions of autism may enhance non-autistic social workers' relational and anti-oppressive practice. This promotes the acceptance of others. Burton and Revill (2018) add to this the concept of professional curiosity in the context of complex and pressured practice demands and the need for supportive practice and organisational environments to enable creativity and curiosity.

Research also focuses on the professional activities of writing and recording (Lillis, 2023). Research by Lillis et al. (2017) indicates that writing-intensive practice contradict social workers' own views as people-focused direct workers. Thus, a debate is opened on the nature of contemporary social work (Lillis et al., 2020). A similar debate relating to professional knowledge development concerns the use of digital technologies (Taylor, 2017). Of course, this activity-based approach to professionalism has come under scrutiny and attack (Hood, 2024).

In response to some of these questions, Rawles (2016) argues that learning research-mindedness in the practice context can enhance professional judgement. This reflects the notion of professional wisdom which is something slippery and undefinable but to be encouraged (Krill, 1996). Professionalism is enhanced by knowledge, values and learning skills through practice. Autonomy and personal agency are important in supporting professional judgement. This interplay is crucial. A similar case is made when considering the role of intuition (Curtis, 2024).

Distilling the key points from the research indicates that professionalism in social work requires the following:

- a secure and updated knowledge base

- bespoke values and ethics

- excellent communication skills

- the capacity for deep critical reflection

- the development of a professional identity that is research-minded, critically questioning and adaptive underpinning professional judgement

There are many elements that we have identified in the research that echo previous understandings of profession and professionalism. The emphasis on critical reflection and research-mindedness, however, add a distinctive feature that should help to ensure that professional social workers remain true to their values and ethics as people-focused practitioners.

The strange case of social work

Let's not be too positive, however. The negative, controlling and excluding aspects of professions and, by consequence, professionals, has plagued social work and still can. Consider the following activity.

ACTIVITY 10.3

Considering 'best interests'

Think of the seemingly innocuous phrase, 'in their best interests'. Can you identify a time when this has been used, how it was used and what you thought it was conveying. Jot down some of your thoughts.

Comment

Let's break that down a little. First of all, we need to ask what interests we are talking about and whether all parties agree on them or not. Centrally, we need to question whose best interests we are serving and how much our own unconscious biases (personal, professional and political) influence our thinking. If we fail to ask these, alongside other important questions, we run the risk of directing our social work practice without paying attention to the wants, needs and wishes of those we are working with. If we are to act professionally, we need to keep a critical and questioning view concerning what we are doing and why we are

---

doing it constantly in mind. On the other side of our social work coin, however, we have a need, as professionals, to use our understanding and authority appropriately and not simply to follow the direction promoted by those who use our services.

However, we can ask a different question that takes us into the arena of good practice encompassing many of those features that we have identified from our overview of the research. That question is: 'What might professional social work practice look like?' For Thompson (2014), this is a matter of developing emotional intelligence through genuine partnerships and empowerment. This means learning to read the emotions of others and one's own, managing these and being able to communicate them appropriately. This necessitates us identifying and negotiating our own unconscious biases. Thompson suggests, in order to work in an emotionally intelligent manner, that professional social workers need to develop:

- Resourcefulness

- Robustness

- Resilience

These are certainly important elements, but we need also to offset the potential for blame which can arise from emphasising resilience too much (see Chapter 11). We would also tweak these three Rs a little and include the following aspects that professional social workers need in their repertoire:

- Relationality

- Resoluteness

- Restorative drivers

Relationality concerns the notion that all things are in some way related to one another in our social work practice. Professional social workers act in a human–relational way to other professionals, to their employers and society and especially to those people they are asked to work with. They need to do this in a strong and determined way, to persevere in order to achieve agreed goals and to work to heal and restore fractured relationships and fragmented lives.

It is in this context that things can get a little difficult. As we have noted earlier, following guidelines, procedures and policies to the letter can ensure practice that meets requirements and expectations and, in many ways, can be considered 'professional'. Also, when we consider the PCF (Professional Capabilities Framework) of English social work, we note that, for experienced social workers, the domain of professionalism concerns identifying and behaving as professional social workers committed to professional development but without defining what is meant and focusing on group identification rather than practice. However, social work is somewhat different and demands more when negotiating the messy worlds of human relations, working within them, and alongside those who inhabit them. Alongside the traits of professionalism that have been identified there needs to be a growing sense of professional judgement that may bend and mould protocols and procedures when this is necessary. This is hard to quantify and fraught as it potentially brings social workers into conflict with their employers and may be possibly thought to infringe employment contracts. Indeed, if anything went wrong in practice and procedures had been flagrantly ignored the social work would rightly be in serious trouble. However, what we are discussing here is a kind of situation ethic that relies on critical reflection and the development of practice wisdom which feeds into social work professionalism.

Situation ethics are contextual and dependent on relationships between time and space and people-in-environment. They were first described by Joseph Fletcher in the 1960s. He was not a social worker but an academic theologian and bioethicist, a man for whom personal integrity was key. This makes Fletcher's work central to contemporary social work which, when undertaken with integrity rooted in personal and professional values and wisdom gained from practice represents professional practice. Situation ethics is closely related to the relational aspects of social work practice and so is driven by those values concerning human relationships which are not always easy to place within the strict boundaries of policy and procedure (Parker, 2025).

Social work ethics are topographically nuanced. Place, in geographical terms and space in relational, hierarchical and positional terms exert an impact on how ethics are perceived and how they are 'performed'. Ethics are not simply written codes referred to at times like a professional touchstone confirming one's belonging to 'social work'. Rather, ethics drive the behaviours and actions of professional social workers. In his academic work, Fletcher explored the importance of context for acting ethically and virtuously and generally encouraged following what was required by the profession (Fletcher, 1966). He did not advocate breaking protocols without very good reason. But, as someone who posited that context was all important, his approach presaged the generalist professional social work concept of person-in-environment (Germain and Gitterman, 1981). His work has been amplified by feminist scholars in respect of care-giving and ethics (see Skeggs, 2012; Gilligan, 1982).

ACTIVITY 10.4

Letter or spirit? Acting professionally in context

Can you think of a time when a strict following of the letter of procedure would have compromised or damaged your professional relationship with a person who uses social work services? Write down your thoughts and concerns about this and think through what you might do in that situation.

Comment

No-one would ever advocate you breaking procedures without very good and justifiable reasons. It would be potentially very dangerous to do so. However, it may be that you need to alter the time of a visit, to work outside normal hours or to provide some form of assistance that you would not usually do. These actions would be done in the context of that individual relationship, based on your critical professional judgement and developing practice wisdom, and would need to be shared as soon as possible with others within the profession to ensure your safety as a practitioner.

What is professional identity as a social worker and how does it interlink with personal professional identity?

Knowing some of the core elements of what being a professional social worker means, we must ask ourselves how we might develop our professional identity as social workers, given we are all different individuals.

Imagine you were meeting a friend for an evening out. You would, most likely, have each other's contact details, specific information of where you were meeting, at what time and probably an inkling of what you were going to do. These represent everyday aspects of being a good friend. However, when you move from the personal to the professional or work sphere there are additional elements to consider especially the setting of appropriate boundaries on your relationship with people using your services. In the same way that our early socialisation inculcates an often unspoken and assumed way of acting as a friend, social work education is a first step in your socialisation as a social worker. In addition, you need to be aware of the structural factors bearing down on you – social ones stemming from your role, occupational ones stemming from the expectations and requirements of employers and political assumptions about your role. The requirements and standards expected by professional bodies are also important. Alongside this, you need an awareness of power and authority that you possess simply by being a social worker. In this context you need a focus on empowerment and working with the independent and creative actions of those with whom you are working alongside. This is very different behaviour to that of acting as a friend.

Professionalism arises at the confluence between you the social worker (your values, beliefs, attitudes and expectations), the organisation in which you work and social context in which you practise (legal, procedural, employment and social perspectives and requirements), and those people you work with as users of social work services or indeed as colleagues and other professionals (their needs and expectations as human beings) (see the Venn diagram below). So, let's look at what that means for being a professional social worker, emphasising the word 'professional'.

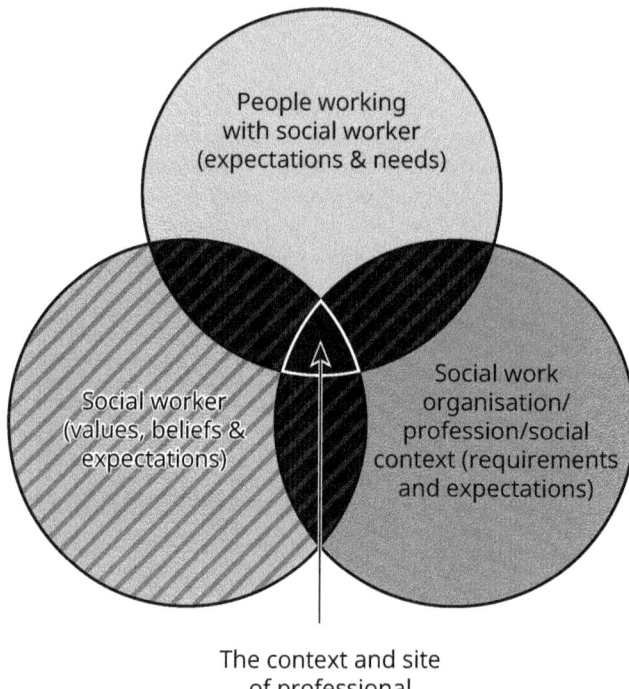

Figure 10.1   The context and site of professional social work

Being a social work professional today – thoughts, reflections and critical questions

Following neatly from our own professional and personal identity we need to ask questions and reflect on what that might mean for the complexities of social work today. Let's consider two things: (1) the importance of not over promising, and (2) your accessibility for people you work with – these questions are important for both colleagues and people using social work services – do they have your number, do they know the limitations in being able to contact you and so on?

What, therefore, are good professional practices? We would like, at this point, to introduce the mnemonic SCoRe – which relates to strengths-based, collaborative and relational social work practice and identity. SCoRe is helpful when we assess our principles and approach. The inculcation of values is central to acting professionally and to the development of a professional identity. Indeed, it is something that you will have been introduced to from the start of your professional education onwards. However, we must also beware of thinking that social workers are the only profession holding clear and bespoke values or, indeed, the only right ones. Our approach must be tempered by an attitude and identity that rests in humility and places the person we are working with centre-stage. By using SCoRe as an approach to practice we can begin to do so and thereby act in a professional manner. So, you need to ensure that you are asking and re-asking the questions: (1) Are you focusing on the strengths of those people you are working with? (2) Are you actively seeking the input of all those you are working with? (3) Are you developing honest, transparent and clear relationships with colleagues, other professional and people who use social work services? Recognising the interactive context and site of professional practice and continually asking these questions will help you to remain on track as a professional social worker.

Who you are as a professional social worker: the important bits!

There are three key elements to remember that underpin this approach to professionalism: communication, genuineness, and knowledge, values and skills.

Communication – this involves developing relationships, and delivering clear, simple and reinforced messages; learning the preferred modes of communication for the people you work with. There are still many people who find reading difficult and you may need to adapt the ways in which you communicate. Also, the more we learn of neurodiversity, the more we recognise different types of communication preference and the problems that some people may face in understanding you. If you cannot communicate in a person's preferred way, for some reason, then, as a professional, you need to explain why that is and seek an acceptable alternative. When I (Jonathan Parker) was in practice it was particularly important to find alternatives to written communications given the still high levels of illiteracy. For today's social workers, alongside the wide range of communication types that may be possible, the question may also concern the type of social media to be used, its security, availability and acceptability to agency, colleagues and other professionals, the person you're working with, and yourself. It is worth remembering as well that the increase in AI assistants to communication may provide quick alternatives in messaging. It is very important here to keep in mind the mistakes that AI can make, the false messages that may ensue and the problems it may cause in forming genuine relationships with people.

Genuineness – your actions and you, yourself, must be honest, clear in your boundaries, and trustworthy. You also need to acknowledge to yourself when you want to throw in the towel or shout and stamp when the job gets a little too much; we all have bad days. Being genuine involves doing what you say you will but never promising what you can't deliver. This is easy to say but not always easy to do in practice. However, by doing so you will be considered trustworthy even if you don't always do what is wanted or don't do it in the way it was wanted. This is especially the case if you explain why it was not possible to act in the way others wanted. This holds true for other professionals as well as people who use social work services.

Knowledge, values and skills – updating yourself through continual professional development is important as we mention below. It is also key to make yourself aware of the latest research in your area and to acknowledge your limitations; find out when you don't know. Acknowledging when you don't know something or someone knows more than you takes courage, but shows you are acting as a relational, collaborative and genuine social worker. Sometimes, we have heard people disparaging training and education as unnecessary and a waste of time that has been taken from working directly with people in need. This is wrong and you should foster the belief that training is key to your role, not shirking or 'having a jolly'. It is a central part of the job and undertaking training is itself a professional act as we shall see next.

The centrality of continuing professional development – a touchstone

Within the drive to update your core knowledge, it is important to acknowledge the critical importance of continued learning for practice in the context of CPD. CPD is a keystone in holding together one's identity and practice as a professional social worker. There has been quite a long history of professional updating and it is now, of course, a recognised element in continued registration as a social worker. There are, however, still attitudes that reflect an older anti-intellectual almost messianic approach to social work that privileges doing without recourse to thinking, questioning, justifying and reflecting: a rushing in to rescue people. This is not professional social work, but is rather a dangerous practice born of the busyness of the work and the unending needs of people who use services, as well as the narcissism of those who suggest they do not need further training and education. However, we do not help people at all if we fall into the trap in believing 'we don't have time' or 'we don't need theory now we're in practice'. It may also indicate something of our own attitudes and if we find ourselves wanting to save and rescue in a heroic way the people we are working with, we need to reflect critically on our own professional identity. For instance, you would probably not want to visit a doctor who has not undertaken any further training since his or her original qualification some 30 years previously. So, why should you impose yourself on others if your knowledge and understanding is out of date. It would be unprofessional.

ACTIVITY 10.5

Updating for professional practice

Have you a clear plan for updating your knowledge? Is it something that is encouraged by your employer? If you haven't yet developed or agreed a plan for CPD, you should look towards doing that now.

Comment

Drawing together a table to keep track of your CPD, updating and training can be useful when it comes to compiling a log for professional registration, for use in supervision and for appraisals. Using the following columns can help.

- Date
- Type of learning
- What I learned and how this will enhance my practice
- What do I need to do now?

Reviewing your own professional journey

Alongside further training and education, there are other ways of reviewing, evaluating and enhancing your own practice as a professional social worker. We will consider some of these here as we review the discussion we have already undertaken.

One part of your responsibility in keeping up your registration and in respect of CPD, is to be up-to-date in your reading and knowledge of current research. You may have included such in your plan. However, this can be time-consuming and incorporating this into very busy practice lives is not easy at all. Nevertheless, it demonstrates a commitment to best practice and can help to ensure your practice is as good as it can be. Many journals are now providing accessible summaries of research that can help in saving time. Another way in which you can maintain your currency in respect of social work research is to meet with other new and recently qualified social workers and take one piece of research each that you agree to summarise and share with everyone else. In this way, five or six pieces of research can be shared almost as easily as reading one for yourself.

Being research-minded and a critical reflective practitioner is an essential part of your professionalism and we have discussed this earlier in Chapters 3, 4 and 7. Being critically reflective, and to a large extent being research-minded, involves you engaging in a reflective cycle akin to action-research. This is something you will know from your qualifying social work education, from practice and from your further studies and reflections as a new social worker. Articulating your learning experiences in an explicit way can help you embed them consciously in your practice where you plan, act, review and evaluate alongside others, replan and repeat, building your practice wisdom and expertise and being able to justify why you are doing what you are doing.

Whilst there is a myriad of reasons why people want to become social workers, a common theme is present: that is, wanting to make life better for those people who social workers work with, whether they want to be involved with social work services or not, and to improve the social world in which we all live. So, remembering these core drivers plays a large part in steering us towards professional practice that respects individuals and families, that puts them centre stage in all that we do and demands that those we work with come before those we work for.

Summary

In this chapter, you have considered how the terms profession, professional and professionalism are defined. You have looked at the negative as well as the positive ways they can be understood and have then examined ways in which these can be applied to social work and especially to your own development as a newly qualified professional social worker. Being a professional social worker is not a one-off act. It is a continual journey of learning and applying that learning and wisdom in practice.

Further reading

Parker, J., & Doel, M. (Eds.). (2014). *Professional social work*. Sage.

Although quite old now, this edited collection offers a number of insights from a range of esteemed academics into what being a professional social worker involves and how you can enhance your own professionalism.

Weekes, A., & Harvey, D. (2025). *Effective personal and professional judgement in social work*. Routledge.

This practical and clearly written book provides useful advice and guidance for social workers at all stages of their careers. Written by experienced practitioners in the field it is invaluable in assisting newly qualified social workers negotiate the complexities of professional social work.

Chapter 11

The monster under the bed: Safeguarding ourselves and others from mental health shame

Andrew Morris

Introduction

This book has aimed to recognise, address and alleviate some of the stresses and strains experienced by newly qualified social workers (and experienced practitioners too). Sometimes these stresses and strains reach tipping point and practitioners go from managing competing demands, navigating complex situations and maintaining their full diaries and equally full heads, to feelings of overwhelm, anxiety, low mood and other negative impacts on their mental and physical wellbeing. The tipping point may be reached due to an accumulation of factors, or it may be a result of a specific event. This chapter alerts readers to the destructive experience of shame, which some practitioners report feeling when they have reached their tipping point and the stresses and strains of practice impact negatively on their mental health. It argues that the motivation of social workers to train and practice is often closely aligned to an individual's values and lived experience, meaning their choice of career is an expression of personal identity (a point echoed in Chapter 1 by the editors' personal stories). This creates psychological jeopardy as the sense of self and identity may be threatened when poor mental health is experienced. This is the opportunity the 'monster under the bed' takes to invite in shame and by describing how and why this occurs the chapter offers readers insight into how to get to know your monster and work with it.

The monster under the bed is a metaphor for social workers' feelings of shame related to poor mental health. It lurks under the bed of our practice and professional identity. It often feels scary and can be psychologically damaging. This chapter will discuss findings from literature to help us understand the monster better: What it is, where it comes from, and how it affects us. By gaining a better understanding, we can begin to engage with our shame in a more constructive way: we may learn to acknowledge it, enter into dialogue with it, and even integrate it into our sense of self, so it no longer undermines our wellbeing. This is particularly relevant to newly qualified social workers, trying to navigate the world of social work while developing their professional identity.

There is currently limited research on shame in social work, especially in relation to experiences of mental health concerns. Some researchers suggest this issue may be difficult to identify and could be hidden in the data of other studies (Scheff 2014; Shen 2018). For example, many studies focus on factors that cause stress (Cleveland 2019; Ravalier et al. 2020; Hollenderer 2022). They identify challenges in working conditions for social workers, such as high caseloads, pressure to meet deadlines, and working with challenging service users. Feelings of shame may not be identified by these studies due to self-reporting bias (Rose and Palattiyil, 2018). Participants may be reluctant to share or even admit feelings of shame, due to the associated stigma (please see below for further details on stigma and the hidden nature of shame). Psychological measures and scales to assess levels of stress are often used, and whilst these can provide quantitative data, they do not ascertain differences between emotions such as stress and shame. These measures may be broad and cover many different aspects of stress and mental health but could miss more subtle thoughts/feelings/behaviours associated with shame (Gilbert 1998; Deonna et al. 2012).

How did the monster under the bed find us? Why do people become social workers?

To understand why some social workers develop a 'monster under the bed' of shame while others do not, it helps to start by exploring what motivates people to enter the profession. Motivation shapes a social worker's values, expectations, and sense of professional identity, which in turn influences how they respond to challenges, stress, and setbacks. By reflecting on why we chose this work, we can better understand the situations that trigger shame, recognise our own vulnerabilities, and begin to manage feelings of self-criticism in a constructive way. Hackett et al. (2003), Norcross and Farber (2005) and Duschinsky (2014) suggest most people join the profession because they want to help people. Indeed, the British Association of Social Workers (BASW) (2022) found this to be the most common reason for entering the profession. This is similar to Furness' (2007) findings from fifteen years previously, when the 696 surveyed social work students identified 14 reasons why they chose this career. These include:

- To help others/improve the quality of life of others 34%

- Challenging/rewarding career 13%

- Personality/aptitude for job 11%

- Work with people 10%

- To make a difference 9%

- Develop skills and knowledge 8%

- Life experiences 6%

- Career opportunities 6%

- Relevant past voluntary/paid work experiences 5%

- Interest in work/concern for others 5%

- Fight social injustices/protection of others 4%

- Work in a team with like-minded people 2%

- To give back to society 2%

- Always wanted to be a social worker 1%

(Furness 2007, p.247).

Personal experiences as motivation

Six per cent of respondents (31 individuals) in Furness' (2007) study described their own life experiences as a motivator for becoming social workers. BASW (2022) found that 6.3 per cent of their respondents also gave this answer, and similar findings were evidenced in a study of Israeli social work students in 2021 (Finklestein and Laufer). Other studies, however, suggest life experience/previous trauma is a *more* common motivator. For example, Sellers and Hunter (2005) found that 69 per cent of their 86 respondents cited personal experience as a main factor that motivated them to train as social workers; Rompf and Royse (1994, p.169) found that social work students were more likely than other students to have 'grown up in a family experiencing psychosocial trauma'; and Daniel (2011, p.899) found that 71 per cent of her social work students surveyed had 'a family history of social services use' (see also Byrne, 2019). The theme of personal experience with adversity was also explored by Gewirtz-Meydan and Even-Zohar (2018), who found issues such as addiction, poor mental health, abuse, and trauma helped influence the Israeli students' decisions to become social workers (see also Rompf and Royce, 1994). In a similar study, Straussner et al. (2018) surveyed over 6000 social workers in the USA and found that more than 40 per cent of the respondents had some kind of mental health condition before they began their training (see also Siebert and Siebert, 2005, p.210). Archer and Burnell (2003) state that many working in the caring professions carry with them experiences of past trauma and shame. Indeed, the prevalence of people living with mental health conditions is higher among the helping professionals compared to the general public (Schernhammer 2005). Nevertheless, social workers who have previous experiences with trauma may be better able to empathise with and understand the needs of their service users (Gewirtz-Meydan and Even-Zohar 2018). These experiences can be used to help strengthen their identity and sense of self.

Social Identity Theory

Social Identity Theory offers potential insights linking an individual's motivation for undertaking social work training with their sense of identity. The theory suggests people classify themselves in various categories related to different values (Terum and Heggen 2016). We attach meaning to these categories and the roles/functions they play in society (Yates and Cahill 2019). This role is an idealised version of oneself where a person perceives themselves (and others perceive them) primarily based on the role they identify with (McCall and Simmons 1966). When it comes to careers, people tend to choose a career based on the category it is associated with, or the identity it can provide for them (Stryker and Burke 2000; Ng and Feldman 2007). This would suggest that social workers want an identity where they are seen as helpers. Social work students and those considering joining the profession generally view the role of social workers as helping people. The idea of the wounded healer, where the past experience of trauma (wound) is also present (Murphy 2021). Being a social worker enables a person to integrate their previous experiences and values into their professional identity, thus strengthening their sense of self (Earls Larrison and Korr 2013). People become part of a group and have a shared identity and values as social workers (Holter 2018). People also find fulfilment in helping, supporting and advocating for others who are experiencing difficulties (Shlomo et al. 2012; Holter 2018).

Caregiver Role Identity Theory

The Caregiver Role Identity (CRI) scale was developed by Seibert and Seibert (2005). Social workers see themselves as caregivers and problem-solvers (Saxena and Chandrapal 2022). As this is an important part of their identity, they may hold themselves to high expectations. However, when stress from the job becomes too much, they are often unwilling to seek help for their difficulties. Seibert and Seibert (2005) suggest that if the social worker were seen as needing support for their mental health, they would no longer be in a *caring role*; they would be in a *cared-for role*. This is the opposite of their identity, and so it creates an internal conflict which threatens their identity and idealised sense of self. This creates an existential crisis as they begin to question their very identity. If they cannot help themselves, how can they help other people? Their sense of who they are as a person is at risk, and this can be a frightening thought for some people whose identity is tied up with being a helper (Stryker and Burke 2000; Ng and Feldman 2007; Terum and Heggen 2016; Yates and Cahill 2019). Siebert and Siebert go on to suggest that people who strongly identify as caregivers, such as social workers, are less likely to seek help for their own physical and mental distress. People try to avoid the role of the *cared-for* person to maintain their sense of self and their identity as a caregiver/social worker. Because a person's support needs related to past experiences can be difficult to identify during the process of social work recruitment and interview (Furness 2007) and social workers may not be open about their needs, some social workers may not get the support they need from their employers. In addition, people may believe they have adequately addressed these issues, but the trauma or pain may be triggered again through vicarious or secondary trauma from working with service users, especially for newly qualified social workers who may not have the same level of emotional resilience as more experienced colleagues. This can be better understood by considering stress in social work.

Why did the monster come here? Stress and social work – factors that make social work stressful

Using the analogy of the monster under the bed for the shame some professionals feel when they experience negative impacts on their mental health and wellbeing, we can say stress attracts the monster, so it takes up residence beneath the bed of our practice. Social workers in the UK are considered an occupational group who are at above-average risk for stress and burnout, with both Adult and Children's Services having some of the most stressful roles (Söderfeldt et al. 1995; Acker 2010; Local Government Association 2014; McFadden et al. 2015; Pentaraki 2017; Rose and Palattiyil 2018; Kagan and Greenblatt Kimron 2021; McFadden et al. 2022). Many factors make social work stressful. It involves challenging personal, organisational, and professional dynamics that are not present in other disciplines (Ellett et al. 2007; Moriarty et al. 2015; Cleveland et al. 2019; Ravalier et al. 2020; Beer et al. 2021; Hollederer 2022). The main stressors are related to organisational issues rather than personal ones, argue Mor Barak et al. (2001). These can include:

- Time constraints to complete work (Dillenburger 2004)

- Unrealistic workloads (McFadden et al. 2015)

- Organisational demands, targets and performance indicators (Lloyd et al. 2002)

- Poor organisational support (Dane 2000)

- And trauma caused by the nature of the work (Choi 2016)

Other factors include poor workforce retention, insufficient staffing levels, high caseloads, verbal abuse, potential violence from service users, and workers feeling they have no voice in the workplace (Mor Barak et al. 2001; Bowers et al. 2009; Totman et al. 2011; Middleton and Potter 2015; Ravalier 2019; Ravalier et al. 2020). Social workers can also experience high levels of uncertainty when working with involuntary service users, as well as experiencing pressures from being subject to intense political and public scrutiny (Ellett et al. 2007). The majority of these studies have focused on social work with children and families, but the issues can easily translate to adult services. Another issue that affects both adult and children's social workers in the UK is highlighted by Gibson (2016, p.559) who asserts that social workers are expected to cope with the high pressures of the job while living and working in a climate/society that does not tolerate mistakes by social workers. Sensationalist reporting in the media has tarnished the profession's reputation, especially in England (Leigh 2018), and all of these issues serve to add to workers' stress levels. Indeed, recent years have seen the pressure on social workers increase disproportionately by the Covid-19 pandemic (McFadden et al. 2022; Ravalier et al. 2022). Owing to these issues, social workers are at a higher risk of trauma and burnout.

Trauma and burnout

The common types of trauma that social workers are exposed to are secondary trauma and vicarious trauma. Secondary trauma is a term used to describe sudden adverse reactions to service users who have experienced wounding (Figley 2002; Jenkins and Baird 2002). It can develop over a relatively short period. Symptoms include poor mental health (Kinman and Grant 2020), depression, poor sleep, social withdrawal and headaches (Showalter 2010), as well as '…intrusive thoughts, images, dreams, and flashbacks about the trauma' (Gil and Weinberg 2015, p.552). Bride (2007) studied secondary traumatic stress and found that many social workers experience these symptoms and are at an increased risk of secondary trauma, which could put their physical and mental health at risk.

Vicarious trauma, on the other hand, occurs over a longer period, resulting from 'empathic engagement with traumatic material' (Jenkins and Baird 2002, p.424). The authors view the main difference between vicarious trauma and secondary trauma as how it is experienced. Secondary trauma is defined by its post-traumatic stress symptoms (Salston and Figley 2003), while vicarious trauma is more related to one's cognitive schemas (Pearlman and Saakvitne 1995). Both vicarious trauma and secondary trauma can impact a social worker's professional life as well as their personal life, and it can lead to burnout (Ashley-Binge and Cousins 2020).

Burnout is common in the caring professions, especially social work (Freudenberger 1974; Sánchez-Moreno et al. 2015; Endriulaitien et al. 2019). Indeed, Grant et al. (2014) and Bunce et al. (2019) found that social workers experience higher levels of burnout compared with other healthcare professionals. These experiences can lead to feelings of being overextended and depleted of emotional and physical resources, as well as feelings of incompetence and a sense of lack of achievement at work (Cordes and Dougherty 1993; Maslach et al. 2001; Horwitz 2006; Hollederer 2022). Added to this is a sense of professional failure (Sánchez-Moreno et al. 2015). To guard against this, one strategy employed by some social workers is stoicism (Beer et al. 2021).

Stoicism

When used positively, stoicism encourages rational thinking, emotional regulation, and resilience, which can help social workers manage their responsibilities more effectively (Watson 2020). Adopting stoic principles can help maintain a level-headed approach, reduce the emotional burden of social workers' caregiving duties and help balance pressures on their caregiver identity with their overall emotional well-being (Cagle and Bunting 2017; Watson 2020). Stoicism can also foster a healthy level of professional detachment, allowing social workers to provide compassionate care without becoming overly identified with their clients' issues, thus protecting their mental health (Moudatsou et al. 2020).

People can, however, become overly reliant on stoicism, and this too can lead to problems (Beer et al. 2021). A team culture of stoicism can be especially damaging to individuals struggling with stress, as it can inadvertently lead to individuals suppressing emotions and being reluctant to seek help (Rose and Palattiyil 2018; Kagan and Itzick 2019). Newly qualified and experienced social workers may fear an *unstoic* response to stress could be perceived as a weakness by colleagues. We feel we must remain strong and composed at all times, so we must put on a façade of coping (Rose and Palattiyil 2018). Adding to this, Kagan and Itzick (2019) and Rogers (2001) point out that the act of being emotionally open and asking for help can be very difficult in teams that are depersonalised or technically focused. An example could be a newly qualified social worker struggling with stress in a team of very stoic professionals, where struggles are seen as a form of weakness. The social workers' difficulty in managing their stress effectively makes them different and somehow inferior to the rest of the team. This illustrates Brown's (2006) assertion that when some social workers begin to struggle with their mental health, they feel inadequate and incompetent because of their perceived shortcomings. It not only harms their well-being, but it also negatively impacts their service users, as the social worker is less emotionally available and alert to their needs (Sánchez-Moreno et al. 2015). Their ability to read emotions and respond in an emotionally appropriate way is likely to be impacted (Walker 2011; Shen 2018). This is due to a lack of insight into their behaviour and other people, as they turn away from potentially damaging emotions.

Continuing with the theme of emotions, Barlow and Hall (2007) argue that Western traditions consider emotions to be impediments to working effectively. The point echoes Miller's (1976) view that society and, by extension, workplaces, seek to neutralise or remove emotions from work, rather than seeing them as strengths. Miller makes an important point about emotions, which is still relevant today, in that removing or minimising emotions in the workplace can lead to an over-reliance on a stoic approach to managing stress. This, in turn, creates a sense of isolation for the social worker. They may avoid discussing their struggles or seeking support for the reasons discussed above, and because of this, their feelings of inadequacy deepen. Their suppression of emotions and lack of expression or release can add to feelings of burnout (Freudenberger 1974; Grant et al. 2014; Sánchez-Moreno et al. 2015; Endriulaitien et al. 2019; Hollederer 2022). This, in turn, can create a sense of isolation and a vicious circle for the individual, where they become reluctant to seek support for their difficulties due to the perceived stigma, and so become more isolated in their pain.

ACTIVITY 11.1

Stoicism

This activity is designed to help newly qualified social workers reflect on their responses to stress and explore the role of stoicism in their professional practice. As social workers, we often feel pressure to remain strong, composed, and unaffected by emotional challenges.

(Continued)

(Continued)

While stoicism can be useful in managing stress, it can also lead to emotional suppression, burnout, and disengagement, which we saw above. This exercise encourages self-awareness and helps find a balance between resilience and healthy emotional expression.

Instructions:

Step 1: Recall Three Stressful Situations

Think of three recent situations in your practice that caused you stress. These could be moments of high emotional intensity, ethical dilemmas, difficult interactions with service users, or workplace pressures. Some examples could be:

- A service user became upset and shouted at you.

- You received negative feedback from a supervisor.

- A heavy caseload left you feeling overwhelmed and behind on work.

Write down each situation in a few sentences.

Step 2: Analyse Your Immediate Reaction

For each situation, reflect on your emotional and physical reactions. Ask yourself:

- What emotions did I feel in that moment? (e.g., frustration, sadness, anxiety)

- How did my body react? (e.g., tense shoulders, fast heartbeat, stomach discomfort)

- What did I do in response? (e.g., push through without acknowledging emotions, vent to a colleague, take deep breaths)

Step 3: Was It a Stoic Response?

Next, assess whether your response was stoic. Remember, stoicism in social work often means suppressing emotions to appear strong and professional.

- Did I downplay or ignore my emotions?

- Did I pretend I wasn't affected?

- Did I carry on without processing the situation?

- Did I think *I just needed to toughen up*?

If your response involved hiding or pushing aside emotions without processing them, it was likely a stoic response.

Step 4: Was This Helpful or Harmful?

Consider whether your response helped or hindered you. Ask yourself:

- Did ignoring my emotions make things worse later?

- Did I experience burnout, frustration, or disengagement afterwards?

- Would a different response have been healthier?

Step 5: Explore Alternative Coping Strategies

Finally, if your response leaned toward stoicism in a way that wasn't helpful, reflect on how you could healthily manage this stress. Maybe:

- Talking to a supervisor or colleague about the situation.
- Taking a short break to reflect and breathe.
- Journaling thoughts and emotions to process them privately.
- Seeking professional supervision or support.
- Practising mindfulness or relaxation techniques.

This exercise encourages self-reflection and helps us recognise when stoicism is useful and when it becomes harmful. By identifying alternative coping strategies, we can develop healthier ways to manage stress while maintaining emotional resilience, which is going to be key in looking after yourselves as newly qualified workers.

Stigma and social work – What is the monster doing under the bed?

Deepening the analogy of the monster under the bed, stigma is what the monster feeds on. It makes it stronger and scarier. Stigma around poor mental health is the reason that the monster lurks in the shadows. Let's use Dudley's (2000) definition of stigma, which includes the presence of stereotypes and negative views attributed to a person/people when their behaviour is viewed as being different or inferior to the rest of the group. This definition is concise and fits well with Araten-Bergman and Werner's (2017) description, which suggests three elements must be present for stigma to take hold. These include stereotypes, prejudice and discrimination. Stereotypes are needed for stigma to exist as they group characteristics and people. Prejudices see people belonging to the other group as being different from themselves. Discrimination occurs when prejudices are acted upon and members of the other group are treated less fairly or negatively because of their membership in that group. To help understand how these elements interact to produce stigma, Corrigan and Rao's (2012) model of stigma illustrates it well. The model draws on social-cognitive theory (Bandura 2001), and has four stages which a person must move through for stigma to take effect (see Box 11.1 below).

BOX 11.1

Corrigan and Rao's (2012) Model of Stigma

Stage 1 – Awareness: The individual social worker becomes aware of negative stereotypes about poor mental health or struggling with stress. Talking about stress could be a taboo

(Continued)

(Continued)

topic. These attitudes can be seen and heard in everyday conversations in the office. For example, colleagues may talk in negative tones about colleagues or people they know who struggle with stress at work. Characteristics or behaviours associated with significant stress, such as anxiety, tiredness, and difficulty sleeping, may be linked with negative stereotypes of *those who can't cope as a social worker!*

Stage 2 – Agreement: The individual accepts either consciously or unconsciously that these negative stereotypes are legitimate or true. It should be noted that this model does not explain why this occurs.

Stage 3 – Application: When the individual experiences poor mental health or they are struggling with stress from their job, they begin to see that the negative attitudes and stereotypes discussed in the team/organisation now apply to them. They now see themselves as part of the stigmatised group due to their poor mental health.

Stage 4 – Harm: The individual may experience an actual or perceived loss of status and discrimination. The individual may begin to perceive themselves as no longer being one of the efficient, capable, *normal* members of the team, but as a weak link – someone who can't cope with the pressure. This quickly results in the individual losing confidence, doubting themselves, and having reduced self-esteem. As this topic is not okay to talk about at work, the person may keep quiet and not seek support, which will exacerbate these feelings of low mood and inability to cope.

Professional Stigma

When trying to understand stigma in social work organisations and teams, Ahmedani (2011) discusses the term professional stigma. He argues that mental health professionals, including social workers, are no less susceptible to stigmatising beliefs than the general public. To illustrate this point, Kotera et al. (2022) studied 84 female social work students and assessed their attitudes towards mental health. The authors explored the relationships between shame, mental health symptoms, self-criticism, self-compassion and role identity. They found that self-criticism, self-compassion and role identity significantly relate to mental health symptoms and directly relate to the prediction of future mental health symptoms. The participants perceived that their peers/communities held negative views of mental health, which negatively impacted their sense of self, self-compassion and identity as social work students.

In another study by Ting (2011), levels of depression and help-seeking beliefs were examined in 215 undergraduate American social work students. Ting identified stigma as the main reason students were reluctant to seek help with their mental health, as well as fear/distrust, and worries around confidentiality, quality of support, and cultural competency.

Social workers can internalise negative stereotypes of mental health and difficulties with stress. This can lead to a sense of stigma being created around someone struggling with their mental health or simply not coping well. Therefore, in a team where social workers should be strong and manage stress well, a social worker struggling with their poor mental health would try to hide their difficulties from the rest of the team by adopting stoic principles. Thus, the vicious cycle continues, creating the ideal conditions for shame to take root (Tangney et al. 1992; Keltner and Buswell 1996; Tangney et al. 1996; Sabini et al. 2001).

ACTIVITY 11.2

Stigma

Instructions:

Step 1: Identifying Unspoken Rules

Reflect on messages that you've encountered in your social work journey so far. They could be subtle or explicit in nature and could come from supervisors, colleagues, university training, or broader societal expectations.

Ask yourself:

- What phrases or ideas have I heard about social workers and mental health?
- Are there expectations that social workers should always be strong, resilient, or self-sacrificing?
- Have I ever felt guilty or hesitant to express stress or ask for support?

Here are five unspoken and untrue rules I have come across:

1. *'Social workers should always be strong for their service users.'*
2. *'Needing support is a sign of weakness.'*
3. *'Talking about burnout means you're not cut out for this job.'*
4. *'Good social workers don't struggle with mental health.'*
5. *'You should be able to handle stress on your own.'*

Step 2: Challenging the Rules

Here are the first three of those unspoken and untrue statements rewritten with a healthier, stigma-free alternative.

1. Unspoken rule: *'Social workers should always be strong for their service users.'*
2. Rewritten: *'Social workers are human too. Acknowledging emotions and seeking support leads to better practice.'*
3. Unspoken rule: *'Needing support is a sign of weakness.'*
4. Rewritten: *'Seeking support is a sign of self-awareness and professionalism.'*
5. Unspoken rule: *'Talking about burnout means you're not cut out for this job.'*
6. Rewritten: *'Burnout is a systemic issue, not an individual failure. Addressing it helps improve working conditions for everyone.'*

Now rewrite the unspoken and untrue rules 4 and 5 with a healthier, stigma-free alternative.

(Continued)

(Continued)

Write down the unspoken and untrue rules you are aware of and rewrite those with a healthier, stigma-free alternative.

This step allows you to reframe harmful beliefs and replace them with positive, constructive alternatives.

Step 3: Reflection and Discussion

If you are completing this activity alone, reflect on the following questions:

- How have these unspoken rules influenced your thoughts, emotions, or actions in practice?
- Have you ever hesitated to speak about mental health because of these rules?
- How could you actively promote a more supportive environment for yourself and your colleagues?

If you are completing it in a group, discuss:

- Did we identify similar unspoken rules?
- How can social work educators, managers, and organisations challenge these hidden expectations?
- What changes could make social work a more open and supportive profession?

This exercise is designed to help newly qualified social workers recognise the hidden pressures that shape their attitudes toward mental health. By actively challenging these norms, you can contribute to reducing stigma, creating a healthier professional culture, and advocating for systemic change in your organisation.

Shame – Understanding the monster under the bed

We know how the monster found us, why it crawled under our bed, and what it's doing there. In order to manage it, we need to get to know it, which can be difficult because the monster is very clever. The monster likes to hide so no one else can see it. As seen above, a social worker struggling with stress may try to cover up their difficulties due to a fear of being seen negatively by colleagues. The motivation to hide one's perceived shortcomings is strong. Indeed, the fear of others becoming aware of one's perceived shortcomings can be much more stressful to some people than the fear of experiencing violence from service users (Gibson 2016). The fear of rejection by teammates and the potential loss of identity and sense of self make people hide their perceived shameful attributes (Walker 2011). This is what helps guard against rejection from others (Daniels and Robinson 2019). Shen (2018) uses the term *shame-drive hiding strategy* to describe this behaviour. To help understand experiences of shame, it is useful to consider the emotion in greater detail.

Shame is often used as an umbrella term to refer to a range of emotions (Dolezal 2017). It is often used interchangeably with terms like humiliation (Elshout et al. 2017), embarrassment and guilt (Gibson 2015). This does not help understand shame because they are all separate emotions: Humiliation involves a sense of being *unjustly put down* and diminished by others and is perceived to affect one's social status negatively (Nussbaum 2006; Deonna et al. 2012). Embarrassment is an emotion related to the response (or perceived response) from others as a result of them witnessing one's behaviour, usually in the form of *breaking a social norm*. Embarrassment is less damaging than guilt, which is associated with the response (or feared response) to an act or behaviour that is considered to be *wrong* in the eyes of others (Walker 2011; Bastin et al. 2016). Guilt differs from shame in that it motivates the individual to make amends for what they have done. Shame, on the other hand, is more destructive. Where guilt focuses on an act or behaviour, shame focuses on the individual's entire character. Shame can be described as the displeasure that a person experiences upon realising they do not measure up to the values with which they embrace (Taylor 1985). This definition fits well with Candiotto's (2019, p.79) assertion that 'shame is experienced in the intersubjective dimension of life…'. It can make a person feel that there is something inherently wrong with them, compared to those around them. When one is experiencing shame, it can be invisible to others, including researchers trying to study the phenomenon (Lewis 1971; Lewis 2003; Schmader and Lickel 2006; Claesson et al. 2007; Scheff 2014; Gibson 2016; Daniels and Robinson 2019; Mun 2019).

Social Shame

Theory and research support the idea that there are two sides to shame – Social Shame and Moral Shame. The concept of social shame is concerned with behaviours and actions as observed by other people. It is usually found within philosophical discussions around how one's behaviours and actions are perceived by others (Mun 2019). It relates to a fear of being seen poorly by others because of what you have done/not done (Deigh 1983; Gilbert and Andrews 1998; Velleman 2001; Gilbert 2003; Calhoun 2004; Gilbert 2007; Hejdenberg and Andrews 2011, Dolezal 2017; Cassidy 2019; Mun 2019). This view relates to the sense that a person's identity is susceptible to criticism from others because they have broken a social norm. Dolezal (2017, p.421) defines this type of shame as 'an emotion of self-assessment that causes the subject to feel anxiety at the thought of how he or she is seen and judged by others'. In other words, this emotion is fundamentally concerned with one's relationships with others and one's connection and sense of belonging to their social world/team. For example, imagine a social worker who believes social workers should be emotionally tough and be able to deal with stress effectively begins to struggle with stress and consequently experiences stress-related symptoms such as tearfulness, short temper, or anxiety attacks. Other people may witness these behaviours, which deviate from the individual's perception of the normal culture of conduct within the team. The individual's self-perceived weaknesses would be on display to their team. They would feel at risk of being negatively judged and possibly rejected by their colleagues because they believe they are now viewed as being weak/less valued. This is the social element of social shame, and it can lead to moral shame.

Moral Shame

Moral shame is concerned with a person's characteristics and values. Indeed, it is seen as a 'value-orientated emotion' (Laing 2022, p.233). Here, shame is defined as a form of adverse self-evaluation, which involves the belief that one falls short of some value or standard (Taylor 1985), which is tied to the individual's identity (Lewis et al. 1992). Similarly, Tangney et al. (1996) and Babcock and Sabini (1990) found that shame is closely linked with violating a personal ideal, rather than public exposure. Daniels and Robinson (2019, p.2454) reiterate this point by describing shame as '… a self-evaluation of failure to meet internalised standards'. In this view, an individual has fallen short of living up to some kind of normative moral standard, such as being able to manage stress as a social worker. When they find themselves struggling and unable to reconcile their experience with their beliefs/team culture, they would likely feel shame due to this *perceived flaw in their character*.

Organisational Shame

There is another form of shame pertinent to NQSWs. Organisational shame is a term used to help understand the relationship between team culture and individual experiences of shame at work. It is defined by Daniels and Robinson (2019) as a painful emotion that arises when an employee identifies a threat to the self after perceiving themselves (or being perceived by others) to have fallen short of an important standard that is closely linked to their professional identity. This concept is closely related to professional stigma and the notion of professional identities and roles discussed earlier in this chapter in Seibert and Seibert's (2005) theory. Professional identities are defined by Dutton et al. (2010) as identities that are tied to particular activities at work or entire careers, such as being a caregiver. If one's professional identity is at risk, the person may experience a form of organisational shame. Daniels and Robinson (2019) assert that for organisational shame to be experienced, two mental processes need to occur related to social and moral shame, respectively. Firstly, there is a belief that one's behaviour has deviated negatively from an important standard related to their work-related identity [social shame], e.g., struggling to manage their stress levels. Secondly, there is a belief that one is faulty/flawed/inadequate because of this deviation [moral shame].

Gaps in knowledge

The literature discussed in this chapter looks at the topic of shame from different perspectives. Some researchers have written about stress, others have written about stigma, and different writers have written about shame. There has been relatively little research carried out specifically on the topic of social workers' experience of shame with Frost et al. (2021) and Gibson (2016) being key contributors to the literature. Gibson notes that shame is something that significantly affects social workers. He concludes that social workers need to become more 'shame resilient' and calls for a culture of more 'empathic relationships' within teams or organisations (2014, p.426). Frost et al.'s (2021) findings were similar to Gibson's in that the profession still needs more understanding of shame and higher levels of self-compassion (Frost et al. 2021).

ACTIVITY 11.3

The Shame Iceberg

This activity is designed to help newly qualified social workers recognise and explore experiences of shame in practice by visualising the difference between what we show to the world and what we feel beneath the surface. You can do this individually or in a group setting.

Instructions:

Step 1: Drawing the Iceberg

- On a piece of paper, draw an iceberg.

- Label the tip of the iceberg (above the water) as 'What I Show' – these are the emotions, behaviours, or statements that others would see if you were feeling shame.

- Label the underwater section as 'What I Feel' – these are the hidden thoughts and emotions that fuel your experience of shame but often remain unspoken. This is what feeds the monster under the bed.

Step 2: Identifying What's Above and Below the Surface

Now, reflect on a time when you felt shame in your social work practice or when you were training (e.g., when you made a mistake, felt judged or struggled emotionally). Fill in the iceberg with the following:

Above the Surface (What I Show)

Write down the ways you *externally present* yourself when you feel shame. These might include:

- Acting confident (even when feeling unsure).

- Staying silent (instead of asking for help).

- Overworking (to compensate for self-doubt).

- Blaming others or external circumstances (to deflect shame).

- Joking or laughing it off (to minimise the seriousness of the feeling).

Below the Surface (What I Feel)

Write down the hidden emotions, thoughts, or fears that exist beneath the behaviours. These might include:

- 'I'm not good enough.'

- 'Everyone else knows what they're doing except me.'

- 'If I ask for help, people will think I'm weak.'

- 'I should have handled that situation better.'

- 'I don't belong in this profession.'

(Continued)

(Continued)

Step 3: Reflection

After completing the iceberg, reflect on these questions:

1. What patterns do I notice? (e.g., Do I always stay silent when I feel ashamed?)
2. How does shame affect my behaviour in social work? (e.g., Does it make me avoid supervision? Does it stop me from learning from my mistakes?)
3. What would help me bring more of my hidden feelings into the open in a safe way?
4. How can I challenge the self-judgement that fuels shame?

The Shame Iceberg helps social workers make the invisible visible. It allows us to see the unspoken rules and self-judgements that shape our experience of shame. By identifying these patterns, we can start to challenge and reframe shame, leading to a more supportive and compassionate professional identity. This will take the fear and power away from the monster under the bed and help us become friends with it by integrating it into our sense of self.

Summary

This chapter has explored the phenomenon of shame experienced by practitioners in relation to their mental health. It has defined shame and discussed how it may be felt in one's social relationships, sense of self or professional identity. The chapter has highlighted how shame about mental health may be hidden and misunderstood, but it can cause profound damage. The message of the chapter is that while social work is challenging and highly skilled work, and you are going to experience the stresses and strains of practice, deeper knowledge about yourself and any monster lurking under your bed will help you seek appropriate support in a timely way. If you find yourself tipping over into anxiety and other symptoms of poor mental health, or find yourself feeling shame, please come back to this chapter, do the exercises and get to know your monster under the bed – they may become your ally.

Further reading

Greer, J. (2016). *Resilience and personal effectiveness for social workers.* Sage.

Greer explores contemporary UK social work and sets it within the political context in which you, as NQSWs, will find yourselves. He provides helpful advice in developing a resilient approach, but without that leading to shame when you don't succeed.

Sand, I. (2022). *Confronting shame: How to understand your shame and gain inner freedom.* Jessica Kingsley Publishers.

This book represents a clear and practical self-help manual that helps you to identify the challenges in your life and at work that can lead to feelings of inadequacy, guilt and shame. It provides a range of exercises and activities to help you develop more positive attitudes to deal with shame.

References

Abrami, P. C., Bernard, R. M., Borokhovski, E., Wade, A., Surkes, M. A., Tamim, R. & Zhang, D. (2008). Instructional interventions affecting critical thinking skills and dispositions: A stage 1 meta-analysis. *Review of Educational Research*, 78 (4), 1102–1134.

Ahmedani, B. K. (2011). Mental health stigma: society, individuals, and the profession. *Journal of Social Work Values and Ethics*, 8 (2), 4–1.

Albano, R., Curzi, Y. & Radin, A. (2020) Social work assessment and information systems: a critique of managerialist models and an agenda for an alternative approach. In Addabbo, T., Ales, E., Curzi, Y., Fabbri, T., Rymkevich, O. & Senatori, I. (Eds.). *Performance appraisal in modern employment relations*. Palgrave Macmillan, 191–223, https://doi.org/10.1007/978-3-030-26538-0_9.

Aldridge, M. (1996). Dragged to market: being a profession in the postmodern world. *British Journal of Social Work*, 26(2), 177–194.

Alla, K. & Joss, N. (2021). What is an evidence-informed approach to practice and why is it important? *Australian Institute of Family Studies*. Available at https://aifs.gov.au/resources/short-articles/what-evidence-informed-approach-practice-and-why-it-important. Retrieved on 18/09/2025.

Andrade, C. (2020). Sample Size and its Importance in Research. *Indian Journal of Psychological Medicine*, 42 (1), 102–103.

Araten-Bergman, T. & Werner, S. (2017). Social workers' attributions towards individuals with dual diagnosis of intellectual disability and mental illness. *Journal of Intellectual Disability Research*, 61 (2), 155–167.

Archer, C. & Burnell, A. (2003). *Trauma, attachment and family permanence: fear can stop you loving*. Jessica Kingsly Publishers.

Argyris, C. & Schön, D. (1974). *Theory in practice: increasing professional effectiveness*. Jossey-Bass.

Argyris, C. & Schön, D. (1978). *Organizational learning: a theory of action perspective*. Addison Wesley.

Ashencaen Crabtree, S., Parker, J., Azman, A. & Carlo, D. P. (2012). Epiphanies and learning in a postcolonial Malaysia context: a preliminary evaluation of international social work placements. *International Social Work*. 57 (6), 618–629, DOI: 10.1177/0020872812448491.

Ashencaen Crabtree, S., Parker, J., Azman, A. & Masu'd, F. (2015). Typologies of learning in international student placements. *Asia Pacific Journal of Social Work and Development*, 25(1): 42–53.

Ashley-Binge, S. & Cousins, C. (2020). Individual and organisational practices addressing social workers' experiences of vicarious trauma. *Practice*, 32 (3), 191–207.

Asimov, I. (1985). *Robots and empire*. Doubleday.

Babcock, M. K. & Sabini, J. (1990). On differentiating embarrassment from shame. *European Journal of Social Psychology*, 20 (2), 151–169.

Bandura, A. (2001). Social cognitive theory: an agentic perspective. *Annual review of psychology*, 52 (1), 1–26.

Banks, S., Tuggle, F. & Coleman, D. (2021). Standardization of human rights–based workforce induction curriculum for social work field supervisors. *Journal of Human Rights and Social Work*, 6 (1), 4–13. https://doi.org/10.1007/s41134-020-00152-y

Barlow, C. & Hall, B. L. (2007). 'What about feelings?': A study of emotion and tension in social work field education. *Social Work Education*, 26 (4), 399–413.

Barnett, R., & Coate, K. (2005). *Engaging the curriculum in higher education*. Society for Research into Higher Education & Open University Press.

Bastin, C., Harrison, B. J., Davey, C. G., Moll, J. & Whittle, S. (2016). Feelings of shame, embarrassment and guilt and their neural correlates: a systematic review. *Neuroscience & Biobehavioral Reviews*, 71, 455–471.

Bates, N., Immins, T., Parker, J., Keen, S., Rutter, L., Brown, K. & Zsigo, S. (2010). 'Baptism of fire': the first year in the life of a newly qualified social worker. *Social Work Education*, 29(2): 152–70.

Beer, O. W. J., Phillips, R. & Quinn, C. R. (2021). Exploring stress, coping, and health outcomes among social workers. *European Journal of Social Work*, 24 (2), 317–330.

Boddy, C. (2016). Sample size for qualitative research. *Qualitative Market Research: An International Journal*, 19 (4), 426–432.

Bronfenbrenner, U. (1979). Ecology of human development. Harvard University Press.

Bostock, L., Bairstow, S., Fish, S. & Macleod, F. (2005). *Managing risk & minimising mistakes in services to children and families*. SCIE. www.scie.org.uk/publications/reports/report06.asp

Bourdieu, P. (1984) Distinction: A Social Critique of the Judgment of Taste. Routledge & Kegan Paul.

Bourdieu, P. (1996). *Distinction: A social critique of the judgement of taste*. Routledge.

Bowers, L., Allan, T., Simpson, A., Jones, J. & Whittington, R. (2009). Morale is high in acute inpatient psychiatry. *Social Psychiatry and Psychiatric Epidemiology*, 44 (1), 39–46.

Bradley, G. (2006). Using research findings to change agency culture and practice. *Research Policy and Planning*, 24(3): 135–48.

Bradley, G. (2008). The induction of newly appointed social workers: some implications for social work educators. *Social Work Education*, 27 (4), 349–365.

Bride, B. E. (2007). Prevalence of secondary traumatic stress among social workers. *Social Work*, 52 (1), 63–70.

British Association of Social Workers (BASW) (2012). *Code of Ethics*. www.basw.co.uk/codeofethics/

British Association of Social Workers (BASW) (2018). *The Professional Capabilities Framework [online]. British Association of Social Workers* www.basw.co.uk/professional-development/professional-capabilities-framework-pcf/the-pcf.

British Association of Social Workers (BASW) (2022). *The BASW Annual Survey of Social Workers and Social Work: 2021 – A summary report*. BASW.

Bronson, D., E. (2000). Progress and problems in social work research and evaluation in the United States. *Journal of Social Work Research and Evaluation*, 1, 125–137.

Brophy, J. (2006). Graham Nuthall and social constructivist teaching: research-based cautions and qualifications. *Teaching and Teacher Education*, 22 (5), 529–537.

Brown, K. & Rutter, L. (2019). *Critical thinking and professional judgement for social work*. Learning Matters.

Bryman, A. (2015). *Social research methods* (5th ed). OUP.

Bunce, L., Lonsdale, A. J., King, N., Childs, J. & Bennie, R. (2019). Emotional intelligence and self-determined behaviour reduce psychological distress: interactions with resilience in social work students in the UK. *The British Journal of Social Work*, 49 (8), 2092–2111.

Burke, P. J., Coffey, J., Gill, R. & Kanai, A. (2022). *Gender in an era of post-truth populism: pedagogies, challenges and strategies.* Bloomsbury Academic.

Burton, V. & Revill, L. (2018). Professional curiosity in child protection: thinking the unthinkable in a neo-liberal world. *British Journal of Social Work.* 48(6), 1508–1523.

Butler, J. (1996). Professional development: practice as text, reflection as process, and self as locus. *Australian Journal of Education*, 40(3): 265–283.

Cagle, J. & Bunting, M. (2017). Patient reluctance to discuss pain: understanding stoicism, stigma, and other contributing factors. *Journal of Social Work in End-of-Life & Palliative Care*, 13 (1), 27–43.

Calhoun, C. (2004). An apology for moral shame. *Journal of Political Philosophy*, 12 (2), 127–146.

Candiotto, L. (2019). The virtues of epistemic shame in critical dialogue, in Mun, C. (ed.) *Interdisciplinary perspectives on shame.* Lexington.

Carden, J., Jones, R. J. & Passmore, J. (2021). Defining self-awareness in the context of adult development: a systematic literature review. *Journal of Management Education*, 46 (1), 140–177.

Care Council for Wales (2008) *Making the most of the first year in practice: A guide for newly qualified social workers.* Cardiff: Care Council for Wales.

Care Council for Wales (2012). Continuing professional education and learning: a framework for social workers in wales. *Requirements for the Consolidation Programme.* Care Council for Wales. http://www.kcl.ac.uk/sspp/policy-institute/scwru/pubs/2012/reports/carpenteretal2012nqswfinal.pdf

Care Council for Wales (2017) *The First three years in practice - A framework for social workers' induction into qualified practice and continuing professional education and learning.* The-First-3-Years-in-Practice-1-1.pdf

Carpenter, J., Patsios, D., Wood, M., Platt, D., Shardlow, S., McLaughlin, H., Scholar, H., Haines, C., Wong, C. & Blewett, J. (2012). *Newly qualified social worker programme final evaluation report* (2008 to 2011). Department for Education.

CASP (2025). *CASP: The critical appraisal skills programme.* https://casp-uk.net/news/different-types-of-research-bias/

Cassidy, L. (2019). Body shaming in the era of social media, in Mun, C. (Ed.) *Body shaming in the era of social media.* Lexington Books.

Centre for Human Services Technology (n.d.). *What is research mindedness.* www.resmind.swap.ac.uk/content/02_what_is/what_is_02.htm

Children Act (2004). www.legislation.gov.uk/ukpga/2004/31/contents

Children and Young Person Act (2008). www.legislation.gov.uk/ukpga/2008/23/contents

Choi, G.-Y. (2016). Secondary traumatic stress and empowerment among social workers working with family violence or sexual assault survivors. *Journal of Social Work*, 17 (3), 358–378.

Chu, W. C. K. & Tsui, M. S. (2008). The nature of practice wisdom in social work revisited. *International Social Work*, 51(1): 47–54.

Claesson, K., Birgegard, A. & Sohlberg, S. (2007). Shame: mechanisms of activation and consequences for social perception, self-image, and general negative emotion. *Journal of Personality*, 75 (3), 595–628.

Cleveland, M., Warhurst, A. & Legood, A. (2019). Experiencing resilience through the eyes of early career social workers. *British Journal of Social Work*, 49 (6), 1434–1451.

Cordes, C. L. & Dougherty, T. W. (1993). A review and an integration of research on job burnout. *The Academy of Management Review*, 18 (4), 621–656.

Corrigan, P. W. & Rao, D. (2012). On the self-stigma of mental illness: stages, disclosure, and strategies for change. *Canadian Journal of Psychiatry*, 57 (8), 464–469.

Council of Europe (1950). *Convention on human rights*. www.hri.org/docs/ECHR50.html

Csiernik, R., Smith, C., Dewar, J., Dromgole, L. & O'Neill, A. (2010). Supporting new workers in a child welfare agency: an exploratory study. *Journal of Workplace Behavioral Health*, 25 (3), 218–232.

Cunningham, J., Cunningham, S. & O'Sullivan, A. (2023). *Sociology and social work* (3rd ed). Sage.

Curtis, C. (2024). The role of intuition in social work practice: differing understandings and attitudes. *Journal of Social Work Practice*, 38(3), 245–258.

D'Cruz, H., Gillingham, P., & Melendez, S. (2007). Reflexivity, its meanings and relevance for social work: a critical review of the literature. *British Journal of Social Work*, 37: 73–90.

Dane, B. (2000). Child welfare workers. *Journal of Social Work Education*, 36 (1), 27–38.

Daniel, B., Eady, S., Engstrom, S., McLenachan, J., Westwood, J. & Yule, N. (2016). *Revised standards in social work education and a benchmark standard for newly qualified social workers*. Dundee: Social Services Council. https://www.sssc.uk.com/knowledgebase/article/KA-01740/en-us

Daniel, C. (2011). The path to social work: Contextual determinants of career choice among racial/ethnic minority students. *Social Work Education*, 30 (8), 895–910.

Daniels, M. A. & Robinson, S. L. (2019). The shame of it all: A review of shame in organizational life. *Journal of Management*, 45 (6), 2448–2473.

Deal, K. H. & Pittman, J. (2009). Examining predictors of social work students' critical thinking skills. *Advances in Social Work*, 10 (1), 87–102.

Deigh, J. (1983). Shame and self-esteem: a critique. *Ethics*, 93 (2), 225–245.

Deonna, J. A., Rodogno, R. & Teroni, F. (2012). *In defense of shame: the faces of an emotion*. Oxford University Press.

Department for Education (DfE) (2014). *Knowledge and skills statement for child and family social work*. www.gov.uk/government/uploads/system/uploads/attachment_data/file/379033/Consultation_on_knowledge_and_skills_for_child_and_family_social_work_-_government_response.pdf

Department for Education (DfE) (2018). *Knowledge and skills statement for child and family social work*. Gov.uk. https://www.basw.co.uk/system/files/resources/basw_90824-6.pdf. Retrieved 27/06/23].

Dewey, J. (2005). *How we think*. Barnes and Noble.

DH (2005). *Mental Capacity Act*. TSO.

DH (2007). *Putting people first: A shared vision and commitment to the transformation of adult social care*. http://webarchive.nationalarchives.gov.uk/20130107105354/http://www.dh.gov.uk/en/Publicationsandstatistics/Publications/PublicationsPolicyAndGuidance/DH_081118

DH (2012). *Caring for our future: Reforming care and support*. www.gov.uk/government/uploads/system/uploads/attachment_data/file/136422/White-Paper-Caring-for-our-future-reforming-care-and-support-PDF-1580K.pdf

DH (2014). *The Care Act*. Department of Health. http://goo.gl/uvShns

DH (2015). *Knowledge and skills statement for social workers in adult services*. Gov.uk. www.basw.co.uk/system/files/resources/basw_115420-2_0.pdf

DH (2022). *Social work workforce review Northern Ireland 2022*. www.health-ni.gov.uk/publications/social-work-workforce-review-northern-ireland-2022

DHSSPS (Department of Health, Social Services and Public Safety) (2015). *Assessed Year in Employment (AYE) of Newly Qualified Social Workers (NQSW): Implementation of the AYE Policy*. Circular HSS (OSS) AYE 2/2015. DHSSPS.

Dillenburger, K. (2004). Causes and alleviation of occupational stress in child care work. *Child Care in Practice*, 10 (3), 213–224.

Dolezal, L. (2017). Shame, vulnerability and belonging: reconsidering Sartre's account of shame. *Human Studies*, 40 (3), 421–438.

Dominelli, L. & Holloway, M. (2008). Ethics and governance in social work research in the UK. *British Journal of Social Work*, 38(5), 1009–1024.

Donnelly, G. F. (2022). Self-care strategies for living artfully: channeling Epictetus. *Journal of Interprofessional Education & Practice*, 29, 100579.

Dreyfus, S. E. (2004). The five-stage model of adult skill acquisition. *Bulletin of Science Technology and Society*, 24(3), 177–181.

Duchscher, J. E. B. (2009). Transition shock: the initial stage of role adaptation for newly graduated registered nurses. *Journal of Advanced Nursing*, 65(5), 1103–1113.

Dudley, J., R. (2000). Confronting stigma within the services system. *Social Work*, 45 (5), 449–455.

Duffy, M., Campbell, C. & Tosone, C. (2019). *Voices of social work through the troubles*. BASW and NISCC. Northern Ireland. https://basw.co.uk/policy-and-practice/resources/voices-social-work-through-troubles#:~:text=The%20key%20objective%20in%20this,Northern%20Ireland

Duffy, M., McConnell, T., Blair, C., Hanna, D., McIlveen, R., O'Donnell,K., O'Hanlon, J., Leavy, G., Fitzmaurice, B., Campbell, A.,McElroy, S. & Quinn, P. (2022). *Conflict, trauma and mental health*. www.cvsni.org/wp-content/uploads/2023/07/FINAL-Trauma-Services-Report.pdf

Duschinsky, R. & Kirk, G. (2014). 'I've come on this course to learn how to be politically minded': political discourses among students entering a social work programme. *European Journal of Social Work*, 17 (4), 587–599.

Dutton, J. E., Roberts, L. M. & Bednar, J. (2010). Pathways for positive identity construction at work: four types of positive identity and the building of social resources. *Academy of Management Review*, 35 (2), 265–293.

Earls Larrison, T. & Korr, W. S. (2013). Does social work have a signature pedagogy? *Journal of Social Work Education*, 49 (2), 194–206.

Ellett, A. J., Ellis, J. I., Westbrook, T. M. & Dews, D. (2007). A qualitative study of 369 child welfare professionals' perspectives about factors contributing to employee retention and turnover. *Children and Youth Services Review*, 29 (2), 264–281.

Elshout, M., Nelissen, R. M. A. & van Beest, I. (2017). Conceptualising humiliation. *Cognition and Emotion*, 31 (8), 1581–1594.

Endriulaitien , A., Žardeckait -Matulaitien , K., Pranckevi ien , A., Markšaityt , R., Tillman, D. R. & Hof, D. D. (2019). Self-stigma of seeking help and job burnout in mental health care providers: The comparative study of Lithuanian and the USA samples. *Journal of Workplace Behavioral Health*, 34 (2), 129–148.

Equality Act (2010). www.legislation.gov.uk/ukpga/2010/15/contents

Everitt, A. & Hardiker, P. (1996). *Evaluating for good practice*. BASW/Macmillan.

Facione, P. A. (1990). *Critical thinking: a statement of expert consensus for purposes of educational assessment and instruction (The Delphi Report)*. California Academic Press.

Fearnley, B. (2022). *Developing knowledge and skills for child and family social work*. Sage/Learning Matters.

Ferguson, G. M. (2022a) The importance of workplace learning for social workers. Insight 67. Glasgow: Institute for Research and Innovation in Social Services. The importance of workplace learning for social workers Iriss

Ferguson, G. M. (2022b) Influences on professional learning in the workplace. *In Scottish Social Services Council (2022) Promoting NQSW learning and development in the supported year*. Dundee: Scottish Social Services Council. https://www.nqsw.sssc.uk.com/promoting-nqsw-professional-learning-and-development-in-the-supported-year/

Figley, C. R. (2002). Compassion fatigue: psychotherapists' chronic lack of self care. *Journal of Clinical Psychology*, 58 (11), 1433–1441.

Finklestein, M. & Laufer, A. (2021). Resilience, growth, and posttraumatic symptoms among social workers who are 'doubly exposed'. *Social Work Research*, 45 (4), 231–242.

Fish, S., Munro, E. & Bairstow, S. (2008). *SCIE Guide 24: Leading together to safeguard children: developing a multi-agency systems approach to case reviews*. SCIE. www.scie.org.uk/publications/guides/guide24/index.asp

Fletcher, J. (1966). *Situation ethics: The new morality*. Westminster Press.

Fletcher, S. (2007). Mentoring adult learners: realizing possible selves, in M. Rossiter (Ed.), *New directions for adult and continuing education*. Jossey-Bass, 75–86.

Fletcher, S. J. & Mullen, C. A. (2012). *Sage handbook of mentoring and coaching in education*. Sage.

Fook, J., & Gardner, F. (2007). *Practising critical reflection: A resource handbook*. Open University Press.

Foucault, M. (1977). *Discipline and punish*. Translated by Sheridan, A. (Ed). Penguin Books.

Foucault, M (1991). 'Governmentality', trans. Rosi Braidotti and revised by Colin Gordon, in Graham Burchell, Colin Gordon and Peter Miller (eds.), *The Foucault effect: studies in governmentality*. University of Chicago Press, 87–104.

Fowler, A. (1996). *Employee induction: a good start*. IPD.

Freire, P. (1970). *Pedagogy of the oppressed*. Penguin Books.

Freudenberger, H. J. (1974). Staff burn-out. *Journal of Social Issues*, 30 (1), 159–165.

Frost, L., Magyar-Haas, V., Holger, S. & Sicora, A. (2021). *Shame and social work: theory, reflexivity and practice*. Policy Press.

Furness, S. (2007). An enquiry into students' motivations to train as social workers in England. *Journal of Social Work*, 7 (2), 239–253.

Gambrill, E. (1993). What critical thinking offers to clinicians and clients. *Behavior Therapist*, 16 (6), 141–147.

Gardner, A. (2011). *Personalisation in social work*. Learning Matters.

Germain, C.B. and Gitterman, A. (1981). *The Life Model of Social Work*. Columbia University Press.

Gewirtz-Meydan, A. & Even-Zohar, A. (2018). Retraining programmes in social work: career considerations, factors influencing the decision to study social work and professional preferences among students. *European Journal of Social Work*, 21 (4), 585–601.

Gibbons, J. & Gray, M. (2004). Critical thinking as integral to social work practice. *Journal of Teaching in Social Work*, 24 (1), 19–38.

Gibbs, G. (1988). *Learning by doing: a guide to teaching and learning methods*. Further Education Unit, Oxford Polytechnic.

Gibbs, L. & Gambrill, E. (1999). *Critical thinking for social workers: exercises for the helping professions*. Sage.

Gibbs, L. E. (1991). *Scientific reasoning for social workers: bridging the gap between research and practice*. Macmillan.

Gibson, F., McGrath, A. & Reid, N. (1989). Occupational stress in social work. *British Journal of Social Work*, 19 (1), 1–16.

Gibson, M. (2014). Social worker shame in child and family social work: inadequacy, failure, and the struggle to practise humanely. *Journal of Social Work Practice*, 28 (4), 417–431.

Gibson, M. (2015). Shame and guilt in child protection social work: new interpretations and opportunities for practice. *Child & Family Social Work*, 20 (3), 333–343.

Gibson, M. (2016). Social worker shame: a scoping review: table 1. *British Journal of Social Work*, 46 (2), 549–565.

Gil, S. & Weinberg, M. (2015). Secondary trauma among social workers treating trauma clients: the role of coping strategies and internal resources. *International Social Work*, 58 (4), 551–561.

Gilbert, P. (1998). *What is shame? Some core issues and controversies. Shame: Interpersonal behavior, psychopathology, and culture*. Oxford University Press, 3–38.

Gilbert, P. (2003). Evolution, social roles, and the differences in shame and guilt. *Social Research: An International Quarterly*, 70 (4), 1205–1230.

Gilbert, P. (2007). *Psychotherapy and counselling for depression* (3rd ed). Sage.

Gilbert, P. & Andrews, B. (1998). *Shame: interpersonal behaviour, psychopathology, and culture*. Oxford University Press.

Gillies, B. (2016). *Implementing a probationary year for social workers in Scotland, February 2016*. Dundee: Scottish Social Services Council. www.sssc.uk.com/knowledgebase/article/KA-01738/en-us

Gilligan, C. (1982). *In a Different Voice: Psychological Theory and Women's Development*. Harvard University Press.

Gilligan, P. (2007). Well motivated reformists or nascent radicals: how do applicants to the degree in social work see social problems, their origins and solutions. *British Journal of Social Work*, 37: 735–60.

Goffman, E. (1959/1990). *The presentation of self in everyday life*. Penguin.

Gordon, J., Gracie, C. and Robertson, L. (2020) Executive Summary of the Evaluation of a Pilot Project for Newly Qualified Social Workers (NQSWs) in Scotland. Dundee: Scottish Social Services Council. https://www.sssc.uk.com/knowledgebase/article/KA02927/

Grant, L. & Kinman, G. (Eds.) (2014). *Developing resilience for social work practice*. Palgrave.

Grant, L., Kinman, G. & Alexander, K. (2014). What's all this talk about emotion? Developing emotional intelligence in social work students. *Social Work Education*, 33 (7), 874–889.

Grant, S., Sharidan, L. & Webb, S. (2014). *Readiness for practice of newly qualified social workers*. Glasgow Caledonian University.

Grant, S., McCulloch, T., Daly, M., Macleod, M. & Kettle, M. (2022). *Newly qualified social workers in Scotland: a five-year longitudinal study*. Scottish Social Services Council. www.sssc.uk.com/knowledgebase/article/KA-03313/en-us

Grant, S., McCulloch, T., Kettle, M., Sheridan, L. & Webb, S. (2017b). *Newly qualified social workers in Scotland: A five-year longitudinal study*. Scottish Social Services Council. www.sssc.uk.com/knowledgebase/article/KA-02259/en-us

Grant, S., Sheridan, L. & Webb, S.A (2017a). Newly qualified social workers' readiness for practice. *British Journal of Social Work*, 47 (2), 487–506. https://doi.org/10.1093/bjsw/bcv146

Gray, D.E. (2009). *Doing Research in the Real World* 3edn. Sage Publications.

Gray, I., Field, R. & Brown, K. (2010). *Effective leadership, management and supervision in health and social care*. Learning Matters.

Gilbert, P. & Andrews, B. (1998). *Shame: interpersonal behaviour, psychopathology, and culture*. Oxford University Press.

Gray, I., Parker, J., Rutter, L. & Williams, S. (2013). Developing communities of practice: a strategy for effective leadership, management and supervision in social work, in Lawler, J. & Hafford-Letchfield, T. (Eds.). *Perspectives on management and leadership in social work*. Whiting and Birch, 118–39.

Greenwood, E. (1957). Attributes of a profession. *Social Work*, 2(3), 45–55.

Guthrie, J. (2023). Swimming with the current but against the tide: reflections of an autistic social worker. *British Journal of Social Work*, 53(3), 1700–1710.

Gwilym, H. (2023). The social policy context for social work in Wales, in Livingston, W., Redcliffe, J. & Quinn Aziz, A. (Eds.). *Social work in Wales*. Policy Press, 5–15.

Hackett, S., Kuronen, M., Matthies, A.-L. & Kresal, B. (2003). The motivation, professional development and identity of social work students in four European countries. *European Journal of Social Work*, 6 (2), 163–178.

Hafford-Letchfield, T., & Engelbrecht, L. (2020). *Contemporary practices in social work supervision: Time for new paradigms?* Routledge.

Halmaghi, E-E. & Elida-Tomita, T. (2023). Creating a Learning Culture in the Organisation. *Scientific Bulletin*. 28(2), 210–214.

Halton, C., Powell, F. & Scandon, M. (2013). *Continuing professional development in social work*. Policy Press.

Hamill, B., Boyle, S. & McFadden, P. (2023). The impact of mentoring interventions to support newly qualified social workers during the COVID-19 pandemic in Northern Ireland. *European Social Work Research*, 1(3), 329–344 DOI: 10.1332/QWBE5026

Hamm, R.M. (1988). Clinical intuition and clinical analysis: expertise and the cognitive continuum, in Dowie, J.A. & Elstein, A. S. (Eds.). *Professional judgement: a reader in clinical decision-making*. Cambridge University Press, 78–105.

Handy, C. (1993). *Understanding organisations* (4th ed). Penguin.

Harris, A., Jones, M., & Ismail, N. (2022). Distributed leadership: taking a retrospective and contemporary view of the evidence base. *School Leadership & Management*, 42(5), 438–456. https://doi.org/10.1080/13632434.2022.2109620

Hart, E. & Bond, M. (1995). *Action research for health and social care*. Open University Press.

Harvey, O., & Oliver, L. (2024). The use of poetry in form of haikus as a tool for critical reflection. *Social Work Education*, 44(3), 636–654. https://doi.org/10.1080/02615479.

Hawkins, P. & Shohet, R. (2007). *Supervising in the helping professions* (3rd ed). OUP.

Healy, K. (2000). *Social work practices: contemporary perspectives on change*. Sage.

Hejdenberg, J. & Andrews, B. (2011). The relationship between shame and different types of anger: A theory-based investigation. *Personality and Individual Differences*, 50 (8), 1278–1282.

Henriksen, Ø. (2023). Coherence and transition. Meaningful connections and challenging transitions in social work. *Social Work Education*, 42:(6) 793–808.

Higham, P. (1999). Vocational qualifications: an opportunity for professional social work education. *Social Work Education*, 18(1), 35–52.

Hollederer, A. (2022). Working conditions, health and exhaustion among social workers in Germany. *European Journal of Social Work*, 25 (5), 792–803.

Holmes, T. H. & Rahe, R. H. (1967). The social re-adjustment rating scale. *Journal of Psychosomatic Research*, 11: 213–18.

Holter, J. (2018). Development of professional identity in social work education. *Doctor of Social Work Banded Dissertation*, 31. https://ir.stthomas.edu/ssw_docdiss/31

Hood, R. (2024). *Inequality and its implications for the social work profession: Reflections on the UK Joint Universities Social Work Association Conference*. British Journal of Social Work, 54(8), 3425–3428.

Horwitz, M. (2006). Work-related trauma effects in child protection social workers. *Journal of Social Service Research*, 32 (1), 1–18.

Houkes, I., Janssen, P. P. M., De Jonge, J. & Nijhuis, F. J. N. (2001). Work and individual determinants of intrinsic work motivation, emotional exhaustion, and turnover intention: a multi-sample analysis. *International Journal of Stress Management*, 8, 257–283.

Howe, D. (2008). *The emotionally intelligent social worker*. Palgrave.

Howe, K. & Gray, I. (2012). *Effective supervision in social work*. Sage/Learning Matters.

Hughes, M. (2019). *A guide to statutory social work interventions: the lived experience*. Palgrave.

Human Rights Act (1998). www.legislation.gov.uk/ukpga/1998/42/contents

Ingram, R. (2015). *Understanding emotions in social work: theory, practice and reflection*. Open University Press.

Innes-Turnill, D. (2023). Child abuse, the narrative of parents living in poverty: a critical analysis of parental and professional explanations of why a child was harmed. *Journal of Social Work Practice*, 37(2), 183–197.

International Federation of Social Workers (IFSW) (2014). *Global definition of the social work profession*. http://ifsw.org/policies/definition-of-social-work/

Jack, G. & Donnellan, H. (2010). Recognising the person within the developing professional: tracking the early careers of newly qualified child care social workers in three local authorities in England. *Social Work Education*, 29(3): 305–18.

Jay, T. and Hersen, M. (eds) (2011). Understanding research in clinical and counselling psychology (2nd ed) pp. 355–376. Routledge.

Jenkins, S. R. & Baird, S. (2002). Secondary traumatic stress and vicarious trauma: a validational study. *Journal of Traumatic Stress*, 15 (5), 423–432.

Johnson, B. (1996). *Polarity management: identifying and managing unsolvable problems* (2nd ed). HRD Press.

Jones, C., Ferguson, I., Lavalette, M. & Penketh, L. (2011). *Social work and social justice: a manifesto for a new engaged practice*. https://socialworkfuture.org/social-work-and-social-justice-a-manifesto-for-a-new-engaged-practice/

Jones, D.N. (2024). The global agenda for social work and social development: a conflicted global concept? *Practice*, 36(2), 101–109.

Jones, K. (2003). The turn to a narrative knowing of persons: One method explored. *Journal of Research in Nursing*, 8(1), 60–71.

Johnson, T.J. (1972). *Professions and Power*. Macmillan.

Kagan, M. & Greenblatt Kimron, L. (2021). Psychological distress among social workers. *Journal of Social Work*, 21 (5), 1243–1260.

Kagan, M. & Itzick, M. (2019). Work-related factors associated with psychological distress among social workers. *European Journal of Social Work*, 22 (1), 30–42.

Kahneman, D. (2011). *Thinking, fast and slow*. Penguin Books.

Kamya, H. (2000). Hardiness and spiritual well being among social work students: implications for social work education. *Journal of Social Work Education*, 36: 231–40.

Keen, S., Galpin, D., Brown, K. & Parker, J. (Eds.) (2016). *Newly-qualified social workers: a practice guide to the assessed and supported year in employment* (3rd ed). Learning Matters/Sage.

Keltner, D. & Buswell, B. N. (1996). Evidence for the distinctness of embarrassment, shame, and guilt: A study of recalled antecedents and facial expressions of emotion. *Cognition and Emotion*, 10, 155–171.

Kinman, G. & Grant, L. (2020). Emotional demands, compassion and mental health in social workers. *Occupational medicine*, 70 (2), 89–94.

Klein, W. C. & Bloom, M. (1995). Practice wisdom. *Social Work*, 40(6): 799–807.

Kolb, D. (1984). *experiential learning: experience as the source of learning and development*. Vol. 1. Prentice-Hall.

Kotera, Y., Tsuda-McCaie, F., Edwards, A.-M., Bhandari, D., Williams, D. & Neary, S. (2022). Mental health shame, caregiver identity, and self-compassion in UK education students. *Healthcare*, 10 (3), 584, doi: 10.3390/healthcare10030584.

Krill, D. (1996). *Practice wisdom*. Sage.

Laal, M. & Salamati, P. (2012). Lifelong learning; why do we need it? *Procedia-Social and Behavioral Sciences*, 31, 399–403.

Laing, J. (2022). Making sense of shame. *Philosophy*, 97 (2), 233–255.

Laming, H. (2003). *The Victoria Climbié Inquiry*. TSO. www.victoria-climbie-inquiry.org.uk

Laming, H. (2009). *The Protection of Children in England: A progress report*. The Stationery Office.

Larkin, G. (1983). *Occupational Monopoly and Modern Medicine*. Tavistock.

Leberman, S. I. & Martin, A. J. (2003). Does pushing comfort zones produce peak learning experiences? *Australian Journal of Outdoor Education*, 7, 10+.

Leigh, J. (2018). Blame, culture and child protection. *Aotearoa New Zealand Social Work*, 30, 93.

Lewis, H. B. (1971). *Shame and guilt in neurosis*. International Universities Press.

Lewis, M. (2003). The role of the self in shame. *Social Research: An International Quarterly*, 70 (4), 1181–1204.

Lewis, M., Alessandri, S. M. & Sullivan, M. W. (1992). Differences in shame and pride as a function of children's gender and task difficulty. *Child Development*, 63 (3), 630–638.

LGA (Local Government Association) (2014). *Standards for Employers of Social Workers in England*. LGA. www.local.gov.uk/documents/10180/6188796/The+Standards+-+updated+July+01+2014/146988cc-d9c5-4311-97d4-20dfc19397bf or http://cdn.basw.co.uk/upload/basw_33012-2.pdf

LGA (Local Government Association) (2014a). *What you should expect as a social worker?* LGA. www.local.gov.uk/documents/10180/6188796/What_should_you_expect_as_social_worker.pdf/8e7fed0c-32d9-4b6a-a213-b06e7c7d1e0d

Liedgren, P. (2020). 'We know what we are, but know not what we may be' – research-minded practitioners and their possible futures in social work. *Nordic Social Work Research*, 12(1), 87–96. https://doi.org/10.1080/2156857X.2020.1793807

Lillis, T. (2023). Professional written voice 'in flux': the case of social work. *Applied Linguistics Review*, 14(3), 615–641.

Lillis, T., Leedham, M. & Twiner, A. (2017). 'If it's not written down it didn't happen': contemporary social work as a writing-intensive profession. *Journal of Applied Linguistics and Professional Practice*, 14(1), 29–52.

Lillis, T., Leedham, M. & Twiner, A. (2020). Time, the written record, and professional practice: the case of contemporary social work. *Written Communication*, 37(4), 431–486.

Lim, L. (2011). Beyond logic and argument analysis: critical thinking, everyday problems and democratic deliberation in Cambridge international examinations' thinking skills curriculum. *Journal of Curriculum Studies*, 43 (6), 783–807.

Lindsey, D., & Schlonsky, A. (Eds.). (2008). Child welfare research: Advances for practice and policy. Oxford University Press.

Lloyd, C., King, R. & Chenoweth, L. (2002). Social work, stress and burnout: a review. *Journal of Mental Health*, 11 (3), 255–265.

Local Government Association (2014). *Open dialogue open doors open minds - HR's role in transforming social work delivery*. LGA.

Macdonald, K.M. (1995). *The Sociology of the Professions*. Sage

Maclean, S. & Harrison, R. (2009). *Making the most of your practice learning opportunities: OR... Everything you ever wanted to know about social work placements*. Kirwin Maclean Associates.

Maclean, S. & Lloyd, I. (2008). *Developing quality practice learning in social work: a straightforward guide for practice teachers and supervisors*. Kirwin Maclean Associates.

Maddock, A. (2024). The relationships between stress, burnout, mental health and well-being in social workers. *The British Journal of Social Work*, 54, (2), 668–686, https://doi.org/10.1093/bjsw/bcad232

Maglajlic, R.A. & Ioakimidis, V. (2022). Deliberately silenced and preferably unheard, Part Two—Discriminatory epistemic injustice and distributive injustice in social work. *British Journal of Social Work*, 52(1), 1–5.

Maher, B., Appleton, C., Benge, D. & Perham, T. (2003). *The criticality of induction training to professional social work care and protection practice*. Paper presented to the ninth Australasian Conference on Child Abuse and Neglect: Sydney.

Mahesh, S., Lowther, J. & Miller, R. (2024). improving quality in social work: the role of peer challenge. *The British Journal of Social Work*, 54(4), 1719–1736, https://doi.org/10.1093/bjsw/bcad252

Management Standards Centre (2015). *Standards*. www.management-standards.org/standards/standards

Manthorpe, J., Moriarty, J., Hussein, S., Stevens, M. & Sharpe, E. (2015). Content and purpose of supervision in social work practice in England: views of newly qualified social workers, managers and directors. *British Journal of Social Work*, 45: 52–68.

Marsh, P. (2006). Promoting children's welfare by inter-professional practice and learning in social work and primary care. *Social Work Education*, 25(2), 148-160.

Maslach, C., Schaufeli, W. B. & Leiter, M. P. (2001). Job burnout. *Annual Review of Psychology*, 52 (1), 397.

Mathias, J. (2015). Thinking like a social worker: examining the meaning of critical thinking in social work. *Journal of Social Work Education*, 51 (3), 457–474.

McBeath, B & Austin, M. J. (2014). The organizational context of research-minded practitioners: challenges and opportunities. *Research on Social Work Practice*, 25(4), 446-459. https://doi.org/10.1177/1049731514536233

McBride, P. (1998). *The assertive social worker*. Ashgate.

McCall, G. J. & Simmons, J. L. (1966). *Identities and interactions*. Free Press.

McDonald, A., Postle, K. & Dawson, C. (2008). Barriers to retaining and using professional knowledge in Local Authority social work practice with adults in the UK. *British Journal of Social Work*, 38(7), 1370–1387.

McFadden, P. (2015). *Measuring burnout among UK social workers: a community care study*. www.qub.ac.uk/schools/media/Media,513723,en.pdf

McFadden, P., Campbell, A. & Taylor, B. (2015). Resilience and burnout in child protection social work: individual and organisational themes from a systematic literature review. *The British Journal of Social Work*, 45 (5), 1546–1563.

McFadden, P., Davies, H., Manthorpe, J.

MacLochlainn, J. McGrory, S. Naylor,R. Mallett, J. Kirby, K. Currie, D. Schroder, H. Nicholl, P. Mullineux, J. & McColgan M. (2024). Safe staffing and workload management in social work: a scoping review of legislation, policy and practice. *The British Journal of Social Work*, 54(5), 2006–2026.

McFadden, P., Mallett, J., Campbell, A. & Taylor, B. (2019). Explaining self-reported resilience in child-protection social work: the role of organisational factors, demographic information and job characteristics. *British Journal of Social Work*, 49(1): 198–216.

McFadden, P., Neill, R., Mallett, J., Manthorpe, J., Gillens, P., Moriarty, J., Currie, D., Schroder, H., Ravalier, J., Nicholl, P. & Ross, J. (2022). Mental well-being and quality of working life in uk social workers before and during the COVID-19 pandemic: a propensity score matching study. *British Journal of Social Work* 52, 2814–2833.

McMahon, A., Jennings, C., & O'Brien, G. (2022). A naturalistic, observational study of the seven-eyed model of supervision. *The Clinical Supervisor*, 41(1), 47–69. https://doi.org/10.1080/07325223.2021.2022060

Mehra, A., Smith, B. R., Dixon, A. L. & Robertson, B. (2006). Distributed leadership in teams: the network of leadership perceptions and team performance. *The Leadership Quarterly*, 17: 232–45.

Mental Health Act (1983). www.legislation.gov.uk/ukpga/1983/20/contents

Mental Health Act (2007). www.legislation.gov.uk/ukpga/2007/12/contents

Middleton, J. S. & Potter, C. C. (2015). Relationship between vicarious traumatization and turnover among child welfare professionals. *Journal of Public Child Welfare*, 9 (2), 195–216.

Miller, J. B. (1976). *Toward a new psychology of women*. Beacon Press.

Miller, J. (2023). Beyond Statistical Significance: A Holistic View of What Makes a Research Finding 'Important'. *Numeracy: Advancing Education in Quantitative Literacy*, 16 (1), 1–21.

Moon, J. (2005). *We seek it here … A new perspective on the elusive activity of critical thinking: a theoretical and practical approach*. ESCalate.

Moorhead, B., Manthorpe, J. & Baginsky, M. (2020). An examination of support and development mechanisms for newly qualified social workers across the UK: implications for Australian social work. *Practice*, 32 (2), 145–159.

Mor Barak, M. E., Nissly, J. & Levin, A. (2001). Antecedents to retention and turnover among child welfare, social work, and other human service employees: What can we learn from past research? A review and metanalysis. *The Social Service Review*, 75, 625–662.

Mor Barak, M., Travis, D., Pyun, H. & Xie, B. (2009). The impact of supervision on worker outcomes: a meta-analysis. *Social Service Review*, 83(1): 3–32.

Mordue, S.J. (2023). *The resilience handbook: exploring the three pillars of resilience*. Shorts Media.

Moriarty, J., Baginsky, M. & Manthorpe, J. (2015). *Literature review of roles and issues within the social work profession in England*. Social Care Workforce Research Unit, KCL.

Moriarty, J., Manthorpe, J., Steven, M. & Hussein, S. (2011). Making the transition: comparing research on newly qualified social workers with other professions. *British Journal of Social Work*, 41: 1340–56.

Moudatsou, M., Stavropoulou, A., Philalithis, A. & Koukouli, S. (2020). The role of empathy in health and social care professionals. *Healthcare*, 8(1), 26, DOI: 10.3390/healthcare8010026

MSH (Management Sciences for Health) and UNICEF (1998). *Welcome to managing for quality*. http://erc.msh.org/quality/

Mun, C. (2019). Unification through the rationalities and intentionalities of shame, in Mun, C. (Ed.) *Interdisciplinary perspectives on shame*. Lexington Books.

Munro, E. (2011). *The Munro review of child protection: final report – a child-centred system*. The Department of Education. www.gov.uk/government/publications/munro-review-of-child-protection-final-report-a-child-centred-system

Murphy, E. (2021). A reflection on social work students as the wounded healer. *Relational Social Work*, 6 (1), 73–83.

Ng, T. W. H. & Feldman, D. C. (2007). The school-to-work transition: a role identity perspective. *Journal of Vocational Behavior*, 71 (1), 114–134.

NHS (2020). *Online library of quality, service improvement and redesign tools, Pareto Analysis*. NHS.

Norcross, J. C. & Farber, B. A. (2005). Choosing psychotherapy as a career: beyond 'I want to help people'. *Journal of Clinical Psychology*, 61 (8), 939–943.

Northern Ireland Social Care Council (2015). *Standards of Conduct and Practice for Social Workers*. NISCC. https://niscc.info/app/uploads/2023/03/Standards-for-Social-Workers.pdf

Northern Ireland Social Care Council (2019). *Standards of conduct and practice for social workers*. https://niscc.info/app/uploads/2023/03/Standards-for-Social-Workers.pdf

Northern Ireland Social Care Council (2021). *The assessed year in employment (AYE) for newly qualified social workers in NI: revised guidance for registrants and their employers*. Northern Ireland Social Care Council.

Northern Ireland Social Care Council (2022a). *The assessed year in employment for newly qualified social workers in Northern Ireland*. https://learningzone.niscc.info/social-worker-assessed-year-in-employment-aye/

Northern Ireland Social Care Council (2022b). *(Registration) Rules*. NISCC. https://niscc.info/app/uploads/2020/09/20250310_Registration-Rules-2025_Final_Signed_CC.pdf

Northern Ireland Social Care Council (2023). *Strategic plan. Supporting safety, quality and improvement in social work and social care 2023–2027*. https://niscc.info/strategic-plan/

Northern Ireland Statistics and Research Agency (NISRA) (2024). *Census 2023* NISRA.gov.uk www.nisra.gov.uk/system/files/statistics/2025-06/MYE23-bulletin_2.pdf

Novell, R. J. (2014). *Starting social work: reflections of a newly qualified social worker*. Critical Publishing.

NSWQB (2004). *Induction study: a study of the induction needs of newly qualified and non-nationally qualified social workers in health boards*. NSWQB.

Nussbaum, M. (2006). *Hiding from humanity: disgust, shame and the Law*. Princeton University Press.

O'Donoghue, K., & Engelbrecht, L. (Eds.). (2023). *The Routledge international handbook of social work supervision*. Routledge.

O'Rourke. M., Maguire, C., Tanner, L, & Mullineux, J. (2020). Testing partnership and preparedness in Northern Ireland during COVID-19. *Social Work Education* 39(8):1084–1093. DOI: 10.1080/02615479.2020.1825664

O'Rourke. M., McVicker, H., & Maguire, C. (2023). Risk and regulation of the social care workforce, in Taylor, B., Fluke, J., Graham, J.C., Keddel, E., Killick, C., Shlonsky, A. & Whittaker, A. (Eds.), *The Sage handbook of decision making, assessment and risk in social work*. Sage, 557–566.

Ovretveit, J. (2014). *Evaluating Improvement and Implementation for Health*. OUP.

Parker, J. (2024). *Analysing the history of british social welfare: compassion, control and ambivalence*. Policy Press.

Parker, J. (2025). *Social work practice: assessment, planning, intervention and review* (7th ed). Sage/Learning Matters.

Parker, J. and Doel, M. (2014). *Professional social work*. Sage/Learning Matters.

Parker, J., Ashencaen Crabtree, S., Azman, A., Carlo, D.P. & Cutler, C. (2014). Problematising international placements as a site of intercultural learning. *European Journal of Social Work*, 18(3): 383–96.

Parker, J., Ashencaen Crabtree, S., Baba, I., Carlo, D. P. & Azman, A. (2012). Liminality and learning: international placements as a rite of passage. *Asia Pacific Journal of Social Work and Development*, 22(3): 146–58.

Parker, J., Whitfield, J. & Doel, M. (2006). *Effective practice learning in local authorities: workforce development, recruitment and retention*. Practice Learning Taskforce.

Pawson, R., Boaz, A., Grayson, L., Long, A. & Barnes, C. (2003). *Types and quality of knowledge in social care, SCIE Knowledge Review 3*. Policy Press. www.scie.org.uk/publications/knowledgereviews/kr03.pdf

Pearlman, L. A. & Saakvitne, K. W. (1995). *Trauma and the therapist: Countertransference and vicarious traumatization in psychotherapy with incest survivors*. WW Norton & Co.

Pearson, G. (1973). Social work as the privatized solution of public ills. *The British Journal of Social Work*, 3(2), 209–227.

Pentaraki, M. (2017). 'I am in a constant state of insecurity trying to make ends meet, like our service users': shared austerity reality between social workers and service users—towards a preliminary conceptualisation. *The British Journal of Social Work*, 47 (4), 1245–1261.

Peters, T. (1989). *The customer revolution*. BBC training videos, BBC.

Phillipson, J. (2002). Supervision and being supervised, in Adams, R., Dominelli, L. & Payne, M. (Eds.). *Critical practice in social work*. Palgrave Macmillan, 244–51.

Postle, K., Edwards, C., Moon, R., Rumsey, H. & Thomas, T. (2002). Continuing professional development after qualification – partnerships, pitfalls and potential. *Social Work Education*, 21(2), 157–169.

Pritchard, C. & Williams, R. (2009). Does Social Work Make a Difference? A Controlled Study of Former `Looked-After-Children' and `Excluded-From-School' Adolescents Now Men Aged 16–24: Subsequent Offences, Being Victims of Crime and Suicide. *Journal of Social Work*, Vol 9(3), pp. 285–307.

Pritchard, C., Davey, J. and Williams, R. (2013). Who Kills Children? Re-Examining the Evidence, *British Journal of Social Work*, 43(7), pp. 1403–1438.

Quinney, A. & Hafford-Letchfield, T. (2012). *Interprofessional social work: effective collaborative approaches* (2nd ed). Sage.

Rai, L., Ferguson, G. & Giddings, L. (2025). Writing as social work: thematic review of the literature. *British Journal of Social Work*, 55(1), 25-44. http://10.1093/bjsw/bcae124

Ratcliff, M. (2024). Social workers, burnout, and self-care: a public health issue. *Delaware Journal of Public Health*, 10(1), 26–29. doi: 10.32481/djph.2024.03.05

Ravalier, J. M. (2019). Psycho-social working conditions and stress in UK social workers. *British Journal of Social Work*, 49 (2), 371–390.

Ravalier, J., McFadden, P., Gillen, P., Mallett, J., Nicholl, P., Neill, R., Manthorpe, J., Moriarty, J., Schroder, H. & Curry, D. (2022). Working conditions and well-being in UK social care and social work during COVID-19. *Journal of Social Work*, 23 (2), 165–188.

Ravalier, J., Wainwright, E., Clabburn, O., Loon, M. & Smyth, N. (2020). Working conditions and wellbeing in UK social workers. *Journal of Social Work*, 21 (5), 1105–1123.

Ravalier, J., Wegrzynek, P., Mitchell, A., McGowan, J., Mcfadden, P. & Bald, C. (2023). A rapid review of reflective supervision in social work. *The British Journal of Social Work*, 53(4), 1945–1962, https://doi.org/10.1093/bjsw/bcac223.

Rawles, J. (2016). Developing social work professional judgement skills: enhancing learning in practice by researching learning in practice. *Journal of Teaching on Social Work*, 36(1), 102–122.

Reeves, T.D., Hamilton, V. & Onder, Y. (2022). Which teacher induction practices work? Linking forms of induction to teacher practices, self-efficacy, and job satisfaction, *Teaching and Teacher Education*, 109, 103546, https://doi.org/10.1016/j.tate.2021.103546

Rogers, A. M. (2001). Nurture, bureaucracy and re-balancing the mind and heart. *Journal of Social Work Practice*, 15 (2), 181–191.

Rogowski, S. (2020). *Social Work: The rise and fall of a profession* (2nd ed). Policy Press.

Rolfe, G., Freshwater, D. & Jasper, M. (2001). *Critical reflection in nursing and the helping professions: a user's guide*. Palgrave Macmillan.

Rolfe, G., Freshwater, D. & Jasper, M. (2011). *Critical reflection in practice: generating knowledge for care* (2nd ed). Palgrave.

Rompf, E., L. & Royse, D. (1994). Choice of social work as a career: possible influences. *Journal of Social Work Education*, 30 (2), 163–171.

Rose, S. & Palattiyil, G. (2018). Surviving or thriving? Enhancing the emotional resilience of social workers in their organisational settings. *Journal of Social Work*, 20 (1), 23–42.

Rossi, P. H., Lispey, M. W. & Freeman, H. E. (2004). *Evaluation: a systematic approach* (7th ed). Sage.

Roulston, A., Hayes, D., Ross, J., Montgomery, L., MacDermott, D., McFadden, P. & Boyle, S. (2022). *Evaluating the motivation, well-being, resilience and employment preferences of social work graduates over time*. Queen's University.

Roulston, A., Ross, J., McFadden, P., Boyle, S., Mackle, D., MacDermott, D., Montgomery, L. & Hayes, D. (2024). A baseline survey of levels of motivation, well-being, and employment preferences of newly qualified social workers in the UK. *Social Work Education*, 1–17. https://doi.org/10.1080/02615479.2024.2380474

Rowlingson, K. & McKay, S. (2009). Income maintenance and taxation, in Bochel, H., Bochel, C., Page, R. & Sykes, R. (Eds.). *Social policy: issues and developments* (2nd ed). Longman.

Ruch, G., Turney, D., & Ward, A. (2010). *Relationship-based social work*. Jessica Kingsley.

Rush, D. (2023). *The essential guide to building your argument*. Sage.

Rutter, L. & Brown, K. (2015). *Critical thinking and professional judgement in social work* (4th ed). Sage/Learning Matters.

Sabini, J., Garvey, B. & Hall, A. L. (2001). Shame and embarrassment revisited. *Personality and Social Psychology Bulletin*, 27 (1), 104–117.

Salston, M. & Figley, C. R. (2003). Secondary traumatic stress effects of working with survivors of criminal victimization. *Journal of Traumatic Stress*, 16, 167–174.

Samson, P. L. (2015). Practice wisdom: the art and science of social work. *Journal of Social Work Practice*, 29(2): 119–131.

Sánchez-Moreno, E., de La Fuente Roldán, I.-N., Gallardo-Peralta, L. P. & Barrón López deRoda, A. (2015). Burnout, informal social support and psychological distress among social workers. *British Journal of Social Work*, 45 (8), 2368–2386.

Saxena, A. & Chandrapal, S. (2022). Social work and policy practice: understanding the role of social workers. *British Journal of Social Work*, 52 (3), 1632–1642.

Scheff, T. (2014). The ubiquity of hidden shame in modernity. *Cultural Sociology*, 8 (2), 129–141.

Schernhammer, E. (2005). Taking their own lives – the high rate of physician suicide. *New England Journal of Medicine*, 352 (24), 2473–2476.

Schmader, T. & Lickel, B. (2006). The approach and avoidance function of guilt and shame emotions: comparing reactions to self-caused and other-caused wrongdoing. *Motivation and Emotion*, 30, 42–55.

Schön, D. (1983). *The reflective practitioner – how professionals think in action*. Basic Books.

SCIE (2012). *At a glance 01: learning together to safeguard children: a systems model for case reviews*. www.scie.org.uk/publications/ataglance/ataglance01.asp

SCIE (2015). *Study resource: organisational change in social care*. www.scie.org.uk/publications/elearning/organisational-change-in-social-care/

SCIE (2022). *Leadership in strengths-based social care*. https://www.scie.org.uk/strengths-based-approaches/leadership/

Scottish Government (2015). *Social services in Scotland: a shared vision and strategy 2015-2020*.

Scottish Government (2018). *Perspectives on the introduction of a mandatory, supported, assessed year for newly qualified social workers*. Scottish Government. www.sssc.uk.com/knowledgebase/article/KA-02732/en-us

Scottish Social Services Council (2016). *Codes of practice for social service workers and employers*. Scottish Social Services Council. www.sssc.uk.com/knowledgebase/article/KA-02412/en-us

Scottish Social Services Council (2019). *Standards in social work education in Scotland*. Scottish Social Services Council. https://learn.sssc.uk.com/siswe/siswe.html

Scottish Social Services Council (2020). *Codes of practice for social service workers and employers*.

Scottish Social Services Council (2022). *Evidencing the NQSW supported year*. Scottish Social Services Council. www.nqsw.sssc.uk.com/implementing-the-approach-resources-for-early-implementation-areas/

Scottish Social Services Council (2023a). *Scottish social service sector: Report on 2022 Workforce Data, September 2023*. Scottish Social Services Council. https://data.sssc.uk.com/images/WDR/WDR2022.pdf

Scottish Social Services Council (2023b). *Overview of NQSW supported year implementation 2023-24, June 2023*. Scottish Social Services Council. www.sssc.uk.com/knowledgebase/article/KA-03507/en-us

Scottish Social Services Council (2024a) Scottish Social Service Sector: Report on 2023 Workforce Data, August 2024. Dundee: Scottish Social Services Council. https://data.sssc.uk.com/images/WDR/WFDR_2023_20240826.pdf

Scottish Social Services Council (2024b) Core Learning Elements for Social Workers: Newly qualified social worker (NQSW) descriptors and mandatory learning activity, January 2024. Dundee: Scottish Social Services Council. https://www.sssc.uk.com/about-us/publications/core-learning-elements-for-social-workers-newly-qualified-social-worker-nqsw-descriptors-and-mandatory-learning-activity/

Scottish Social Services Council (2024c) NQSW Supported Year: Overview and guidance, January 2024. Dundee: Scottish Social Services Council. https://www.sssc.uk.com/about-us/publications/nqsw-supported-year-overview-and-guidance-2024/

Scottish Social Services Council (2024a). *Continuous professional learning (CPL)*. www.sssc.uk.com/supporting-the-workforce/continuous-professional-learning/

Scottish Social Services Council (2024b). *Newly qualified social worker (NQSW)*. www.nqsw.sssc.uk.com/about/

Sellers, S. L. & Hunter, A. G. (2005). Private pain, public choices: influence of problems in the family of origin on career choices among a cohort of MSW students. *Social Work Education*, 24 (8), 869–881.

Senge, P. M. (1990). *The fifth discipline: The art and practice of the learning organisation*. Random House.

Senge, P.M. (2006). *The fifth discipline: the art and practice of the learning organization* (2nd ed.). Random House Business Books.

Shen, L. (2018). The evolution of shame and guilt. *PloS one*, 13 (7), e0199448.

Sheppard, M., Charles, M., Rees, P., Wheeler, M. & Williams, R. (2018). Inter-personal and critical-thinking capabilities in those about to enter qualified social work: a six-centre study. *The British Journal of Social Work*, 48 (7), 1855–1873.

Shlomo, S., Levy, D. & Itzhaky, H. (2012). Development of professional identity among social work students: contributing factors. *The Clinical Supervisor*, 31, 240–255.

Showalter, S. E. (2010). Compassion fatigue: what is it? Why does it matter? Recognizing the symptoms, acknowledging the impact, developing the tools to prevent compassion fatigue, and strengthen the professional already suffering from the effects. *American Journal of Hospice and Palliative Medicine*, 27 (4), 239–242.

Showell Nicholas, W. & Kerr, J. (2015). *Practice educating social work students: supporting qualifying students on their placements*. Open University Press.

Siebert, D. & Siebert, C. (2005). The caregiver role identity scale: a validation study. *Research on Social Work Practice*, 15, 204–212.

Simpson, M., Daly, M. & Smith, M. (2020). The social work regulator and professional identity: A narrative of lord and bondsman. *British Journal of Social Work*, 50(6), 1909–1925.

Skeggs, B. and Wood, H. (2012). *Reacting to Reality Television: Audience, performance and value*. Routledge.

Skills for Care (2011a). *NQSW framework in adult services*. Skills for Care.

Skills for Care (2011b). *Newly qualified social worker (NQSW) resource pack*. Skills for Care.

Skills for Care (2024). *AYSE*. www.skillsforcare.org.uk/Regulated-professions/Social-work/ASYE/ASYE. aspx?gad_source=1&gclid=EAIaIQobChMIwMWEve63hAMVq4xQBh1gzgXsEAAYASAAEgIOg_D_BwE

Skills for Care/Children's Workforce Development Council (2007). *Providing effective supervision*. SfC/CWDC. www.skillsforcare.org.uk/Document-library/Finding-and-keeping-workers/Supervision/Providing-Effective-Supervision.pdf

Skoura-Kirk, E., Brown, S. & Mikelyte, R. (2021). Playing its part: an evaluation of professional skill development through service user-led role-plays for social work students. *Social Work Education*, 40(8), 977–993.

Smith, R. A. & Pilling, S. (2007). Allied health graduate program – supporting the transition from student to professional in an interdisciplinary program. *Journal of Interprofessional Care*, 21 (3), 265–276.

Social Care Wales (2011). *National occupational standards for social work*. socialcare.http://wales/nos-areas/social-work

Social Care Wales (2012). *Consolidation programme for newly qualified social workers: your questions answered*. https://socialcare.wales/cms-assets/documents/Consolidation-Programme-FAQ.pdf

Social Care Wales (2017). *Code of professional practice for social care*. https://socialcare.wales/cms-assets/documents/Code-of-Professional-Practice-for-Social-Care-web-version.pdf.

Social Care Wales (2018a). *Code of practice for social care employers*. https://Employers-code.pdf

Social Care Wales (2018). Continuing professional education and learning: a framework for social workers in Wales. *Requirements for the consolidation programme for newly qualified social workers*. https://Requirements-for-the-Consolidation-Programme-for-Newly-Qualified-Social-Workers.pdf

Social Care Wales (2019a). *The first three years in practice: a framework for newly qualified social workers' induction and continuing professional development*. (socialcare.wales).

Social Care Wales (2019b). *The social worker: practice guidance for social workers registered with social care Wales*. https://Practice-guidance-social-workers.pdf

Social Care Wales (2023). *Consolidation programme for newly qualified social workers – your questions answered*. Social Care Wales.

Social Care Wales (2023). *The first three years in practice A framework for newly - Qualified social workers' induction and continuing professional development*. https://socialcare.wales/cms-assets/documents/First-three-years-in-practice.pdf

Social Work England (2019). *Professional standards*. www.socialworkengland.org.uk/standards/professional-standards/

Social Work England (2024). *What Counts as CPD?* www.socialworkengland.org.uk/cpd/what-counts-as-cpd/#:~:text=CPD%20is%20not%20just%20about,practice%20in%20a%20particular%20area..

Social Work England (2022). *Continuing professional development (CPD) guidance for social workers.* www.socialworkengland.org.uk/cpd/cpd-guidance/#:~:text=Standard%204%20is%20about%20CPD,worker%20can%20do%20as%20CPD..

Social Work Task Force (2009). *Building a safe and confident future.* http://webarchive.nationalarchives.gov.uk/20130401151715/https://www.education.gov.uk/publications/standard/publicationdetail/page1/dcsf-01114-2009

Söderfeldt, M., Söderfeldt, B. & Warg, L.-E. (1995). Burnout in social work. *Social Work*, 40 (5), 638–646.

Starwars: The Empire Strikes Back. (1980). Film, USA.

Stein, J. (1956). *William Faulkner, the art of fiction.* The Paris Review.

Stevenson, L. (2018). *49% of ASYE social workers promised a protected caseload don't have one, a survey finds.* Community Care.

Stone, K., Vicary, S., Scott, C. & Buckland, R. (2020). Ethical approval and being a virtuous social work researcher. The experience of multi-site research in UK health and social care: An Approved Mental Health Professional case study. *Ethics and Social Welfare*, 14(2), 156–171.

Storey, J. & Billingham, J. (2001). Occupational stress and social work. *Social Work Education*, 20: 659–70.

Straussner, S. L. A., Senreich, E. & Steen, J. T. (2018). Wounded healers: a multistate study of licensed social workers' behavioral health problems. *Soc Work*, 63 (2), 125–133.

Stryker, S. & Burke, P. (2000). The past, present, and future of an identity theory. *Social Psychology Quarterly*, 63, 284–297.

SWRB (2010). *Building a safe and confident future: one year on.* Social Work Reform Board. www.education.gov.uk/swrb

SWRB (2012a). *Standards for employers of social workers in England and supervision framework.* SWRB. www.education.gov.uk

Tangney, J. P., Miller, R. S., Flicker, L. & Barlow, D. H. (1996). Are shame, guilt, and embarrassment distinct emotions? *Journal of Personality and Social Psychology*, 70 (6), 1256.

Tangney, J. P., Wagner, P. & Gramzow, R. (1992). Proneness to shame, proneness to guilt, and psychopathology. *Journal of Abnormal Psychology*, 101, 469–478.

Taylor, A. (2017). Social work and digitalisation: bridging the knowledge gaps. *Social Work Education*, 36(8), 869–879.

Taylor, G. (1985). *Pride, shame, and guilt: emotions of self-assessment.* Oxford University Press.

Teater, B. (2024). *An introduction to applying theories and methods in social work* (4th ed). McGraw-Hill.

Terum, L. I. & Heggen, K. (2016). Identification with the social work profession: the impact of education. *The British Journal of Social Work*, 46 (4), 839–854.

The Law Commission (2011). *Adult social care.* The Stationery Office.

The Poverty Site (ed. Palmer, G.) (2011). *Indicators of poverty in the UK based on Joseph Rowntree Foundation Annual Monitoring Poverty and Social Exclusion Reports.* www.poverty.org.uk/index.htm

The Poverty Site (ed. Palmer, G.) (2011). *Poverty and social exclusion.* www.poverty.org.uk/summary/social%20exclusion.shtml

The Social Workers Regulations. (2018). https://www.legislation.gov.uk/uksi/2018/893/part/6/made

Thomas, I. (2023). The regulation of social work in Wales, in Livingston, W., Redcliffe, J. & Quinn Aziz, A. (Eds.). *Social work in Wales*. Policy Press.

Thompson, N. (2011). *Promoting equality: working with diversity and difference* (3rd ed). Palgrave Macmillan.

Thompson, N. (2014). The emotionally competent professional, in Parker, J. and Doel, M. (eds) *Professional Social Work*. Sage, pp. 68–80.

Thompson, N. (2016). *Anti-discriminatory practice* (6th ed). Palgrave Macmillan.

Thompson, N. (Ed.). (2002). *Loss and grief*. Palgrave.

Ting, L. (2011). Depressive symptoms in a sample of social work students and reasons preventing students from using mental health services: an exploratory study. *Journal of Social Work Education*, 47, 253–268.

Totman, J., Hundt, G. L., Wearn, E., Paul, M. & Johnson, S. (2011). Factors affecting staff morale on inpatient mental health wards in England: a qualitative investigation. *BMC Psychiatry*, 11 (1), 68.

UK Human Rights Act (1998).

United Nations (UN) (1948). *Declaration of Universal Human Rights*. www.un.org/en/universal-declaration-human-rights/index.html

Unrau, Y. A., Gabor, P. A. & Grinnell, R. M. (2007). *Evaluation in social work: the art and science of practice* (4th ed). Oxford University Press.

Walker, J. (2011). The relevance of shame in child protection work. *Journal of Social Work Practice*, 25 (4), 451–463.

Walker, J., Crawford, K., & Parker, J. (2008). *practice education in social work: a handbook for practice researchers, assessors and educators*. Learning Matters.

Walker, P. & Finney, N. (1999). Skill development and critical thinking in higher education. *Teaching in Higher Education*, 4 (4), 531–547.

Watson, C. (2020). *Exploring the application of the principles of Stoic philosophy in the workplace*. James Cook University.

Watson, T. J. (2002). *Organising and managing work: organisational, managerial and strategic behaviour in theory and practice*. Pearson Education.

Welsh Assembly Government (2011). *Sustainable social services: a Framework for Action*. Crown Copyright.

Wenger, E. (1998). *Communities of practice: learning, meaning and identity*. Cambridge University Press.

Wenger, E. (2015). *Introduction to communities of practice*. http://wenger-trayner.com/introduction-to-communities-of-practice/

Wenger, E. (2000). *Communities of practice: learning, meaning, and identity* (2nd ed). Cambridge University Press.

Wenger-Traynor, E., Wenger-Traynor, B., Reid, P. & Bruderlein, C. (2023). *Communities of practice within and across organizations: a guidebook* (2nd ed). Social Learning Lab.

West, M., Eckert, R., Steward, K. & Pasmore, B. (2014). *Developing collective leadership for health care*. King's Fund. www.kingsfund.org.uk/insight-and-analysis/reports/developing-collective-leadership-for-health-care

Williams, C. (2011). *Social policy for social welfare practice in a devolved Wales* (2nd ed.). Venture Press.

Williams, S. & Rutter, L. (2010). *The practice educator's handbook*. Learning Matters.

Williams, S. & Rutter, L. (2023). *The practice educator's handbook* (6th ed.). Learning Matters.

Wenger-Traynor, E., Wenger-Traynor, B., Reid, P. & Bruderlein, C. (2023). *Communities of Practice Within and Across Organizations: A guidebook* (2nd ed). Social Learning Lab.

Witkin, S. L. (1990). The implications of social constructionism for social work education. *Journal of Teaching in Social Work*, 4 (2), 37–48.

Witz, A. (1992). *Professions and Patriarchy*. Routledge.

World Health Organization (2001). *The World Health Report: 2001: Mental health: new understanding, new hope*. World Health Organization.

Yates, J. & Cahill, S. (2019). What kind of shoes does a social worker wear? A Content analysis of four occupational prototypes. *British Journal of Guidance & Counselling*, 47 (3), 355–370.

Index

Page numbers followed by "f" indicate figures; those followed by "t" indicate tables.